APPLIED STATISTICS FOR SOFTWARE MANAGERS

ISBN 0-13-041789-0

90000

9 780130 417893

Software Quality Institute Series

The Software Quality Institute Series is a partnership between the Software Quality Institute (SQI) at The University of Texas at Austin and Prentice Hall Professional Technical Reference (PHPTR). The books discuss real-life problems and offer strategies for improving software quality and software business practices.

Each publication is written by highly skilled, experienced practitioners who understand and can help solve the problems facing software professionals. SQI series topic areas include software development practices and technologies, management of software organizations, integration of high-quality software into other industries, business issues with reference to software quality, and related areas of interest.

TITLES IN THE SOFTWARE QUALITY INSTITUTE SERIES

APPLIED STATISTICS FOR SOFTWARE MANAGERS

Katrina D. Maxwell

Prentice Hall PTR
Upper Saddle River, NJ 07458
www.phptr.com

Library of Congress Cataloging-in-Publication Data is available.

Editorial/Production Supervision: *Donna Cullen-Dolce*
Executive Editor: *Paul Petralia*
Editorial Assistant: *Richard Winkler*
Marketing Manager: *Debby van Dijk*
Manufacturing Manager: *Alexis Heydt-Long*
Cover Design Director: *Jerry Votta*
Cover Design: *Nina Scuderi*

© 2002 by Pearson Education, Inc.
Publishing as Prentice Hall PTR
Upper Saddle River, New Jersey 07458

Prentice Hall books are widely used by corporations and government
agencies for training, marketing, and resale.

For information regarding corporate and government bulk discounts please contact:
Corporate and Government Sales (800) 382-3419 or corpsales@pearsontechgroup.com. Or write:
Prentice Hall PTR, Corporate Sales Dept., One Lake Street, Upper Saddle River, NJ 07458.

Printed in the United States of America

10 9 8 7 6 5 4 3 2 1

ISBN 0-13-041789-0

Pearson Education LTD.
Pearson Education Australia PTY, Limited
Pearson Education Singapore, Pte. Ltd.
Pearson Education North Asia Ltd.
Pearson Education Canada, Ltd.
Pearson Educación de Mexico, S.A. de C.V.
Pearson Education—Japan
Pearson Education Malaysia, Pte. Ltd.

To Hervé Balloux,
and
to our daughters,
Caroline, Emilie, and Olivia

Contents

Chapter   4
Case Study: Developing a Software Development Cost Model

Chapter   5
Case Study: Software Maintenance Cost Drivers   183

Preface

You've implemented a measurement program and have collected some software metrics data. Great, but do you know how to make the most of this valuable asset? Categorical variables such as language, development platform, application type, and tool use can be important factors in explaining the cost, duration, and productivity of your company's software projects. However, analyzing a database containing many non-numerical variables is not a straightforward task.

Statistics, like software development, is as much an art as it is a science. Choosing the appropriate statistical methods, selecting the variables to use, creating new variables, removing outliers, picking the best model, detecting confounded variables, choosing baseline categorical variables, and handling influential observations all require that you make many decisions during the data analysis process. Decisions for which there are often no clear rules. What should you do? Read on.

Using real software project data, this book leads you through all the steps necessary to extract the most value from your data. In Chapter 1, I describe my methodology for analyzing software project data. You do not need to understand statistics to follow the methodology. I simply explain what to do, why I do it, how to do it, and what to watch out for at each step.

Common problems that occur when analyzing real data are thoroughly covered in four case studies of gradually increasing complexity. Each case study is based around a business issue of interest to software managers. In Chapter 2, you will learn how to determine which variables explain differences in software development productivity. In Chapter 3, you will look at factors that influence time to market. In Chapter 4, you will learn how to develop and measure the accuracy of cost estimation models. In Chapter 5, you will study the cost drivers of software maintenance, with an emphasis on presenting results. Finally, in Chapter 6, you will learn what you need to know about descriptive statistics, statistical tests, correlation analysis, regression analysis, and analysis of variance.

Intended audience

I wrote this book for current and future software managers. In particular, the unique combination of statistics applied to software business issues should help every future software engineer/manager understand why software measurement is useful and what to do with the data.

This book could be used as the basis for a corporate training program, and in the software engineering and information systems curricula of universities. Additionally, it could be used in statistics courses taught to computer scientists as it contains examples of interest to them.

Prerequisites

Anyone who wants to analyze data will need to know how to use a statistical software tool. As far as mathematics go, a basic knowledge of algebra is sufficient.

Acknowledgments

I would like to thank Shari Lawrence Pfleeger, who not only encouraged me to write this book, but also read every word of it. I also thank Pekka Forselius of Software Technology Transfer Finland (*www.sttf.fi*) for allowing me to publish the data he collected, and for spending many hours with me validating it and discussing how the results should be interpreted. Finally, I thank Barbara Kitchenham, Hervé Balloux, and Mark Standing for reviewing various chapters.

Katrina D. Maxwell

Data Analysis
Methodology

1

Suppose you inherited the database in Table 1.1 and needed to find out what could be learned from it—fast. Say your boss entered your office and said, "Here's some software project data your predecessor collected. Is there anything interesting about it? I'd like you to present the results at next week's management meeting." Given that it usually takes a number of years to collect enough software project data to analyze, plus the software industry's high job turnover rate, and more often than not, you probably will be analyzing data that was collected by others.

What is this data? What do the abbreviations mean? What statistical methods should you use? What should you do first? Calm down and read on. After eight years of collecting, validating, analyzing, and benchmarking software projects, I've written the book that I wish had been available the day I was told to "find something interesting" about the European Space Agency software project database.

In this chapter, I will share with you my data analysis methodology. Each step is demonstrated using the software project data in Table 1.1. You do not need to understand statistics to follow the "recipe" in Sidebar 1.1. I simply

TABLE 1.1
Software Project Data

id	effort	size	app	telonuse	t13	t14
2	7871	647	TransPro	No	4	4
3	845	130	TransPro	No	4	4
5	21272	1056	CustServ	No	3	2
6	4224	383	TransPro	No	5	4
8	7320	209	TransPro	No	4	2
9	9125	366	TransPro	No	3	2
15	2565	249	InfServ	No	2	4
16	4047	371	TransPro	No	3	3
17	1520	211	TransPro	No	3	3
18	25910	1849	TransPro	Yes	3	3
19	37286	2482	TransPro	Yes	3	1
21	11039	292	TransPro	No	4	2
25	10447	567	TransPro	Yes	2	2
26	5100	467	TransPro	Yes	2	3
27	63694	3368	TransPro	No	4	2
30	1745	185	InfServ	No	4	5
31	1798	387	CustServ	No	3	3
32	2957	430	MIS	No	3	4
33	963	204	TransPro	No	3	3
34	1233	71	TransPro	No	2	4
38	3850	548	CustServ	No	4	3
40	5787	302	MIS	No	2	4
43	5578	227	TransPro	No	2	3
44	1060	59	TransPro	No	3	3
45	5279	299	InfServ	Yes	3	2
46	8117	422	CustServ	No	3	2
50	1755	193	TransPro	No	2	4
51	5931	1526	InfServ	Yes	4	3
53	3600	509	TransPro	No	4	2
54	4557	583	MIS	No	5	3
55	8752	315	CustServ	No	3	3
56	3440	138	CustServ	No	4	3
58	13700	423	TransPro	No	4	2
61	4620	204	InfServ	Yes	3	2

Ingredients:
As much high-quality data as possible
One package statistical analysis software
A good dose of common sense

Step 1: Validate your data
Step 2: Select the variables and model
Step 3: Perform preliminary analyses (using graphs, tables, correlation and stepwise regression analyses)
Step 4: Build the multi-variable model (using analysis of variance)
Step 5: Check the model
Step 6: Extract the equation

After you fully understand Steps 1 through 6, which are explained in this chapter, read the case studies in Chapters 2 through 5 to gain experience analyzing more complicated databases and to learn how to transform your equations into management implications. See Chapter 5 for an example of how to serve your results to your guests. If you have time, refer to Chapter 6 to learn more about the different statistical methods used in the recipe.

explain what to do, why we do it, how to interpret the statistical output results, and what to watch out for at each stage.

Data Validation

The most important step is data validation. I spend much more time validating data than I do analyzing it. Often, data is not neatly presented to you in one table as it is in this book, but it is in several files that need to be merged and which may include information you do not need or understand. The data may also exist on different pieces of paper.

What do I mean by data validation? In general terms, I mean finding out if you have the right data for your purpose. It is not enough to write a questionnaire and get people to fill it out; you need to have a vision. Like getting the requirement specifications right before starting to develop the software. Specifically, you need to determine if the values for each variable make sense.

Why Do It? You can waste months trying to make sense out of data that was collected without a clear purpose, and without statistical analysis requirements in mind. It is much better to get a precise idea of exactly what data you have and how much you trust it before you start analyzing. Regardless of whether the data concerns chocolate bar sales, financial indicators, or software projects, the old maxim "garbage in equals garbage out" applies. If you find out that something is wrong with the raw data after you have analyzed it, your conclusions are meaningless. In the best case, you may just have to correct something and analyze it all again. However, if the problem lies with the definition of a variable, it may be impossible to go back and collect the data needed. If you are collecting the data yourself, make sure you ask the right questions the first time. You may not have a second chance.

How to Do It   Start off by asking these questions:

- What is this data?
- When was the data collected?
- Why was the data collected?
- Who collected it?
- How did that person ensure that everyone understood the definitions?
- What is the definition of each variable?
- What are the units of measurement of each variable?
- What are the definitions of the values of each variable?

Example   The software development project data in Table 1.1 describes 34 COBOL applications running in a mainframe environment at a bank. Most of these applications used other languages in addition to COBOL. The project's manager collected the data upon completion of each project. One person entered all project data into a company database and validated it. The purpose of the data collection was to help manage project portfolios at the bank. Table 1.2 defines the variables. I recommend that you create a table like this for each database you analyze. It is important to be very organized so you can return to your work later and understand it (or leave it for someone else to understand).

Once we understand what the variables are, we need to check that the values make sense. One easy way to do this is to use a data summary function for all variables with numerical values. Example 1.1 shows the number of observations (*Obs*), the average (*Mean*), the standard deviation (*Std. Dev.*), the minimum (*Min*), and the maximum (*Max*) value for each variable. For the moment, we are just interested in the number of observations and range of values. If the number of observations is not the same for each variable, this

TABLE 1.2
Variable Definitions

Variable	Full Name	Definition
id	identification number	Each completed project has a unique identification number. (Originally, each project was given a name instead of a number, but I replaced these names for data confidentiality reasons.)
effort	effort	Work carried out by the software supplier from specification until delivery, measured in hours.
size	application size	Function points measured using the Experience method.
app	application type	CustServ = Customer service MIS = Management information system TransPro = Transaction processing InfServ = Information/on-line service
telonuse	Telon use	Telon is a tool that generates code. No = No Telon used Yes = Telon used
t13	staff application knowledge	Knowledge of application domain in project team (supplier and customer): 1 = Very low; team application experience <6 months on average 2 = Low; application experience low; some members have experience; 6-12 months on average 3 = Nominal; application experience good; 1-3 years on average 4 = High; application experience good both at supplier and customer sites; 3-6 years on average; business dynamics known 5 = Very high; both supplier and customer know application area well, including the business; >6 years' average experience
t14	staff tool skills	Experience level of project team (supplier and customer) in regard to development and documentation tools at project kick-off: 1 = Very low; team has no experience in necessary tools; team's average experience <6 months

(*continued*)

TABLE 1.2 (*continued*)

Variable	Full Name	Definition
		2 = Low; tools experience less than average; some members have experience with some tools; 6-12 months on average
		3 = Nominal; tools experience good in about half the team; some members know development and documentation tools well; 1-3 years on average
		4 = High; most team members know tools well; some members can help others; 3-6 years on average
		5 = Very high; team knows all tools well; support available for specific needs of project; >6 years' average experience

means that data is missing. This may be normal as all variables may not have been collected for each project, or it may point to a problem. See if you can find these missing values and add them to the database before you go any further. Also, check to see if the maximum and minimum values make sense. In this case, they do. But if *t13* or *t14* had 7 as a maximum value, we would immediately know there was a problem because by definition, 5 is the highest value possible.

This is also a useful exercise to undertake when someone transfers a very large database to you via the Internet. When it is impossible to check each value individually, check the summary values with the person who sent you the data. I also recommend checking all the variables one-by-one for the first project, the last project, and a few random projects from the middle of the database to make sure nothing got altered during the transfer.

Example 1.1

```
                       . summarize

    Variable     Obs        Mean    Std. Dev.     Min       Max
    id            34        31.5     17.9059        2        61
    effort        34    8734.912    12355.46      845     63694
    size          34    578.5882    711.7584       59      3368
    t13           34    3.235294    .8548905        2         5
    t14           34    2.911765    .9000891        1         5
```

Next, I tabulate each variable that has words or letters as values. Besides providing valuable information about how many projects are in each category, it is also an easy way to check for spelling mistakes. For example, if there was one observation for *CustSer* and five observations for *CustServ*, you should check if there are really two different categories.

In Examples 1.2 and 1.3, *Freq.* is the number of observations in each category, *Percent* is the percentage of observations in each category, and *Cum.* is the cumulative percentage. We can see that the majority of the applications (about 59%) are transaction processing (*TransPro*) applications. Seven applications used Telon in addition to COBOL. For business presentations, this type of information would look good displayed in a pie chart.

Example 1.2

. tabulate app

Application Type	Freq.	Percent	Cum.
CustServ	6	17.65	17.65
MIS	3	8.82	26.47
TransPro	20	58.82	85.29
InfServ	5	14.71	100.00
Total	34	100.00	

Example 1.3

. tabulate telonuse

Telon Use	Freq.	Percent	Cum.
No	27	79.41	79.41
Yes	7	20.59	100.00
Total	34	100.00	

What to Watch Out For

- What does a blank mean? (Missing? Don't know? None?)
- What does a 0 mean? (0? Missing? A number close to 0 that has been rounded to 0?)
- If there is an *"Other"* category, what does it include? If the *"Other"* category is extremely diverse, it can't be analyzed as a homogenous category.
- Can you cross-check any variables to see if they make sense? For example, if you have the start date, end date, and duration of a project, you can check if *end date − start date = duration*.

Variable and Model Selection _____

Once we understand what data we actually have, we need to determine what we can learn from it. What possible relationships could we study? What possible relationships should we study? What relationship will we study first? Your answers to the last two questions will depend on the overall goals of the analysis.

Why Do It?   The data may have been collected for a clearly stated purpose. Even so, there might be other interesting relationships to study that occur to you while you are analyzing the data, and which you might be tempted to investigate. However, it is important to decide in advance what you are going to do first and then to complete that task in a meticulous, organized manner. Otherwise, you will find yourself going in lots of different directions, generating lots of computer output, and becoming confused about what you have tried and what you have not tried; in short, you will drown yourself in the data. It is also at this stage that you may decide to create new variables or to reduce the number of variables in your analysis. Variables of questionable validity, variables not meaningfully related to what you want to study, and categorical variable values that do not have a sufficient number of observations should be dropped from the analysis. (See the case studies in Chapters 2 through 5 for examples of variable reduction/modification.) In the following example, we will use all the variables provided in Table 1.1.

Example   The smallest number of observations for a categorical variable is 3 for the *MIS* (management information systems) category of the application type (*app*) variable (see Example 1.2). Given that our data set contains 34 observations, I feel comfortable letting *MIS* be represented by three projects. No matter how many observations the database contains, I don't believe it is wise to make a judgment about something represented by less than three projects. This is my personal opinion. Ask yourself this: If the *MIS* category contained only one project and you found in your statistical analysis that the *MIS* category had a significantly higher productivity, would you then conclude that all *MIS* projects in the bank have a high productivity? I would not. If there were two projects, would you believe it? I would not. If there were three projects, would you believe it? Yes, I would in this case. However, if there were 3000 projects in the database, I would prefer for *MIS* to be represented by more than three projects. Feel free to use your own judgment.

Even with this small sample of software project data, we could investigate a number of relationships. We could investigate if any of the factors collected influenced software development effort. Or we could find out which factors influenced software development productivity (i.e., *size/effort*). We could also look at the relationship between application size (*size*) and Telon use (*telonuse*), between size and application type (*app*), or between application type (*app*) and staff application knowledge (*t13*), just to name a few more possibilities. In this example, we will focus on determining which factors affect effort. That is, do size, application type (*app*), Telon use (*telonuse*), staff application knowledge (*t13*), staff tool skills (*t14*), or a combination of these factors have an impact on effort? Is effort a function of these variables? Mathematically speaking, does:

$$effort = f \, (size, \, app, \, telonuse, \, t13, \, t14)?$$

In this equation, effort is on the left-hand side (LHS) and the other variables are on the right-hand side (RHS). We refer to the LHS variable as the dependent variable and the RHS variables as independent variables.

What to Watch Out For

- To develop a predictive model, make sure that the independent variables are all factors that you know or can predict with reasonable accuracy in advance.
- Category values with less than three observations should be dropped from any multi-variable analysis.

Preliminary Analyses

Before running "blind" statistical tests, I check that the assumptions underlying them are true. In addition, I like to get some first impressions of the data. My objective is not a complete understanding of all possible relationships among all the variables. For example, in Step 2, variable and model selection, I decided that my first goal was to determine which of the variables collected had an influence on effort. To achieve that goal, I follow the steps described in this section before building the multi-variable model (Step 4).

Graphs

Histograms   To start, I look at a graph of each numerical variable individually to see how many small values, large values, and medium values there are, that is, the distribution of each variable. These are also called histograms.

Why Do It?   I want to see if the variables are normally distributed. Many statistical techniques assume that the underlying data is normally distributed, so you should check if it is. A normal distribution is also known as a bell-shaped curve. Many of us were graded on such curves at large competitive universities. In a bell-shaped curve, most values fall in the middle, with few very high and very low values. For example, if an exam is graded and the results are fit to a normal distribution (Figure 1.1), most students will get a C. Less students will get a B or a D. And even fewer students will receive an A or an F. The average test score will be the midpoint of the C grade, whether the score is 50, or 90, out of 100. That does not always seem very fair, does it? You can learn more about normal distributions and why they are important in Chapter 6.

How to Do It   To create a histogram for the variable *t13* manually, you would count how many 1s there are, how many 2s, etc. Then, you would make a bar chart with either the number of observations or the percentage of observations on the y-axis for each value of *t13*. However, you don't need to waste your time doing this by hand.

Let a statistical analysis tool do it for you. You will need to learn how to use a statistical analysis tool to analyze data. I have used SAS, Excel, and

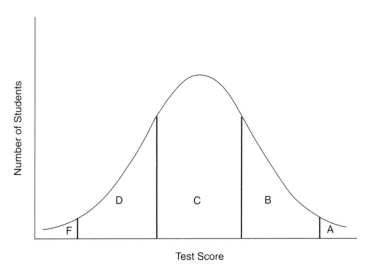

FIGURE 1.1
Example of a normal distribution

Stata in my career. My opinions regarding each are: SAS was fine when I worked for large organizations, but far too expensive when I had to pay for it myself. Excel is not powerful or straightforward enough for my purposes. Stata is relatively inexpensive (no yearly licensing fee), does everything I need, and is very easy to use (see *www.stata.com*). However, no matter which statistical software you use, the output should always look the same, and it is the interpretation of that output on which this book focuses.

Example The distributions of effort and size show that they are not normally distributed (Figures 1.2 and 1.3). The database contains few projects with a very high effort, or a very big size. It also contains many low effort, and small size projects. This is typical in a software development project database. Not only are the efforts and sizes not normally distributed in this sample, but we would not expect them to be normally distributed in the population of all software development projects.

To approximate a normal distribution, we must transform these variables. A common transformation is to take their natural log (*ln*). Taking the natural log makes large values smaller and brings the data closer together. For example, take two project sizes of 100 and 3000 function points. 3000 is much bigger than 100. If I take the *ln* of these numbers, I find that *ln*(100) = 4.6 and

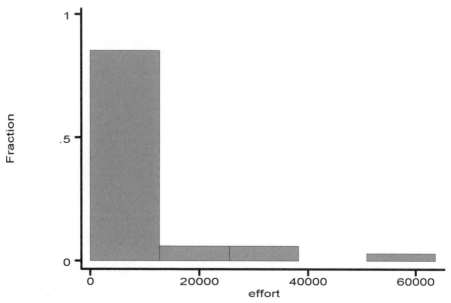

FIGURE 1.2
Distribution of *effort*

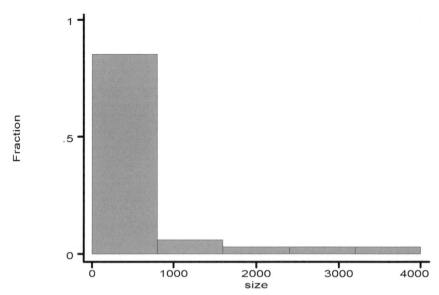

FIGURE 1.3
Distribution of *size*

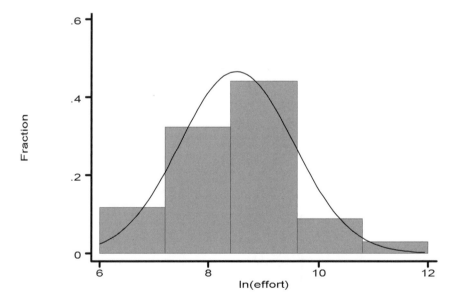

FIGURE 1.4
Distribution of *ln(effort)*

ln(3000) = 8.0. These transformed sizes are much closer together. As you can see, taking the natural log of effort and size more closely approximates a normal distribution (Figures 1.4 and 1.5).

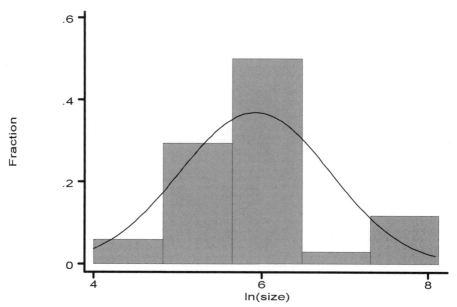

FIGURE 1.5
Distribution of *ln(size)*

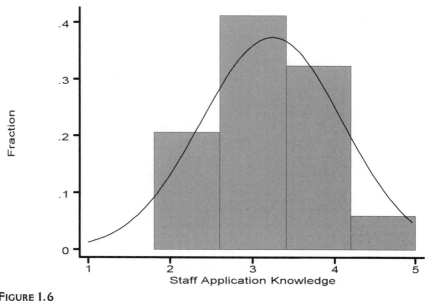

FIGURE 1.6
Distribution of *t13*

Graphs of staff application knowledge (*t13*) and staff tool skills (*t14*) look more normally distributed (Figures 1.6 and 1.7). Most projects have an average value of 3. Additionally, in the larger multi-company database from

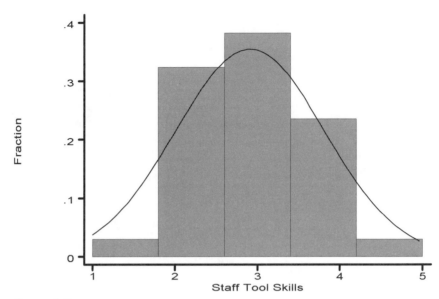

FIGURE 1.7
Distribution of *t14*

which this subset was taken, the distributions of these factors are approximately normal. In fact, the definitions of the factors were chosen especially so that most projects would be average. These variables do not need any transformation.

What to Watch Out For

- Just because the values of variables are numbers, it does not imply that they have any numerical sense. For example, application type (*app*) might have been coded as 1, 2, 3, and 4 instead of *CustServ*, *MIS*, *TransPro*, and *InfServ*. Application type (*app*) is a categorical variable with a nominal scale; that is, its values cannot be arranged in any meaningful order. I can arrange the values in any order I want: *MIS* before *CustServ*, for example. I suggest giving these types of variables meaningful names instead of numbers before you start analyzing the data. It will help you remember what they are. (You will learn more about variable types in Chapter 6.)

- On the other hand, there may be categorical variables with meaningful names that do have numerical sense. For example, staff application knowledge (*t13*) could have been coded as very low, low, average, high, and very high instead of 1, 2, 3, 4, and 5 (often referred to as a Likert scale). Staff application knowledge (*t13*) is a categorical variable whose values can be arranged in a meaningful order. I suggest transforming these types of variables into ordered numbers before you start analyzing the data. Then, check to see if they are normally distributed. If they are approximately normally distributed, I treat them as numerical variables for the rest of the analysis. If they are not normally distributed, and I have no good reason to expect that in the population of all software development projects they would be, I treat them as categorical variables. It is common practice in the market research profession to treat Likert-type variables as numerical data. As you will see, it is easier to analyze numerical-type data than true categorical data.

Two-Dimensional Graphs I also make graphs of the dependent variable against each independent numerical variable. In this example, I am interested in the relationships between effort and size, effort and staff application knowledge (*t13*), and effort and staff tool skills (*t14*).

Why Do It? A picture is worth a thousand words. I highly recommend visualizing any relationship that might exist between the dependent and independent variables before running "blind" statistical tests. It is important to see if the relationship is linear as our statistical tests are based on linear relationships and will "ignore" non-linear relationships. A relationship is linear if you can fit one straight line through the data points, and this represents them well.

Example I plot these graphs using the transformed data. We can see in Figure 1.8 that there appears to be a linear relationship between *ln(effort)* and *ln(size)*. As project size increases, the amount of effort needed increases. Figure 1.9 gives the impression that there is no relationship between effort and staff application knowledge (*t13*). Conversely, Figure 1.10 seems to suggest that less effort is required for projects with higher levels of staff tool skills (*t14*). These are first impressions that will be verified through statistical tests.

Another good reason to use a log transformation is to make a non-linear relationship more linear. Figure 1.11 shows the relationship between the variables *effort* and *size* before the log transformation. As you can see, the relationship in Figure 1.8 is much more linear than the relationship in Figure 1.11.

What to Watch Out For

- Non-linear relationships.
- Outliers—that is, any data points (projects) far away from the others. In an extreme case, an outlier can distort the scale, causing all the other

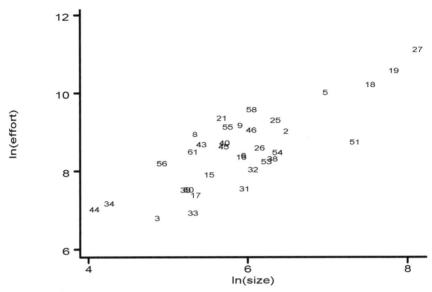

FIGURE 1.8
ln(effort) vs. *ln(size)*

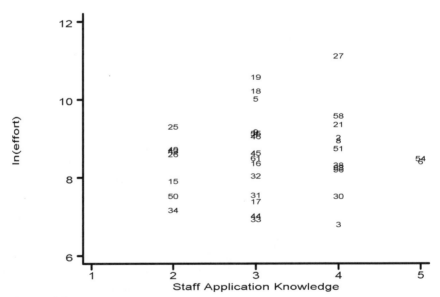

FIGURE 1.9
ln(effort) vs. *t13*

projects to look as if they are grouped together in a little cloud. All the straight lines fit to the data will try to go through the outlier, and will treat the cloud of data (that is, all the other projects) with less impor-

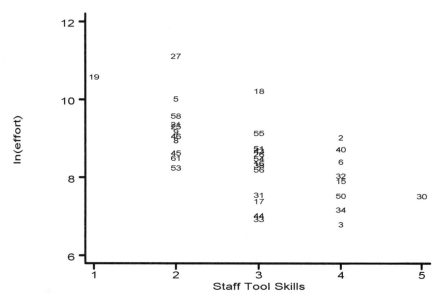

FIGURE 1.10

ln(effort) vs. *t14*

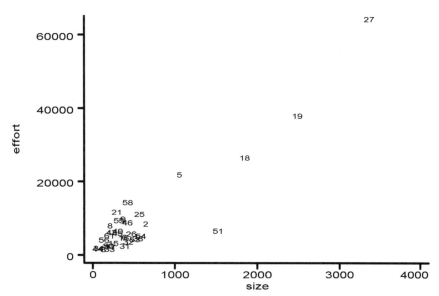

FIGURE 1.11

effort vs. *size*

tance. Remove the outlier(s) and re-plot the data to see if there is any relationship hidden in the cloud. See Chapter 2 for an example where an outlier is detected and removed.

Tables

I make tables of the average value of the dependent variable and the number of observations it is based on for each value of each categorical variable. In this example, the tables will show the average value of effort for each application type, and for Telon use.

Why Do It? We make tables to see if there is a big difference in the effort needed by category and to start formulating possible reasons for this.

Example From Example 1.4, we learn that on average, transaction processing (*TransPro*) applications require the highest effort, then customer service (*CustServ*) applications, then *MIS* applications, and finally, information service (*InfServ*) applications. Why is this? Answering this question will be important for the interpretation phase of the analysis. Example 1.5 tells us that, on average, projects that used Telon required almost twice as much effort as projects that did not. Is this because they were bigger in size, or could there be another explanation?

Example 1.4

```
. table app, c(n effort mean effort)
```

Application Type	N(effort)	mean(effort)
CustServ	6	7872
MIS	3	4434
TransPro	20	10816
InfServ	5	4028

Example 1.5

```
. table telonuse, c(n effort mean effort)
```

Telon Use	N(effort)	mean(effort)
No	27	7497
Yes	7	13510

What to Watch Out For Remember that we still need to check the relationships in Examples 1.4 and 1.5 to see if they are statistically significant.

Even if there appears to be a big difference in the average values, it may not really be true because one project with a high effort could have influenced a category's average.

Correlation Analysis

Another assumption of the statistical procedure I use to build a multi-variable model is that independent variables are independent; that is, they are not related to each other. In our example, there should be no strong relationships among the variables: *size*, *t13*, *t14*, *app*, and *telonuse*. There is a very quick way to check if the numerical variables, *size*, *t13*, and *t14*, are independent: correlation analysis. If some of the numerical variables were collected using an ordinal or quasi-interval Likert scale (like *t13* and *t14*), I use Spearman's rank correlation coefficient because it tests the relationships of orders rather than actual values. (See Chapter 6 for scale definitions.) Another important feature of Spearman's rank correlation coefficient is that it is less sensitive to extreme values than the standard Pearson correlation coefficient.

Two variables will be highly positively correlated if low ranked values of one are nearly always associated with low ranked values of the other, and high ranked values of one are nearly always associated with high ranked values of the other. For example, do projects with very low staff tool skills always have very low staff application knowledge, too; are average tool skills associated with average application knowledge, high tool skills with high application knowledge, etc.? If such a relationship is nearly always true, the correlation coefficient will be close to 1.

Two variables will be highly negatively correlated if low ranked values of one are nearly always associated with high ranked values of the other, and vice-versa. For example, do the smallest projects (smallest in size) always have the highest staff application knowledge, and do the biggest projects always have the lowest staff application knowledge? If such a situation is nearly always true, the correlation coefficient will be close to -1. Variables that are not correlated at all will have a correlation coefficient close to zero. You will learn more about correlation analysis in Chapter 6.

Why Do It?   Perform a correlation analysis as a quick check to see if there are possible violations of the independence assumption. Later, as I build the multi-variable model, I will use this information. For the moment, I only make note of it.

Example   Example 1.6 shows the statistical output for the Spearman's rank correlation coefficient test between the variables *size* and *t13*. The number of observations equals 34. The correlation coefficient is *"Spearman's rho,"* which is 0.1952. Already it is clear that these two variables are not very correlated as this number is closer to 0 than 1. The *"Test of H$_o$"* tests if *size* and *t13* are independent (i.e., not correlated). If $Pr > |t|$ = a number greater than 0.05, then *size* and *t13* are independent. Because 0.2686 > 0.05, we conclude that this is indeed the case. (*Pr* is an abbreviation for probability; *t* means that the t distribution was used to determine the probability. You will learn more about this in Chapter 6.)

Example 1.6

```
                     . spearman size t13

 Number of obs = 34
Spearman's rho = 0.1952
Test of Ho: size and t13 independent
      Pr > |t| = 0.2686
```

From Example 1.7, we learn that the variables *size* and *t14* have a Spearman's correlation coefficient of −0.3599. We cannot accept that *size* and *t14* are independent because 0.0365 is less than 0.05. Thus, we conclude that *size* and *t13* are negatively correlated.

Example 1.7

```
                     . spearman size t14

 Number of obs = 34
Spearman's rho = -0.3599
Test of Ho: size and t14 independent
      Pr > |t| =  0.0365
```

We conclude from the results in Example 1.8 that *t13* and *t14* are not correlated.

Example 1.8

```
                     . spearman t13 t14

 Number of obs = 34
Spearman's rho = -0.0898
Test of Ho: t13 and t14 independent
      Pr > |t| = 0.6134
```

What to Watch Out For

- If the absolute value of Spearman's rho is greater than or equal to 0.75, and the $Pr > |t|$ value equals 0.05 or less, then the two variables are strongly correlated and should not be included in the final model together.
- Many statistical analysis packages will automatically calculate the standard Pearson correlation coefficient unless you state otherwise. Make sure you request Spearman's correlation.
- It does not matter if you use the original variable (for example, *size*) or the transformed variable (*ln(size)*) to calculate Spearman's correlation; the results will be the same.

Categorical Variable Tests   Now that we have checked the numerical variables' independence with correlation analysis, perhaps you are asking: What about the categorical variables? It takes much more time to check the independence of every possible relationship between the categorical variables and between the categorical variables and numerical variables, especially in a large database. It is for this reason that I only carry out these checks on the independent variables present in the final multi-variable model in Step 5, when I check the model.

Stepwise Regression Analysis

Performing multiple regression analyses allows us to determine the relative importance of each independent, numerical variable's relationship (*ln(size)*, *t13, t14*) to the dependent variable (*ln(effort)*).

Why Do It?   Because stepwise regression analysis is automatic and very simple to run, I always like to see how good of a model can be built just with the numerical data. In addition to learning if the non-categorical variables collected are very important indicators of effort, this also gives me a quick idea of what performance the categorical data is going to have to beat.

Example   The output in Example 1.9 shows the results of running a forward stepwise regression procedure on our data set. Forward stepwise regression means that the model starts "empty" and then the variables most related to *leffort* (abbreviation of *ln(effort)* in statistical output) are added one by one in order of importance until no other variable can be added to improve the model. You must run this procedure using the transformed variables.

You can see that first, *lsize* (abbreviation of *ln(size)* in statistical output) is added, then *t14* is added. No further variation in *leffort* is explained by *t13*, so it is left out of the model. In Chapter 6, you will learn how to interpret every part of this output; for now, I will just concentrate on the values in bold. These are the values that I look at to determine the performance and significance of the model. I look at the number of observations (*Number of obs*) to see if the model was built using all the projects. The model was built using all 34 observations. I look at *Prob > F* to determine if the model is significant, in other words, can I believe this model? (*Prob* is an abbreviation for probability; *F* means that the F distribution was used to determine the probability. You will learn more about this in Chapter 6.) If *Prob > F* is a number less than or equal to 0.05, then I accept the model. Here it is 0, so the model is significant. I look at the adjusted R-squared value (*Adj R-squared*) to determine the performance of the model. The closer it is to 1, the better. The *Adj R-squared* of 0.7288 means that this model explains nearly 73% (72.88%) of the variation in *leffort*. This is a very good result. This means that even without the categorical variables, I am sure to come up with a model than explains 73% of the variation in effort. I am very interested in finding out more about which variables explain this variation.

I can see from the output that *lsize* and *t14* are the RHS explanatory variables. I also check the significance of each explanatory variable and the constant (*_cons*) in the column $P > |t|$. If $P > |t|$ is a number less than or equal to 0.05, then the individual variable is significant; that is, it is not in the model by chance. (*P* is yet another abbreviation for probability; *t* means that the t distribution was used to determine the probability.)

Example 1.9

```
                    . sw regress leffort lsize t13 t14, pe(.05)
begin with empty model

            p = 0.0000 < 0.0500    adding    lsize
            p = 0.0019 < 0.0500    adding    t14
```

Source	SS	df	MS		
Model	25.9802069	2	12.9901035		
Residual	8.88042769	31	.286465409		
Total	34.8606346	33	1.05638287		

Number of obs =	34			
$F(2,31)$	=	45.35		
Prob > F	**= 0.0000**			
R-squared	= 0.7453			
Adj R-squared	**= 0.7288**			
Root MSE	= .53522			

leffort	Coef.	Std. Err.	t	**P>|t|**	[95% Conf. Interval]	
lsize	.7678266	.1148813	6.684	**0.000**	.5335247	1.002129
t14	−.3856721	.1138331	−3.388	**0.002**	−.6178361	−.153508
_cons	5.088876	.8764331	5.806	**0.000**	3.301379	6.876373

The output in Example 1.10 shows the results of running a backward stepwise regression procedure on our data set. Backward stepwise regression means that the model starts "full" (with all the variables) and then the variables least related to effort are removed one by one in order of unimportance until no further variable can be removed to improve the model. You can see here that *t13* was removed from the model. In this case, the results are the same for forward and backward stepwise regression; however, this is not always the case. Things get more complicated when some variables have missing observations.

Example 1.10

```
                          . sw regress leffort lsize t13 t14, pr(.05)
begin with full model

p = 0.6280 >= 0.0500   removing t13

Source          SS        df       MS              Number of obs =       34
Model      25.9802069     2    12.9901035          F(2,31)        =    45.35
Residual   8.88042769    31    .286465409          Prob > F       = 0.0000
                                                    R-squared      = 0.7453
Total      34.8606346    33    1.05638287          Adj R-squared  = 0.7288
                                                    Root MSE       = .53522

leffort       Coef.    Std. Err.      t      P>|t|    [95% Conf. Interval]
lsize       .7678266    .1148813    6.684    0.000    .5335247    1.002129
t14        -.3856721    .1138331   -3.388    0.002   -.6178361    -.153508
_cons       5.088876    .8764331    5.806    0.000    3.301379    6.876373
```

What to Watch Out For   Watch out for variables with lots of missing values. The stepwise regression procedure only takes into account observations with non-missing values for **all** variables specified. For example, if *t13* is missing for half the projects, then half the projects will not be used. Check the number of observations used in the model. You may keep coming up with models that explain a large amount of the variation for a small amount of the data. If this happens, run the stepwise procedures using only the variables available for nearly every project.

Building the Multi-Variable Model

I call the technique I've developed to build the multi-variable model "stepwise ANOVA" (analysis of variance). It is very similar to forward stepwise regression except I use an analysis of variance procedure to build models with categorical variables. You will learn more about analysis of variance in Chapter 6. For the moment, you just need to know that this procedure allows us to determine the influence of numerical **and** categorical variables on the dependent variable, *leffort*. The model starts "empty" and then the variables most related to *leffort* are added one by one in order of importance until no other variable can be added to improve the model. The procedure is very labor-intensive because I make the decisions at each step myself; it is not automatically done by the computer. Although I am sure this could be automated, there are some advantages to doing it yourself. As you carry out the steps, you will develop a better understanding of the data. In addition, in the real world, a database often contains many missing values and it is not always clear which variable should be added at each step. Sometimes you need to follow more than one path to find the best model. In the following example, I will show you the simplest case using our 34-project, 6-variable database with no missing values. My goal for this chapter is that you understand the methodology. The four case studies in Chapters 2 through 5 present more complicated analyses, and will focus on interpreting the output.

Example
Determine Best One-Variable Model   First, we want to find the best one-variable model. Which variable, *lsize*, *t13*, *t14*, *app*, or *telonuse*, explains the most variation in *leffort*? I run regression procedures for the numerical variables and ANOVA procedures for the categorical variables to determine this. In practice, I do not print all the output. I save it in output listing files and record by hand the key information in a summary sheet. Sidebar 1.2 shows a typical summary sheet. I note the date that I carried out the analysis, the directory where I saved the files, and the names of the data file, the procedure file(s), and the output file(s). I may want to look at them again in the future, and if I don't note their names now, I may never find them again! We are going to be creating lots of procedures and generating lots of output, so it is important to be organized. I also note the name of the dependent variable.

Now I am ready to look at the output file and record the performance of the models. In the summary sheet, I record data only for significant variables. For the regression models, a variable is highly significant if its $P > |t|$ value is 0.05 or less. In this case, I do not record the actual value; I just note the number of observations, the variable's effect on effort, and the adjusted R-squared value. If the significance is borderline, that is, if $P > |t|$ is a number between 0.05 and 0.10, I note its value. If the constant is not significant, I note it in the *Comments* column. If you are analyzing a very small database, you might like to record these values for every variable—significant or not.

Personally, I have found that it is not worth the effort for databases with many variables. If I need this information later, I can easily go back and look at the output file.

For the ANOVA models, I do the same except I look at a variable's *Prob > F* value to determine if the variable is significant. The effect of a categorical variable depends on the different types. For example, using Telon (*telonuse* = Yes) will have one effect on *leffort* and not using Telon (*telonuse* = No) will have a different effect on *leffort*. You cannot determine the effect from the ANOVA table.

In Example 1.11, I have highlighted the key numbers in bold. I see that there is a very significant relationship between *leffort* and *lsize* ($P > |t|$ = *0.000*): *lsize* explains 64% of the variation in *leffort*. The coefficient of *lsize* (*Coef.*) is a positive number (0.9298). This means that *leffort* increases with increasing *lsize*. The model was fit using data from 34 projects. I add this information to the summary sheet (Sidebar 1.2).

Example 1.11

. regress leffort lsize

Source	SS	df	MS			
Model	22.6919055	1	22.6919055	**Number of obs** =		**34**
Residual	12.1687291	32	.380272786	F(1,32)	=	59.67
				Prob > F	=	0.0000
Total	34.8606346	33	1.05638287	R-squared	=	0.6509
				Adj R-squared =		**0.6400**
				Root MSE	=	.61666

leffort	**Coef.**	Std. Err.	t	**P>|t|**	[95% Conf.	Interval]
lsize	**.9297666**	.1203611	7.725	**0.000**	.6845991	1.174934
_cons	3.007431	.7201766	4.176	**0.000**	1.54048	4.474383

In Example 1.12, I see that there is not a significant relationship between *leffort* and *t13*. Therefore, I do not even look at the coefficient of *t13*. I note nothing and move on to the next model.

Example 1.12

. regress leffort t13

Source	SS	df	MS			
Model	.421933391	1	.421933391	Number of obs =		34
Residual	34.4387012	32	1.07620941	F(1,32)	=	0.39
				Prob > F	=	0.5357
Total	34.8606346	33	1.05638287	R-squared	=	0.0121
				Adj R-squared	=	0.0188
				Root MSE	=	-1.0374

```
leffort      Coef.     Std. Err.       t      P>|t|    [95% Conf. Interval]
t13        .1322679    .2112423      0.626   0.536   -.2980186    .5625544
_cons      8.082423    .706209      11.445   0.000    6.643923    9.520924
```

In Example 1.13, I see that there is a very significant relationship between *leffort* and *t14* : *t14* explains 36% of the variation in *leffort*. The coefficient of *t14* is negative. This means that *leffort* decreases with increasing *t14*. The model was fit using data from 34 projects. I add this information to the summary sheet (Sidebar 1.2).

Example 1.13

```
                                . regress leffort t14

Source         SS        df      MS              Number of obs =       34
Model      13.1834553    1   13.1834553          F(1,32)        =    19.46
Residual   21.6771793   32   .677411853          Prob > F       =   0.0001
                                                  R-squared      =   0.3782
Total      34.8606346   33   1.05638287          Adj R-squared  =   0.3587
                                                  Root MSE       =   .82305

leffort      Coef.     Std. Err.       t      P>|t|    [95% Conf. Interval]
t14       -.7022183    .1591783     -4.412   0.000   -1.026454   -.3779827
_cons     10.55504     .4845066     21.785   0.000    9.568136   11.54195
```

In Example 1.14, I see that there is no significant relationship between *leffort* and *app*. I note nothing and move on to the next model.

Example 1.14

```
                                . anova leffort app

                 Number of obs =       34       R-squared      =  0.0210
                 Root MSE      = 1.06659         Adj R-squared  = -0.0769

        Source      Partial SS    df      MS           F       Prob > F
        Model      .732134098     3   .244044699      0.21      0.8855
        app        .732134098     3   .244044699      0.21      0.8855
        Residual   34.1285005    30   1.13761668
        Total      34.8606346    33   1.05638287
```

In Example 1.15, I see that there is a borderline significant relationship between *leffort* and *telonuse* : *telonuse* explains 8% of the variation in *leffort*. The model was fit using data from 34 projects. I add this information to the summary sheet (Sidebar 1.2).

Example 1.15

```
. anova leffort telonuse

      Number of obs = 34              R-squared = 0.1094
             Root MSE = .984978   Adj R-squared = 0.0816

  Source     Partial SS   df      MS        F     Prob > F
  Model      3.81479355    1   3.81479355   3.93    0.0560
  telonuse   3.81479355    1   3.81479355   3.93    0.0560
  Residual   31.0458411   32   .970182533
  Total      34.8606346   33   1.05638287
```

SIDEBAR 1.2
STATISTICAL OUTPUT SUMMARY SHEET

Date: 01/03/2001
Directory: C:\my documents\data analysis book\example34\
Data File: bankdata34.dta
Procedure Files: *var.do (* = one, two, three, etc.)
Output Files: *var.log
Dependent Variable: *leffort*

Variables	Num Obs	Effect	Adj R²	Significance of Added Variable	Comments
1-variable models					
*lsize	34	+	0.64		
t14	34	–	0.36		
telonuse	34		0.08	.056	
2-variable models					
with *lsize*					
t14	34	–	0.73		best model, sign. = 0.0000
3-variable models					
with *lsize, t14*					
none significant					no further improvement possible

Once I have recorded all of the output in the summary sheet, I select the variable that explains the most variation in *leffort*. In this step, it is obviously *lsize*. There is no doubt about it. Then I ask myself: Does the relationship between *leffort* and *lsize* make sense? Does it correspond to the graph of *leffort* as a function of *lsize* (Figure 1.8)? Yes, it does, so I add *lsize* to the model and continue with the next step.

Determine Best Two-Variable Model   Next I want to determine which variable, *t13*, *t14*, *app*, or *telonuse*, in addition to *lsize*, explains the most variation in *leffort*. I add *lsize* to my regression and ANOVA procedures and run them again. I record the output in the same summary sheet (Sidebar1.2). What I am principally concerned with at this stage is if the additional variable is significant. So first I look at $P > |t|$ value of this variable. If it is not significant, I record nothing and move on to the next model.

In Example 1.16, I see that *t13* is not significant (0.595).

Example 1.16

```
. regress leffort lsize t13
```

Source	SS	df	MS		
Model	22.8042808	2	11.4021404		
Residual	12.0563538	31	.388914638		
Total	34.8606346	33	1.05638287		

Number of obs =		34
F(2,31)	=	29.32
Prob > F	=	0.0000
R-squared	=	0.6542
Adj R-squared =		0.6318
Root MSE	=	.62363

leffort	Coef.	Std. Err.	t	P>|t|	[95% Conf. Interval]	
lsize	.943487	.1243685	7.586	0.000	.6898359	1.197138
t13	-.0697449	.1297491	-0.538	0.595	-.33437	.1948801
_cons	3.151871	.7763016	4.060	0.000	1.568593	4.735149

In Example 1.17, I learn that *t14* is significant (0.002): *lsize* and *t14* together explain 73% of the variation in *leffort*. The coefficient of *t14* is a negative number. This means that *leffort* decreases with increasing *t14*. This is the same effect that we found in the one-variable model. If the effect was different in this model, that could signal something strange going on between *lsize* and *t13*, and I would look into their relationship more closely. *lsize* and the constant (*_cons*) are still significant. If they were not, I would note this in the *Comments* column. Again, this model was built using data from 34 projects.

Example 1.17

```
. regress leffort lsize t14
```

Source	SS	df	MS		
Model	25.9802069	2	12.9901035		
Residual	8.88042769	31	.286465409		
Total	34.8606346	33	1.05638287		

Number of obs =		**34**
F(2,31)	=	45.35
Prob > F	=	0.0000
R-squared	=	0.7453
Adj R-squared =		**0.7288**
Root MSE	=	.53522

leffort	Coef.	Std. Err.	t	P>|t|	[95% Conf. Interval]	
lsize	.7678266	.1148813	6.684	0.000	.5335247	1.002129
t14	-.3856721	.1138331	-3.388	0.002	-.6178361	-.153508
_cons	5.088876	.8764331	5.806	0.000	3.301379	6.876373

In Examples 1.18 and 1.19, I see that *app* and *telonuse* are not significant (0.6938 and 0.8876).

Example 1.18

. anova leffort lsize app, category (app)

Number of obs =   34   R-squared   = 0.6677
Root MSE   = .63204   Adj R-squared = 0.6218

Source	Partial SS	df	MS	F	Prob > F
Model	23.2758606	4	5.81896516	14.57	0.0000
lsize	22.5437265	1	22.5437265	56.43	0.0000
app	.583955179	3	.194651726	0.49	**0.6938**
Residual	11.584774	29	.399474964		
Total	34.8606346	33	1.05638287		

Example 1.19

. anova leffort lsize telonuse, category (telonuse)

Number of obs =   34   R-squared   = 0.6512
Root MSE   = .626325   Adj R-squared = 0.6287

Source	Partial SS	df	MS	F	Prob > F
Model	22.6998727	2	11.3499363	28.93	0.0000
lsize	18.8850791	1	18.8850791	48.14	0.0000
telonuse	.007967193	1	.007967193	0.02	**0.8876**
Residual	12.1607619	31	.392282644		
Total	34.8606346	33	1.05638287		

Again, the decision is obvious: The best two-variable model of *leffort* is *lsize* and *t14*. Does the relationship between *t14* and *leffort* make sense? Does it correspond to the graph of *leffort* as a function of *t14*? If yes, then we can build on this model.

Determine Best Three-Variable Model   Next I want to determine which variable, *t13*, *app*, or *telonuse*, in addition to *lsize* and *t14*, explains the most variation in *leffort*. I add *t14* to my regression and ANOVA procedures from the previous step and run them again. I record the output in the same summary sheet (Sidebar 1.2). As in the previous step, what I am principally concerned with at this stage is if the additional variable is significant. If it is not significant, I record nothing and move on to the next model. Let's look at the models (Examples 1.20, 1.21, and 1.22).

Example 1.20

. regress leffort lsize t14 t13

Source	SS	df	MS		Number of obs = 34
Model	26.0505804	3	8.68352679		F(3, 30) = 29.57
Residual	8.81005423	30	.293668474		Prob > F = 0.0000
					R-squared = 0.7473
Total	34.8606346	33	1.05638287		Adj R-squared = 0.7220
					Root MSE = .54191

leffort	Coef.	Std. Err.	t	P>|t|	[95% Conf. Interval]	
lsize	.7796095	.118781	6.563	0.000	.5370263	1.022193
t14	-.383488	.1153417	-3.325	0.002	-.6190471	-.1479289
t13	-.055234	.1128317	-0.490	**0.628**	-.285667	.175199
_cons	5.191477	.9117996	5.694	0.000	3.329334	7.05362

Example 1.21

. anova leffort lsize t14 app, category (app)

Number of obs = 34   R-squared   = 0.7478
Root MSE   = .560325   Adj R-squared = 0.7028

Source	Partial SS	df	MS	F	**Prob > F**
Model	26.0696499	5	5.21392998	16.61	0.0000
lsize	12.3571403	1	12.3571403	39.36	0.0000
t14	2.79378926	1	2.79378926	8.90	0.0059
app	.089442988	3	.029814329	0.09	**0.9622**
Residual	8.7909847	28	.313963739		
Total	34.8606346	33	1.05638287		

Example 1.22

. anova leffort lsize t14 telonuse, category(telonuse)

Number of obs = 34   R-squared   = 0.7487
Root MSE   = .540403   Adj R-squared = 0.7236

Source	Partial SS	df	MS	F	**Prob > F**
Model	26.099584	3	8.69986134	29.79	0.0000
lsize	12.434034	1	12.434034	42.58	0.0000
t14	3.39971135	1	3.39971135	11.64	0.0019
telonuse	.119377093	1	.119377093	0.41	**0.5274**
Residual	8.7610506	30	.29203502		
Total	34.8606346	33	1.05638287		

None of the additional variables in the three models (Examples 1.20, 1.21, and 1.22) are significant.

The Final Model The stepwise ANOVA procedure ends as no further improvement in the model is possible. The best model is the two-variable model: *leffort* as a function of *lsize* and *t14*. No categorical variables were significant in this example, so this model is the same model found by the automatic stepwise regression procedure. I check one final time that the relationships in the final model (Example 1.23) make sense. We see that *lsize* has a positive coefficient. This means that the bigger the application size, the greater the development effort required. Yes, this makes sense to me. I would expect bigger projects to require more effort. The coefficient of *t14*, staff tool skills, is negative. This means that effort decreases with increasing staff tool skills. Projects with very high staff tool skills required less effort than projects with very low staff tool skills, everything else being constant. Yes, this makes sense to me, too. Print the final model's output and save it.

Example 1.23

```
. regress leffort lsize t14
```

Source	SS	df	MS			Number of obs =	34
Model	25.9802069	2	12.9901035			F(2, 31) =	45.35
Residual	8.88042769	31	.286465409			**Prob > F** **= 0.0000**	
						R-squared =	0.7453
Total	34.8606346	33	1.05638287			Adj R-squared =	0.7288
						Root MSE =	.53522

leffort	**Coef.**	Std. Err.	t	P>|t|	[95% Conf.	Interval]
lsize	**.7678266**	.1148813	6.684	0.000	.5335247	1.002129
t14	**-.3856721**	.1138331	-3.388	0.002	-.6178361	-.153508
_cons	**5.088876**	.8764331	5.806	0.000	3.301379	6.876373

On the summary sheet, I note the significance of the final model. This is the *Prob > F* value at the top of the output. The model is significant at the 0.0000 level. This is Stata's way of indicating a number smaller than 0.00005. This means that there is less than a 0.005% chance that all the variables in the model (*lsize* and *t14*) are not related to *leffort*. (More information about how to interpret regression output can be found in Chapter 6.)

What to Watch Out For

- Be sure to use an ANOVA procedure that analyzes the variance of unbalanced data sets, that is, data sets that do not contain the same number of observations for each categorical value. I have yet to see a "balanced" software development database. In Stata, the procedure is called "ANOVA."

- Use the transformed variables in the model.
- Some models may contain variables with lots of missing values. It might be better to build on the second best model if it is based on more projects.
- If the decision is not obvious, follow more than one path to its final model (see Chapters 4 and 5). You will end up with more than one final model.
- Always ask yourself at each step if a model makes sense. If a model does not make sense, use the next best model.

Checking the Model

Before we can accept the final model found in the previous step, we must check that the assumptions underlying the statistical tests used have not been violated. In particular, this means checking that:

- Independent numerical variables are approximately normally distributed. (We did this in the preliminary analyses.)
- Independent variables are not strongly related to each other. (We did this partially during the preliminary analyses; now, we need to complete it.)
- The errors in our model should be random and normally distributed. (We still need to do this.)

In addition, we also need to check that no single project or small number of projects has an overly strong influence on the results.

Numerical Variable Checks

We already calculated the correlation coefficients of numerical variables in our preliminary analyses and noted them. Now that I have my final model, I need to check that all the independent numerical variables present in the final model are not strongly linearly related to each other. In other words, I need to check for multicollinearity problems. Why would this cause a problem? If two or more explanatory variables are very highly correlated, it is sometimes not possible for the statistical analysis software to separate their independent effects and you will end up with some strange results. Exactly when this will happen is not predictable. So, it is up to you to check the correlations between all numerical variables. Because my model only depends on *lsize* and *t14*, I just need to check their correlation with each other. To avoid multicollinearity problems, I do not allow any two variables with an absolute value of Spearman's rho greater than or equal to 0.75 in the final model together. From our preliminary correlation analysis, we learned that *size*[1] and *t14* are slightly negatively correlated; they have a significant Spearman's correlation coefficient of –0.3599. Thus, there are no multicollinearity problems with this model.

You should also be aware that there is always the possibility that a variable outside the analysis is really influencing the results. For example, let's say I have two variables, my weight and the outdoor temperature. I find that my weight increases when it is hot and decreases when it is cold. I develop a model that shows my weight as a function of outdoor temperature. If I did not use my common sense, I could even conclude that the high outdoor temperature causes my weight gain. However, there is an important variable that I did not collect which is the real cause of any weight gain or loss—my ice cream consumption. When it is hot outside, I eat more ice cream, and when it is cold, I eat much less. My ice cream consumption and the outdoor temperature are therefore highly correlated. The model should really be my weight as a function of my ice cream consumption. This model is also more useful because my ice cream consumption is within my control, whereas the outdoor temperature is not. In this case, the outdoor temperature is confounded[2] with my ice cream consumption and the only way to detect this is to think about the results. Always ask yourself if your results make sense and if there could be any other explanation for them. Unfortunately, we are less likely to ask questions and more likely to believe a result when it proves our point.

Categorical Variable Checks

Strongly related categorical variables can cause problems similar to those caused by numerical variables. Unfortunately, strong relationships involving categorical variables are much more difficult to detect. We do not have any categorical variables in our final effort model, so we do not need to do these checks for our example. However, **if** we had found that *telonuse* and *app* were both in the model, how would we check that they are not related to each other or to the numerical variables in the model?

To determine if there is a relationship between a categorical variable and a numerical variable, I use an analysis of variance procedure. Let's take *app* and *t14* in Example 1.24. Does *app* explain any variance in *t14*?

---

1. Remember that the Spearman's correlation coefficients of *size* and *t14*, and *lsize* and *t14*, are identical.
2. Confound means to mistake one variable's effect for another's.

Example 1.24

```
                        . anova t14 app
            Number of obs =      34    R-squared      = 0.1023
            Root MSE      =.894427    Adj R-squared = 0.0125
```

Source	Partial SS	df	MS	F	Prob > F
Model	2.73529412	3	.911764706	1.14	0.3489
app	2.73529412	3	.911764706	1.14	**0.3489**
Residual	24.00	30	.80		
Total	26.7352941	33	.810160428		

Example 1.24 shows that there is no significant relationship between *app* and *t14* (the *Prob > F* value for *app* is a number greater than 0.05). I run ANOVA procedures for every categorical/numerical variable combination in the final model. (Note that the numerical variable must be the dependent LHS variable.) If I find a very strong relationship, I will not include the two variables together in the same model. I define "very strong relationship" as one variable explaining more than 75% of the variation in another.

I would like to point out here that we can get a pretty good idea about which variables are related to each other just by looking at the list of variables that are significant at each step as we build the one-variable, two-variable, three-variable, etc. models. In the statistical output sheet, Sidebar 1.2, we see that *telonuse* is an important variable in the one-variable model. However, once *lsize* has been added to the model, *telonuse* does not appear in the two-variable model. This means that there is probably a relationship between *telonuse* and *lsize*. Let's check (Example 1.25):

Example 1.25

```
                        . anova lsize telonuse
            Number of obs =      34    R-squared      = 0.1543
            Root MSE      =.832914    Adj R-squared = 0.1279
```

Source	Partial SS	df	MS	F	Prob > F
Model	4.04976176	1	4.04976176	5.84	0.0216
telonuse	4.04976176	1	4.04976176	5.84	**0.0216**
Residual	22.1998613	32	.693745665		
Total	26.2496231	33	.795443123		

Yes, there is a significant relationship between *lsize* and *telonuse*. The use of Telon explains about 13% of the variance in *lsize*. Example 1.26 shows that applications that used Telon were much bigger than applications that did not. So, the larger effort required by applications that used Telon (Example 1.5) may not be due to Telon use per se, but because the applications were bigger. Once size has been added to the effort model, Telon use is no longer important; size is a much more important driver of effort. I learn as I analyze. Had this all been done automatically, I may not have noticed this relationship.

Example 1.26

```
              . table telonuse, c(mean size)

Telon Use        mean(size)
No                      455
Yes                    1056
```

It is more difficult to determine if there is an important relationship between two categorical variables. To check this, I first calculate the chi-square statistic to test for independence. From this I learn if there is a significant relationship between two categorical variables, but not the extent of the relationship. (You will learn more about the chi-square test in Chapter 6.) In Example 1.27, I am interested in the *Pr* value (in bold). *Pr* is the probability that we are making a mistake if we say that there is a relationship between two variables. If the value of *Pr* is less than or equal to 0.05, we can accept that there is a relationship between the two variables. Here, *Pr* = 0.069, so I conclude that there is no significant relationship between the two variables.

Example 1.27

```
            . tabulate app telonuse, chi2

Application Type       Telon Use
                      No      Yes        Total
     CustServ          6        0            6
     MIS               3        0            3
     TransPro         16        4           20
     InfServ           2        3            5
     Total            27        7           34
```
              Pearson chi2(3) = 7.0878   **Pr = 0.069**

If there is a significant relationship, I need to look closely at the two variables and judge for myself if they are so strongly related that there could be a problem. For example, if application type (*app*) and Telon use (*telonuse*) had been significantly related, I would first look closely at Example 1.27. There I would learn that no customer service (*CustServ*) or *MIS* application used

Telon. Of the seven projects that used Telon, there is a split between transaction processing (*TransPro*) applications (a high-effort category; see Example 1.4) and information service (*InfServ*) applications (a low-effort category). Thus, the high effort for Telon use (see Example 1.5) is not due to an over-representation of high-effort transaction processing applications. In fact, the majority of projects that did not use Telon are transaction processing applications. I conclude that any relationship between Telon use and effort cannot be explained by the relationship between application type and Telon use; i.e. application type and Telon use are not confounded.

If I find any problems in the final model, I return to the step where I added the correlated/confounded variable to the variables already present in the model, take the second best choice, and rebuild the model from there. I do not carry out any further checks. The model is not valid, so there is no point. We have to start again. (See Chapter 5 for an example of confounded categorical variables.)

Testing the Residuals

In a well-fitted model, there should be no pattern to the errors (residuals) plotted against the fitted values. The term "fitted value" refers to the *leffort* predicted by our model; the term "residual" is used to express the difference between the actual *leffort* and the predicted *leffort* for each project. Your statistical analysis tool should calculate the predicted values and residuals automatically for you. The errors of our model should be random. For example, we should not be consistently overestimating small efforts and underestimating large efforts. It is always a good idea to plot this relationship and take a look. If you see a pattern, it means that there is a problem with your model. If there is a problem with the final model, then try the second best model. If there is a problem with the second best model, then try the third best model, and so on. In Figure 1.12, I see no pattern in the residuals of our final model.

In addition, the residuals should be normally distributed. We can see in Figure 1.13 that they are approximately normally distributed. You will learn more about residuals in Chapter 6.

Detecting Influential Observations

How much is our final model affected by any one project or subset of our data? If we dropped one project from our database, would our model be completely different? I certainly hope not. But we can do better than hope; we can check the model's sensitivity to individual observations. Projects

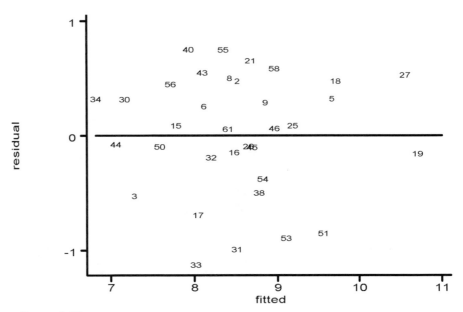

FIGURE 1.12
Residuals vs. fitted values

with large predicted errors (residuals) and/or projects very different from other project's values for at least one of the independent variables in the model can exert undue influence on the model (leverage).

Cook's distance summarizes information about residuals and leverage into a single statistic. Cook's distance can be calculated for each project by dropping that project and re-estimating the model without it. My statistical analysis tool does this automatically. Projects with values of Cook's distance, D, greater than $4/n$ should be examined closely (n is the number of observations). In our example, $n = 34$, so we are interested in projects for which $D > 0.118$. I find that one project, 51, has a Cook's distance of 0.147 (Example 1.28).

Example 1.28

```
. list id size effort t14 cooksd if cooksd>4/34

          id     size     effort     t14      cooksd
   28.     51     1526      5931        3     .1465599
```

Why do I use Cook's distance? I use it because my statistical analysis tool calculates it automatically after ANOVA procedures. Other statistics, DFITS and Welsch distance, for instance, also summarize residual and leverage

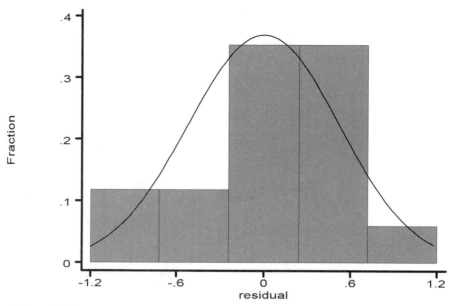

FIGURE 1.13
Distribution of residuals

information in a single value. Of course, the cut-off values are different for DIFTS and Welsh distance. Do not complicate your life; use the influence statistic that your statistical analysis tool provides.[3]

Referring back to Figure 1.8, I see that the influence of Project 51 is due to its effort being slightly low for its size compared to other projects, so it must be pulling down the regression line slightly (leverage problem). After looking closely at this project, I see no reason to drop it from the analysis. The data is valid, and given the small number of large projects we have, we cannot say that it is an atypical project. If we had more data, we could, in all likelihood, find more projects like it. In addition, 0.15 is not that far from the 0.12 cut-off value.

If a project was exerting a very high influence, I would first try to understand why. Is the project special in any way? I would look closely at the data and discuss the project with anyone who remembered it. Even if the project is not special, if the Cook's distance is more than three times larger than the cut-off value, I would drop the project and develop an alternative model using the reduced data set. Then I would compare the two models to better understand the impact of the project.

---

3. If you use Stata, see the "fit" procedure for these and other diagnostics.

Extracting the Equation

Our model has passed all our checks. So far, everything has been calculated automatically. We have not been forced to extract the equation and calculate effort ourselves. What is the actual equation? From the final model (Example 1.23), I see that the equation to calculate *leffort* is:

$$ln\,(\mathit{effort}) = 5.088876 + 0.7678266 \times ln\,(\mathit{size}) - 0.3856721 \times t14$$

How did I read the equation off the output? The equation is a linear equation of the form $y = a + bx_1 + cx_2$. y is $ln(\mathit{effort})$, x_1 is $ln(\mathit{size})$, and x_2 is $t14$. a, b, and c are the coefficients (*Coef.*) from the output. The constant (*_cons*), a, is 5.088876, the coefficient of $ln\,(\mathit{size})$, b, is 0.7678266, and the coefficient of $t14$, c, is –0.3856721.

In a presentation or report, I give the results in the form of an equation for *effort*, not $ln\,(\mathit{effort})$. I find it is easier for people to understand. Keep in mind that most people don't want to know how you analyzed the data or the equation; they just want to know the management implications. I almost never include an equation in an oral presentation. By all means, prepare some slides about the methodology and the equation, but do not show them unless specifically asked to go into the details in public.

To transform $ln\,(\mathit{effort})$ into *effort*, I take the inverse natural log (or e) of each side of the equation. To do this accurately, I use all seven significant digits of the coefficients from the output. However, when I present the equation, I round the transformed coefficients to four digits. This results in about a 0.025% difference in total predicted *effort* (between a one- to two-hour difference) in this example compared with using the seven-digit coefficients. Rounding the coefficients to two digits resulted in a 100-hour difference in predicted *effort* for some projects in this sample, which I consider unacceptable. If I were to use the equation in practice to calculate *effort*, I would retain all seven significant digits. Try to always simplify as much as possible what you present to others, but be sure to use all the accuracy of the initial equations for your own calculations.

$$\mathit{effort} = 162.2074 \times \mathit{size}^{0.7678} \times e^{-0.3857 \times t14}$$

To prove to yourself that these two equations are the same, transform the *effort* equation back to the initial $ln(\mathit{effort})$ equation by taking the ln of both sides and applying the following three rules from algebra:

$$ln(xyz) = ln(x) + ln(y) + ln(z), \quad ln(x)^a = aln(x), \quad \text{and} \quad ln(e) = 1$$

In Chapters 3, 4, and 5, you will see how to extract the equation from models that include categorical variables. The impact of categorical variables in an equation is simply to modify the constant term (a).

Final Comments

Now that you've learned the basics of my methodology for analyzing software project data, you are ready to attack some more complicated databases. In the following four case studies (Chapters 2-5), you will learn how to deal with common problems that occur when analyzing software project data (see Table 1.3). You will also learn how to interpret data analysis results and turn them into management implications.

TABLE 1.3
Common Problems and Where to Learn How to Deal with Them

	Chapter 2 Productivity	Chapter 3 Time to Market	Chapter 4 Development Cost	Chapter 5 Maintenance Cost
Detecting invalid data	X			
Transforming data before use	X			X
Categories with too few observations	X		X	X
Outliers	X			
Choice of best model not obvious		X	X	X
Relationships that don't make sense	X	X	X	
Confounded categorical variables				X
Choosing baseline categorical variables				X
Influential observations	X	X	X	X

Case Study: Software Development Productivity

Many companies would like to benchmark the software development productivity of their projects. If your company has a well-established metrics program and a high project turnover, you have a definite advantage. You can benchmark your projects internally and avoid many of the measurement comparability problems associated with multi-company databases. In addition, through the analysis of your own software project data, you can identify the factors that influence the productivity of projects in **your** company. You may find that some of these important factors are given and unchangeable; for example, certain applications of a particular type may always be more difficult and associated with low productivity ratings. However, some variables, such as choice of tool, may be within your control. Learn as much as you can from your valuable data. Use this knowledge to guide, and defend, your future actions. Always keep in mind that data collection and analysis should be tied to business as well as technical goals. Recommendations backed up by hard data carry more weight with upper management.

In this chapter, you will learn how to determine which variables explain the productivity differences among software development applications. To do this, I will show you how I analyzed real data from one bank. The initial database contained 29 variables for 63 completed software development applications (see Appendix A).

Data Validation

As the project data had already been entered into a software management data collection tool, which included definitions of all the variables, I did not have to spend too much time trying to understand the data and correcting mistakes. (See Chapter 5 for an example where this was not the case.) The bank collected this data to help manage project portfolios. The project's manager provided data at the end of each project. One person entered all project data into the database and validated it. In addition to the data file, I received a copy of the Experience software tool (*www.sttf.fi*), a database parameter file, and a productivity factor definition file. The database parameter file defined each categorical variable value's code. For example, *app = 406* corresponded to a transaction processing application. Nonetheless, an initial face-to-face meeting with the data provider was necessary to fully understand everything I was given. I then consolidated all the information I needed to understand the data into a variable definition table (Table 2.1).

TABLE 2.1
Variable Definitions

Variable	Full Name	Definition
id	identification number	Each completed project has a unique identification number. (Originally, each project was given a name instead of a number, but I replaced these names for data confidentiality reasons.)
size	application size	Function points measured using the Experience method.
effort	effort	Work carried out by the software supplier from specification until delivery, measured in hours.
duration	duration	Duration of project from specification until delivery, measured in months.
start	exact start date	Month/day/year application specification started.
app	application type	401 = Customer service (CustServ)[1] 402 = Management information system (MIS)

[1] *The text in parentheses is the category definition's abbreviation in the statistical output (maximum length of eight characters).*

Variable	Full Name	Definition
		406 = Transaction processing (TransPro) 407 = Production control, logistics, order processing (ProdCont) 408 = Information/on-line service (InfServ)
har	hardware platform	1001 = Networked (Network) 1002 = Mainframe (Mainfrm) 1003 = Personal computer (PC) 1004 = Mini computer (Mini) 1005 = Multi-platform (Multi)
dba	DBMS architecture	1602 = Relational (Relatnl) 1604 = Other (Other) 1605 = Sequential (Sequentl)
ifc	user interface	2001 = Graphical user interface (GUI) 2002 = Text user interface (TextUI)
source	where developed	7001 = In-house (Inhouse) 7004 = Outsourced (Outsrced)
lan1	language used	Up to four languages were used per application. They could be used in any order; thus, lan1 is not necessarily the most important language. Too many codes to list here; however, codes
lan2 *lan3* *lan4*	language used language used language used	of special interest include: 2617 = COBOL 2660 = Telon

t01	customer
	participation
		How actively customer took part in
		development work:
		1 = Very low; none
		2 = Low; passive; client defined or approved
		  <30% of all functions
		3 = Nominal; client defined and approved
		  30-70% of all functions
		4 = High; active; client defined and approved
		  all of most important functions, and over
		  70% of others

Continued

TABLE 2.1 (*Continued*)

Variable	Full Name	Definition
		5 = Very high; client participated very actively, thus most functions were slightly volatile and changes had to be made
t02	development environment adequacy	Performance level of tool resources and equipment during project: 1 = Very low; continuous shortcomings in devices, building of test environments and testing required special arrangements 2 = Low; shared equipment/machine resources; delays in some work stages (e.g., compiling and testing) 3 = Nominal; enough during development work; a workstation for everybody 4 = High; enough to deal with capacity peaks (efficiency, storage, response time) 5 = Very high; dedicated, over-dimensioned development environments, in practice only for this project
t03	staff availability	Availability of software personnel during project: 1 = Very low; big problems with key personnel availability; lots of simultaneous customer and maintenance responsibilities; special know-how required 2 = Low; personnel involved in some other simultaneous projects and/or maintenance responsibilities 3 = Nominal; key members involved in only one other project 4 = High; project members involved almost full-time 5 = Very high; qualified personnel available when needed; full-time participation
t04	standards use	Level and use of standards: 1 = Very low; standards developed during project 2 = Low; some standards, but not familiar ones; more must be developed for some tasks

Variable	Full Name	Definition
		3 = Nominal; generally known standards applied in environment before; some tailoring needed 4 = High; detailed standards applied in same environment for some time 5 = Very high; stable and detailed standards; already familiar to team; use controlled
t05	methods use	Level and use of methods: 1 = Very low; no modern design methods; mostly meetings; used by individuals 2 = Low; use beginning; traditional concepts employed (structural analysis and design, top-down design, etc.) 3 = Nominal; generally known methods used 4 = High; methods integrated in detail and most activities covered; support existed; used by everyone 5 = Very high; methods used during entire lifecycle; methods tailored for specific needs of project; methods supported for individual projects
t06	tools use	Level and use of tools: 1 = Very low; minimal tools: editors, compilers, and testing tools 2 = Low; basic tools: interpreters, editors, compilers, debuggers, databases, and libraries 3 = Nominal; development environment, database management system (DBMS), and support for most phases 4 = High; modern tools like CASE, project planners, application generators, and standardized interfaces between phases 5 = Very high; integrated CASE environment over entire lifecycle; all tools support each other
t07	software's logical complexity	Computing, I/O needs, and user interface requirements: 1 = Very low; only routines; no need for user interface; simple databases 2 = Low; functionally clear; no algorithmic tasks; database solution clear

Continued

TABLE 2.1 *(Continued)*

Variable	Full Name	Definition
		3 = Nominal; functionally typical; normal, standard database; no algorithms
		4 = High; processing more demanding; database large and complex; new requirements for user interfaces
		5 = Very high; functionally and technically difficult solution; user interface very complex; distributed databases
t08	requirements volatility	Volatility of customer/user requirements during project: 1 = Very low; no new features; standard components; conversions only 2 = Low; some changes to specifications; some new or adapted functions; some minor changes in data contents 3 = Nominal; more changes to specifications, but project members could handle them; impact minor (<15% new or modified functions) 4 = High; some major changes affecting total architecture and requiring rework; 15-30% of functions new or modified 5 = Very high; new requirements added continuously; lots of rework; more than 30% new or modified functions compared to original requirements
t09	quality requirements	Quality goals of software: 1 = Very low; no quality requirements; "quick-and-dirty" allowed 2 = Low; basic requirements satisfied (documentation, implementation testing, system testing, and module testing); no statistical controls or reviews 3 = Nominal; proper documentation of critical features; design- and implementation-tested; modules/job flows tested; walkthroughs; maintenance work planned 4 = High; formal reviews and inspections between all phases; attention to documentation, usability, and maintenance

Variable	Full Name	Definition
		5 = Very high; quantified quality requirements; 100% satisfaction of technical and functional goals; maintenance work minimal
$t10$	efficiency requirements	Efficiency goals of software: 1 = Very low; no efficiency requirements needing attention or planning 2 = Low; efficiency goals easy to reach; requirements below average 3 = Nominal; capacity level of software stable and predictable; response time, transaction load, and turnaround time typical 4 = High; specific peaks in capacity, response time, transaction processing, and turnaround time reached by specific design and implementation techniques 5 = Very high; efficiency essential; strict efficiency goals needing continuous attention and specific skills
$t11$	installation requirements	Training needs for users and variants of platform: 1 = Very low; no training needs; <10 users 2 = Low; some training; about 10 users; creation of basic data only minor 3 = Nominal; typical training; 10-50 users; some conversions of old data 4 = High; large-scale training for several organizations; <1000 users; extra software for conversions; possible parallel runs; several platforms 5 = Very high; >1,000 users; long expected lifetime; several user organizations; several different platforms
$t12$	staff analysis skills	Analysis skills of project staff at kick-off: 1 = Very low; no experience in requirements analysis or similar projects 2 = Low; <30% of project staff with analysis and design experience in similar projects 3 = Nominal; 30-70% of project staff with analysis experience; one experienced member

Continued

TABLE 2.1 (*Continued*)

Variable	Full Name	Definition
		4 = High; most members of staff with experience in specifications and analysis; analysis professional in charge 5 = Very high; project staff composed of first-class professionals; members have strong vision and experience with requirements analysis
t13	staff application knowledge	Knowledge of application domain in project team (supplier and customer): 1 = Very low; team application experience <6 months on average 2 = Low; application experience low; some members have experience; 6-12 months on average 3 = Nominal; application experience good; 1-3 years on average 4 = High; application experience good both at supplier and customer sites; 3-6 years on average; business dynamics known 5 = Very high; both supplier and customer know application area well, including the business; >6 years' average experience
t14	staff tool skills	Experience level of project team (supplier and customer) with development and documentation tools at project kick-off: 1 = Very low; team has no experience in necessary tools; team's average experience <6 months 2 = Low; tools experience less than average; some members have experience with some tools; 6-12 months on average 3 = Nominal; tools experience good in about half the team; some members know development and documentation tools well; 1-3 years on average 4 = High; most team members know tools well; some members can help others; 3-6 years on average 5 = Very high; team knows all tools well; support available for specific needs of project; >6 years' average experience

Variable	Full Name	Definition
t15	staff team skills	Ability of project team to work effectively according to best project practices: 1 = Very low; scattered team; minimal project and management skills 2 = Low; some members with previous experience on similar projects; not united as a group 3 = Nominal; most members with experience on similar projects; commitment on project goals good; no motivation to utilize real team spirit 4 = High; group very active and knows how to exploit team effectiveness 5 = Very high; very anticipatory team; team can solve in an innovative way most personal and team problems; superior spirit

Once I understood the variable definitions, I was ready to start my analysis. First, I used the summary function (Example 2.1) to quickly see if there were any missing values, to check that the values made sense, and to begin understanding the data better.

Example 2.1

```
                              .  summarize[2]
    Variable        Obs         Mean      Std. Dev.        Min         Max
    id               63           32        18.3303          1          63
    size             63      671.3968       777.3081         48        3634
    effort           63      8109.54        10453.89        583       63694
    duration         63      17.15873       10.57265          4          54
    app              63      404.6825       2.693034        401         408
    har              63      1002.714       1.419093       1001        1005
    dba              61      1602.082       .4580787       1602        1605
    ifc              63      2001.921       .2724789       2001        2002
    source           63      7001.429       1.058213       7001        7004
    lan1             61      2616.754       9.406834       2601        2660
    lan2             52      2635.019       18.33938       2601        2668
    lan3             32      2645.313       13.41265       2617        2660
    lan4             13      2653.385       10.1451        2622        2660
    t01              63      3.079365       1.020777          1           5
    t02              63      3.047619       .7054756          1           5
    t03              63      3.031746       .8793006          2           5
```

2. *start* is not included because it has a date format.

t04	63	3.174603	.7080114	2	5
t05	63	3.047619	.7054756	1	5
t06	63	2.920635	.7025664	1	4
t07	63	3.253968	.8974562	1	5
t08	63	3.809524	.9479544	2	5
t09	63	4.047619	.749808	2	5
t10	63	3.603175	.8897206	2	5
t11	63	3.396825	.9925478	2	5
t12	63	3.825397	.6848518	2	5
t13	63	3.063492	.9482244	1	5
t14	63	3.285714	1.022782	1	5
t15	63	3.333333	.7405316	1	5

The minimum (*Min*) and maximum (*Max*) values for all of the variables make sense. There are no strange numbers for which I have no definition. I note that some of the productivity factors do not use the full range from 1 through 5 and are missing either the very low or very high values. This is probably because these values would never be allowed in banking applications. The summary statistics for size, effort, and duration are of special interest. The size of projects in this database range from 48 function points to 3634 function points; the average project size is 671 function points. Effort ranges from 583 hours to 63694 hours, with an average of 8110 hours. Project duration ranges from 4 months to 54 months; the average project duration is 17 months.

Whatever we are going to find out from our data analysis, it is important to remember that it is only true for similar projects, that is, projects with sizes, efforts, and durations within the domain of this database. My conclusions will not apply to projects in this bank that are smaller than 48 function points, or that used less than 583 hours of effort, or that were less than four months in duration. They will also not apply to projects bigger than 3634 function points, or projects that used more than 63694 hours of effort, or projects longer than 54 months in duration.

Some variables, *dba* and *lan1-4*, for example, have missing values. The DBMS architecture (*dba*) is missing for two projects. It also looks as though two projects do not have any language data. On closer inspection of the data, I found out that Project 12, which does not have a value for *lan1*, does have one for *lan2*. Project 24 has no language at all. I contacted the data provider for more information. First of all, I learned that the two projects with a missing *dba* value were "client application" development projects and did not have a database. Thus, they did not have any DBMS architecture. So in this case, missing data means "none." I was told that the project with no language at all actually used a development tool called *Clipper*. It had not been entered in the database because it was not one of the choices in the list.

I created a new code, *2670*, for *Clipper*. Finally, I learned that for the project with a *lan2* and no *lan1*, there was only one language used, the language listed in *lan2*. Until this conversation, I had assumed that *lan1* was the most important language, *lan2* the second most important language, etc.; however, I learned that this was not the case. The languages were input in any order, not in order of importance. There was no information about the percentage use of each language. This was bad news for me; from previous research, I knew that language was important and it would have been interesting to look at the effect of language on productivity in the bank. I was planning to use *lan1* as the principal language to do this.

Variable and Model Selection

Now that the data has been validated, we can proceed to Step 2 of our recipe, variable and model selection, which includes the creation of new variables, data modifications, identification of categorical variables subsets, and the selection of the model to be studied.

Creation of New Variables

Because I couldn't make use of the language variable in the traditional way, I needed to find a way to transform the language information I did have into something useful. First, I decided to try grouping projects that used the same combinations of languages together. I found 32 different language combinations for 63 projects. This meant that, on average, there were two projects per language combination—not enough to make any meaningful conclusions. In addition, most language combinations containing enough observations to analyze used COBOL, so perhaps they weren't really that different. I then decided it might be interesting to see if productivity was different for projects that used one language, two languages, three languages, or four languages, so I created the variable *nlan*—number of languages used. I thought that perhaps it might be less productive to use many languages in a project. In addition, as some research has suggested that using Telon can improve productivity, I decided to create a new categorical variable, *telonuse*, which was 1 if Telon was one of the languages used and 0 if it was not.

I also created the following new variables:

- *syear*—As it could be interesting to see if productivity had increased or decreased over time, I decided to create one new variable by extracting the year from the exact start date of the project. I used this variable for making graphs and tables.

- *time*—This is the variable I used in the regression and ANOVA models to represent time. I calculated it from the start year:

$$time = syear - 1985 + 1$$

  thus *time* is 1 in 1985, 2 in 1986, etc. Why do I do this? Why not just put *syear* in the models? First of all, it is common practice in time series analysis to do this. It is not the actual year that matters, just the fact that a year is one year more than the previous year (or one year less than the following year). In addition, should I have to transform *syear* by taking its natural log, *ln*, I will find that the natural logs of large numbers like 1985, 1986, etc. are not very different (*ln*(1985) = 7.5934; *ln*(1990) = 7.5959, *ln*(1993) = 7.5973). It will look like time does not vary very much. This will have a bizarre influence on the results. The logs of smaller numbers are more differentiated. In addition, if time has an exponential effect on productivity and I try to calculate e^{syear}, I will get a number so big that it will overload the computer.

- *prod*—If I want to study productivity, I must have a variable that measures productivity. Productivity is typically defined as output divided by the effort required to produce that output. Although not perfect, application size is traditionally used to measure the output of a software project. Thus:

$$prod = size/effort$$

Data Modifications

Before analyzing the data further, I corrected the data, added the new variables I created, and replaced the meaningless (to me) categorical variable codes with more meaningful words (see Appendix B). I did this by attaching descriptive labels to each value using my statistical analysis tool.[3] The labels are automatically printed on the tables and graphs of the statistical output instead of the variable code, making it easier for me to interpret the output.

Identifying Subsets of Categorical Variables

Because the categorical variables are actually numbers in the database, I did not need to tabulate them to check their spelling in the data validation step. However, because I want to know the number of projects in each category, I will print them out now (Example 2.2).

---

3. See the label command in Stata.

Example 2.2

```
                    . tabulate app

    Application Type    Freq.      Percent      Cum.
    CustServ            .  18       28.57       28.57
    MIS                    4         6.35       34.92
    TransPro              29        46.03       80.95
    ProdCont               1         1.59       82.54
    InfServ               11        17.46      100.00

    Total                 63       100.00
```

We can see that nearly half of the projects were transaction processing (*TransPro*) applications. There was only one production control (*ProdCont*) application in this database. As I do not believe that one project is enough to base any conclusions on, I will create a subset of application type (*subapp*), which excludes the *ProdCont* application type. As a rule of thumb, I exclude any category with less than three observations.

Example 2.3

```
                    . tabulate har

    Hardware Type    Freq.      Percent      Cum.
    Network             7        11.11       11.11
    Mainfrm            37        58.73       69.84
    PC                  2         3.17       73.02
    Mini                1         1.59       74.60
    Multi              16        25.40      100.00

    Total              63       100.00
```

As shown in Example 2.3, the majority of projects were mainframe (*Mainfrm*) applications. Because the personal computer (*PC*) and mini computer (*Mini*) categories do not include enough observations to be analyzed, I will create a subset of hardware type (*subhar*), which excludes these categories.

Example 2.4

```
                    . tabulate dba

    DBMS
    Architecture    Freq.      Percent      Cum.
    None               2         3.17        3.17
    Relatnl           59        93.65       96.83
    Other              1         1.59       98.41
    Sequentl           1         1.59      100.00

    Total             63       100.00
```

Example 2.4 shows that nearly all the applications used a relational DBMS architecture (*Relatnl*). It is impossible to look at the effect on productivity due to changes in this variable. Thus, I decided to drop the variable *dba* from my analysis.

Example 2.5

```
                          . tabulate ifc

        User Interface     Freq     Percent      Cum.
        GUI                   5        7.94       7.94
        TextUI               58       92.06     100.00
        Total                63      100.00
```

Example 2.5 shows that most projects used a text user interface (*TextUI*).

Example 2.6

```
                         . tabulate source

        Where Developed    Freq.    Percent      Cum.
        Inhouse              54       85.71      85.71
        Outsrced              9       14.29     100.00
        Total                63      100.00
```

From Example 2.6, we see that most projects were developed in-house (*Inhouse*); 14% of the projects were outsourced (*Outsrced*).

Example 2.7

```
                        . tabulate telonuse

        Telon Use      Freq.     Percent       Cum.
        No                48       76.19       76.19
        Yes               15       23.81      100.00
        Total             63      100.00
```

Nearly 24% of the applications were developed using Telon (Example 2.7).

Only hardware platform and application type required the creation of new variables, *subhar* and *subapp*, which are subsets of the original variables. Table 2.2 summarizes all of the new variables I added to the original database.

TABLE 2.2
Summary of Variables Created

Variable	Full Name	Definition
nlan	number of different development languages used	1 = One language used 2 = Two languages used 3 = Three languages used 4 = Four languages used
telonuse	Telon use	0 = No 1 = Yes
syear	start year of project	1985-1993
time	time	*time = syear – 1985 + 1*
prod	productivity	*prod = size/effort* (in units of function points per hour)
subapp	subset application type	Contains categories with three or more observations
subhar	subset hardware platform	Contains categories with three or more observations

I also printed out the summary data for the new numerical variables (Example 2.8). Productivity (*prod*) ranged from approximately 0.03 function points per hour to 0.53 function points per hour; the average productivity was 0.11 function points/hour.

Example 2.8

```
            . summarize nlan syear time prod

Variable    Obs       Mean     Std. Dev.       Min         Max
nlan         63    2.52381     1.029518           1           4
syear        63   1989.603     2.121622        1985        1993
time         63   5.603175     2.121622           1           9
prod         63   .1080363     .0787779    .0264517    .5291902
```

Model Selection

My goal in this study is to determine which variables explain the productivity differences among software development projects in this bank.

$$prod = f(size,\ effort,\ duration,\ subapp,\ subhar,\ ifc,\ source,$$
$$t01\text{-}t15,\ nlan,\ telonuse,\ time)$$

What are the relationships between productivity (*prod*) and application size (*size*), the amount of effort spent (*effort*), the duration of a project (*duration*), the type of application (*subapp*), the type of hardware (*subhar*), the user interface (*ifc*), whether or not the development was outsourced (*source*), the 15 different productivity factors (*t01-t15*), the number of languages used (*nlan*), whether or not Telon was used (*telonuse*), and time (*time*)?

Preliminary Analyses

In all the case studies, the assumption is that you are already familiar with my data analysis methodology presented in Chapter 1. The focus in the case studies is on **interpreting** the output results.

Graphs

I always look at two types of graphs: histograms and two-dimensional graphs.

Histograms   Effort, size, duration, and productivity are not normally distributed (Figures 2.1 through 2.4). To approximate the normal distribution, I must transform these variables by taking their natural log (see Chapter 1). These transformed variables more closely approximate a normal distribution (Figures 2.5 through 2.8).

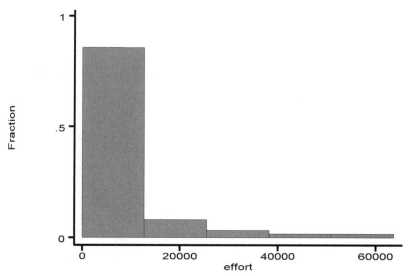

FIGURE 2.1
Distribution of *effort*

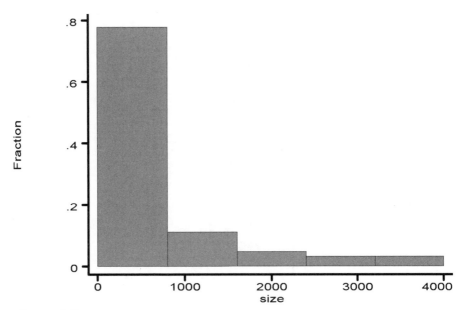

FIGURE 2.2
Distribution of *size*

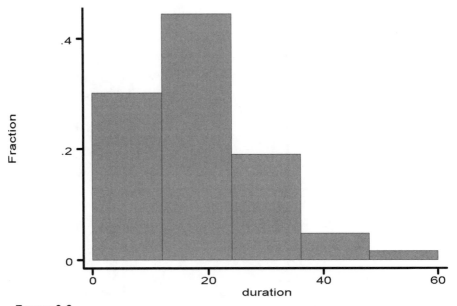

FIGURE 2.3
Distribution of *duration*

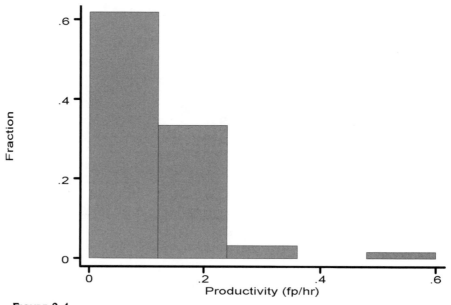

FIGURE 2.4
Distribution of *prod*

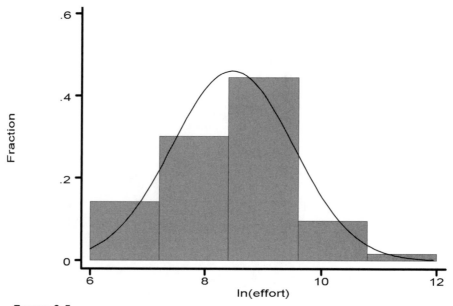

FIGURE 2.5
Distribution of *ln(effort)*

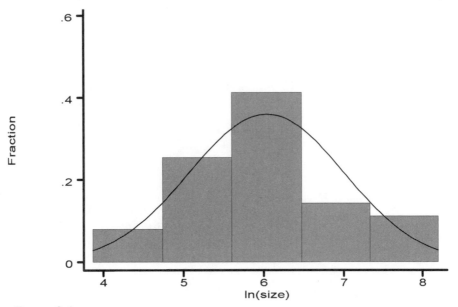

FIGURE 2.6
Distribution of *ln(size)*

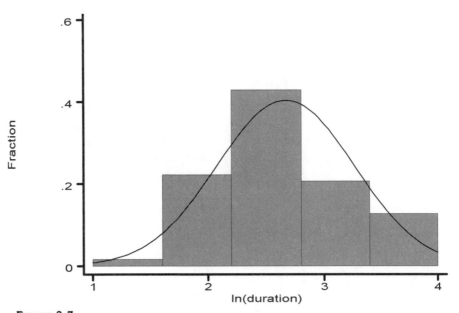

FIGURE 2.7
Distribution of *ln(duration)*

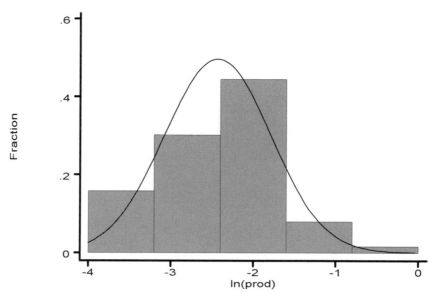

FIGURE 2.8
Distribution of *ln(prod)*

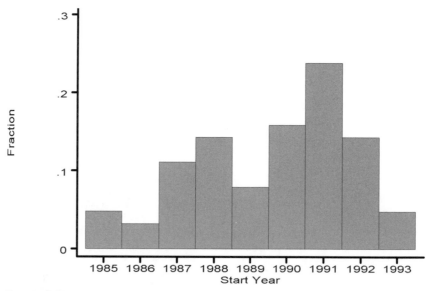

FIGURE 2.9
Distribution of *syear*

About 25% of the applications started development in 1991 (Figure 2.9). Most projects used two or three development languages (Figure 2.10); many used one or two.

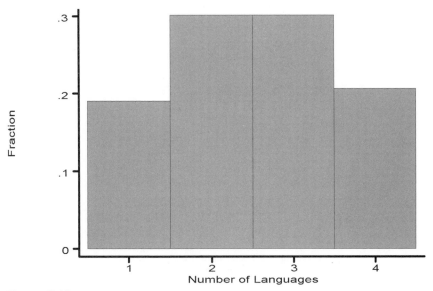

FIGURE 2.10
Distribution of *nlan*

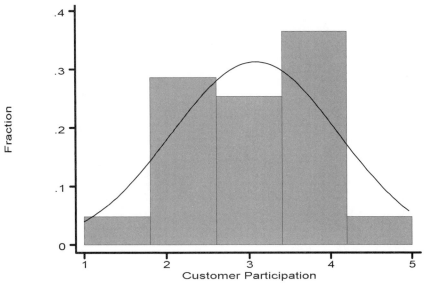

FIGURE 2.11
Distribution of *t01*

The productivity factors are approximately normally distributed in the sample (Figures 2.11 through 2.25). The definitions of these factors were chosen especially so that most projects from a diverse group of companies and

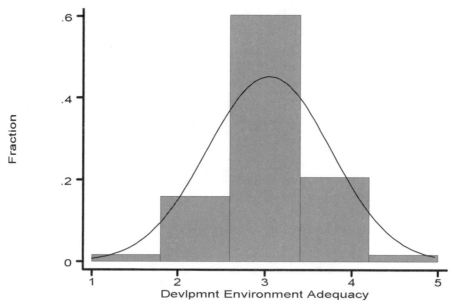

FIGURE 2.12
Distribution of *t02*

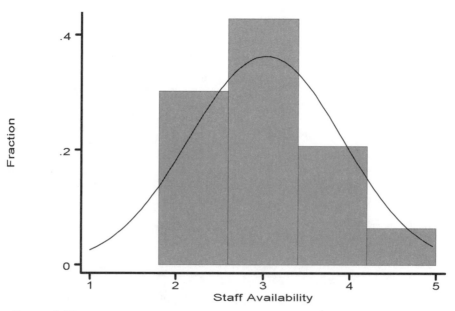

FIGURE 2.13
Distribution of *t03*

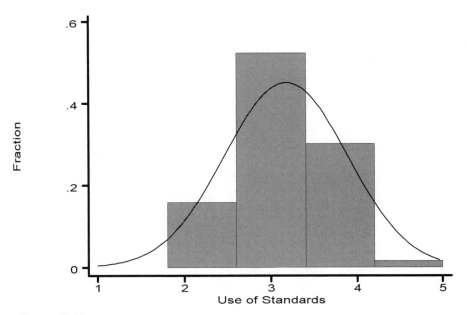

FIGURE 2.14
Distribution of *t04*

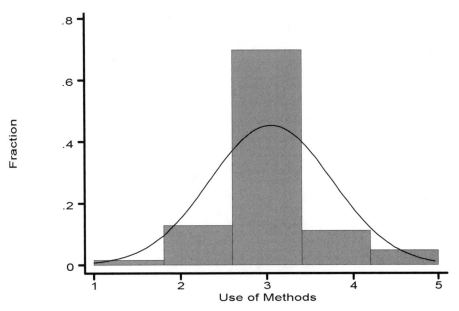

FIGURE 2.15
Distribution of *t05*

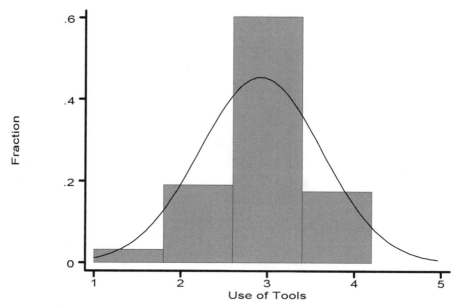

FIGURE 2.16
Distribution of *t06*

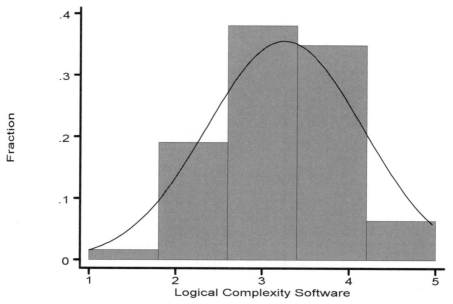

FIGURE 2.17
Distribution of *t07*

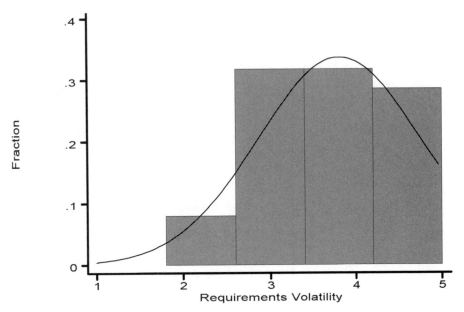

FIGURE 2.18
Distribution of *t08*

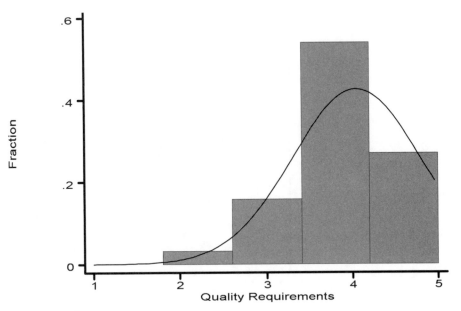

FIGURE 2.19
Distribution of *t09*

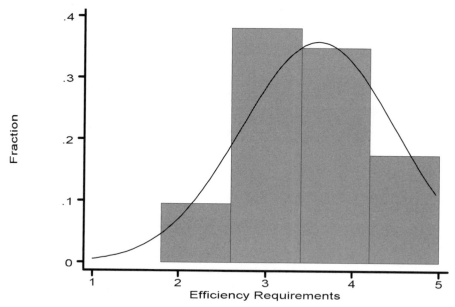

FIGURE 2.20
Distribution of *t10*

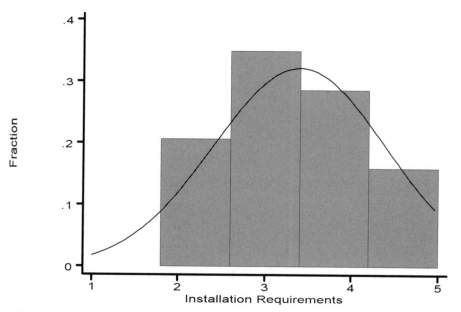

FIGURE 2.21
Distribution of *t11*

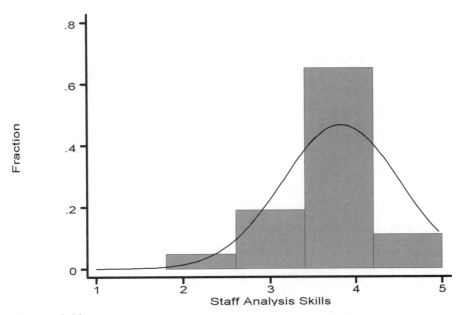

FIGURE 2.22
Distribution of *t12*

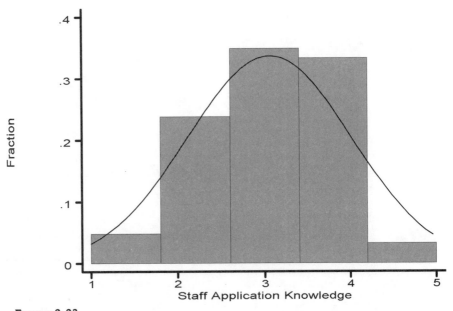

FIGURE 2.23
Distribution of *t13*

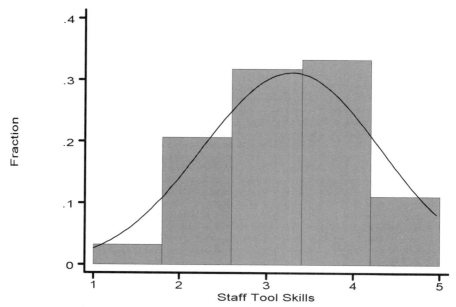

FIGURE 2.24
Distribution of *t14*

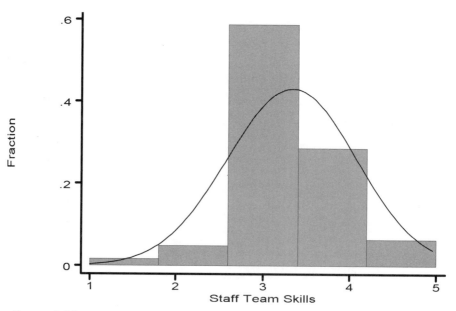

FIGURE 2.25
Distribution of *t15*

industries would be average and the distributions would be normal. This is the case in the larger multi-company database from which this subset was taken. However, in this bank, we note some differences.

From the preceding graphs, I learned that in this bank:

- Most applications had high customer participation (*t01*).
- No application had big problems with key personnel availability (*t03*).
- No project needed standards development (*t04*).
- No application used an integrated CASE environment (*t06*).
- The logical complexity of the software was on the high side (*t07*).
- Requirements volatility was quite high. Half the applications had high or very high requirements volatility. No application had very low requirements volatility (*t08*).
- No application had zero quality requirements—"quick-and-dirty" would never be allowed in a bank. About 75% of the applications had high to very high quality requirements (*t09*).
- Some level of attention and planning was needed for the efficiency requirements of all applications. Efficiency requirements were also on the high side (*t10*).
- All applications required some kind of user training (*t11*).
- For most projects, the analysis skills of the project staff at the time of kick-off were high. Most people had experience with specification and analysis, and the project manager was a professional analyst (*t12*).
- Tools experience was on the high side (*t14*).

Two-Dimensional Graphs I plotted the relationships between the transformed productivity variable, *ln*(*prod*), and each independent numerical variable. The independent variables were transformed as described in the previous section.

Figure 2.26 shows a linear relationship between *ln*(*prod*) and *ln*(*effort*); productivity appears to decrease with an increasing amount of effort. Figure 2.27 suggests that productivity increases slightly with increasing size. In Figure 2.28, it looks like short projects have a higher productivity than lengthy projects. In all graphs, Project 1 looks suspiciously like an outlier.

In Figure 2.29, I don't see any clear relationship between start year (*syear*) and productivity. The productivity of Project 1 again appears high.

Figure 2.30 shows that there is no clear relationship between productivity and the number of languages used (*nlan*).

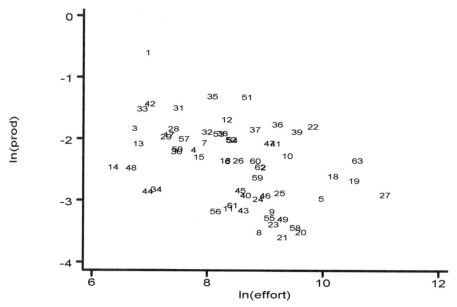

FIGURE 2.26
ln(prod) vs. *ln(effort)*

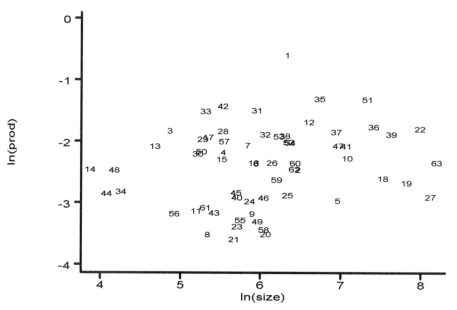

FIGURE 2.27
ln(prod) vs. *ln(size)*

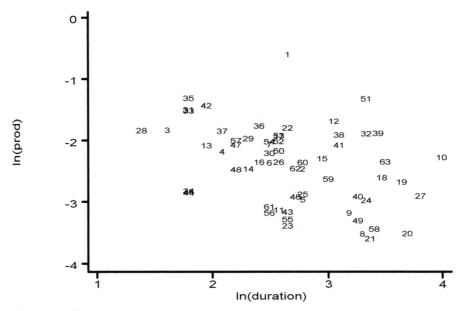

FIGURE 2.28
ln(prod) vs. *ln(duration)*

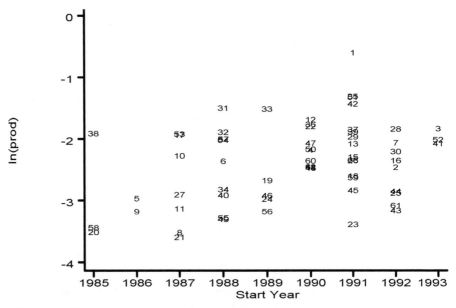

FIGURE 2.29
ln(prod) vs. *syear*

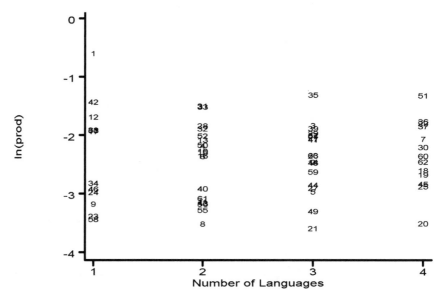

Figure 2.30

ln(prod) vs. *nlan*

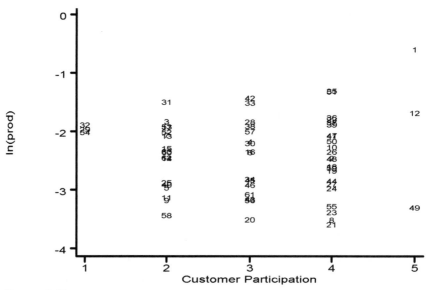

Figure 2.31

ln(prod) vs. *t01*

In Figures 2.31 through 2.34, I don't see any clear relationships between productivity and customer participation (*t01*), development environment adequacy (*t02*), staff availability (*t03*), or use of standards (*t04*).

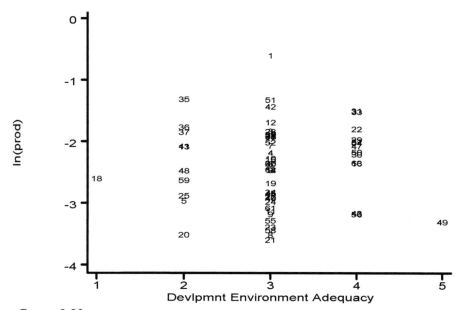

FIGURE 2.32
ln(prod) vs. *t02*

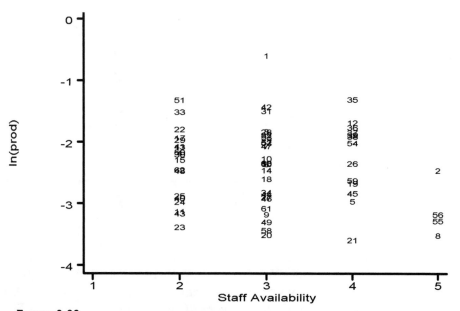

FIGURE 2.33
ln(prod) vs. *t03*

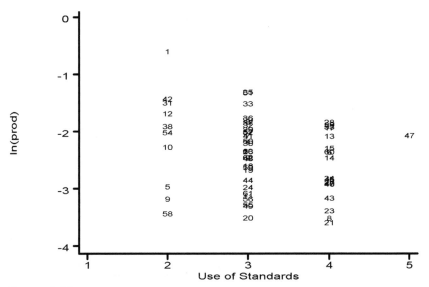

FIGURE 2.34

ln(prod) vs. *t04*

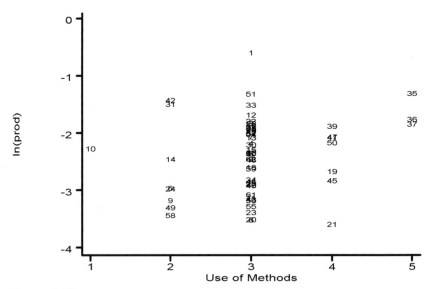

FIGURE 2.35

ln(prod) vs. *t05*

In Figures 2.35 through 2.37, there are no obvious relationships between productivity and use of methods (*t05*), use of tools (*t06*), or the logical complexity of the software (*t07*). In Figure 2.38, it looks like productivity decreases with increasing requirements volatility (*t08*). This makes sense.

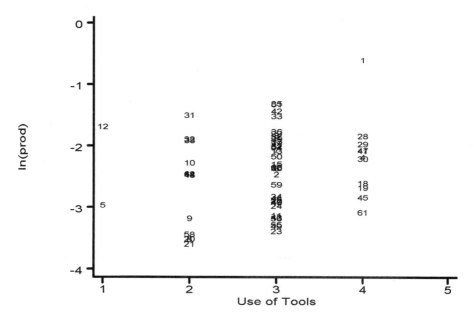

FIGURE 2.36
ln(prod) vs. *t06*

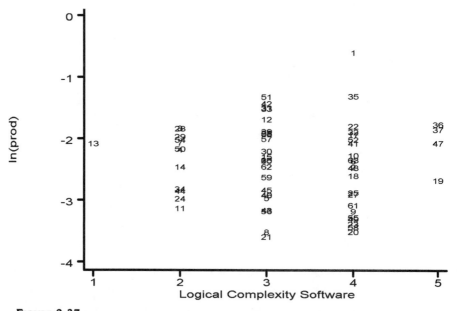

FIGURE 2.37
ln(prod) vs. *t07*

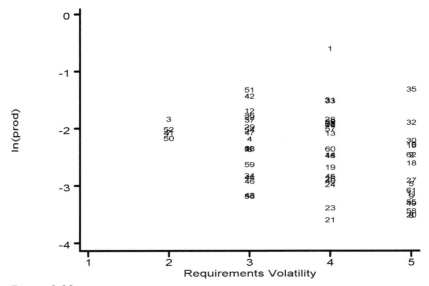

FIGURE 2.38
ln(prod) vs. *t08*

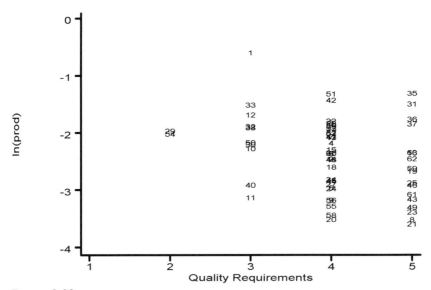

FIGURE 2.39
ln(prod) vs. *t09*

Looking at Figures 2.39 and 2.40, productivity appears to decrease with increasing quality requirements (*t09*) and efficiency requirements (*t10*). And, in Figures 2.41 and 2.42, I don't see any clear relationships between productivity and installation requirements (*t11*) or staff analysis skills (*t12*).

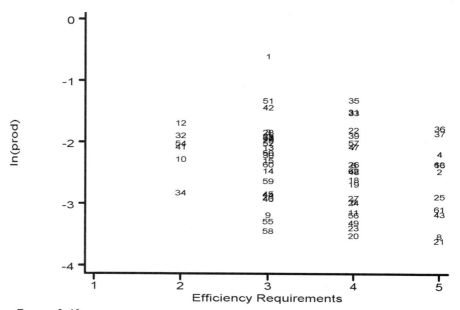

FIGURE 2.40
ln(prod) vs. *t10*

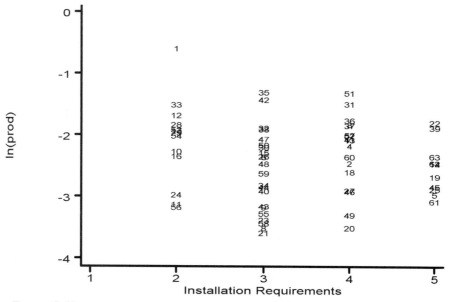

FIGURE 2.41
ln(prod) vs. *t11*

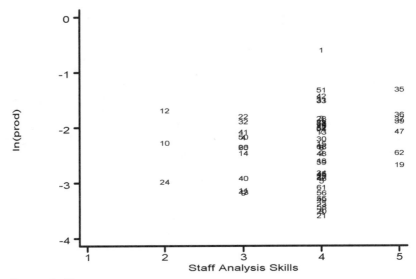

FIGURE 2.42

ln(prod) vs. *t12*

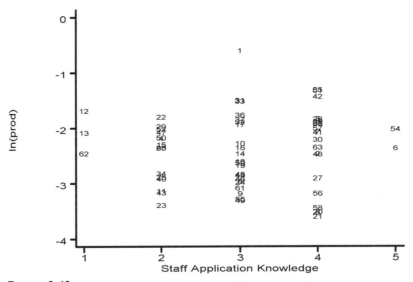

FIGURE 2.43

ln(prod) vs. *t13*

In Figure 2.44, it looks like productivity increases with increasing staff tool skills (*t14*). However, if I ignore Project 1, there appears to be no relationship. Figures 2.43 and 2.45 indicate no obvious relationships between productivity and staff application knowledge (*t13*) or staff team skills (*t15*).

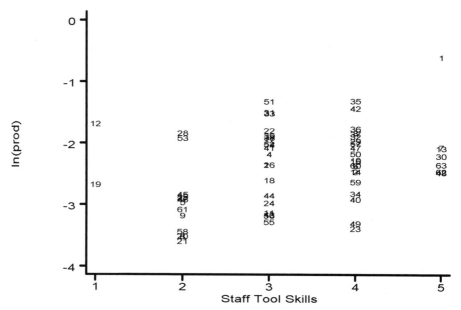

FIGURE 2.44

ln(prod) vs. *t14*

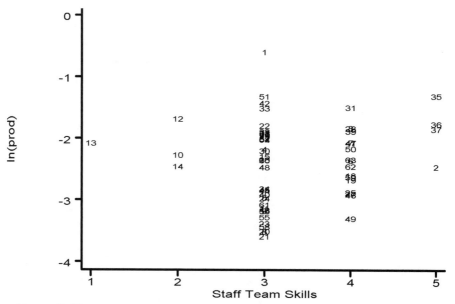

FIGURE 2.45

ln(prod) vs. *t15*

Handling Outliers   In many of the two-dimensional graphs, Project 1 (*id* = 1) really stands out as being different from the other projects. I printed out an ordered list of each project's productivity to get a better look (Example 2.9).

Example 2.9

```
.  list id prod

          id        prod
  1.      21    .0264517
  2.       8    .0285519
  3.      20    .0288334
  4.      58    .0308759
  5.      23    .0324474
  6.      49    .0353806
  7.      55    .0359918
  8.       9    .0401096
  9.      56    .0401163
 10.      43    .0406956
 11.      11     .042093
 12.      61    .0441558
 13.      24     .049137
 14.       5    .0496427
 15.      46    .0519897
 16.      40    .0521859
 17.      27    .0528778
 18.      25     .054274
 19.      44    .0556604
 20.      45    .0566395
 21.      34    .0575831
 22.      19    .0665665
 23.      59    .0696692
 24.      18    .0713624
 25.      48    .0816583
 26.       2    .0822005
 27.      14    .0823328
 28.      62    .0826735
 29.       6    .0906724
 30.      60    .0912559
 31.      26    .0915686
 32.      16    .0916728
 33.      63    .0920489
 34.      15     .097076
 35.      10    .0992437
 36.      30    .1060172
 37.       4    .1090129
 38.      50    .1099715
 39.      13         .12
 40.      41    .1208247
 41.      47    .1214696
```

42.	7	.1220807
43.	54	.1279351
44.	52	.1290395
45.	57	.1297325
46.	29	.1351724
47.	17	.1388158
48.	53	.1413889
49.	38	.1423377
50.	32	.1454177
51.	39	.1467143
52.	37	.1522059
53.	28	.1532405
54.	3	.1538462
55.	22	.1596757
56.	36	.1648
57.	12	.1780723
58.	33	.211838
59.	31	.2152392
60.	42	.23
61.	51	.2572922
62.	35	.2592593
63.	1	.5291902

Project 1 has the highest productivity by far, approximately 0.53 function points/hour. It is over twice as productive as the next highest rated project in the database. Why is this? I contacted the data provider to find out more about Project 1. I learned that this project was an **exceptional** project. Project 1 was the only Macintosh project the bank ever had. More importantly, it was outsourced at a fixed price. It was the only project in the database where the actual effort was not really known. The effort input in the database was derived from the outsourcing price. As this price was fixed, and it was impossible to know if the developing company made or lost a lot of money on it, the derived effort value was not comparable with the other projects' efforts. As Project 1 was neither a typical project for this bank, nor was its productivity reliable, I dropped it from the analysis.

What about the other high productivity projects? Was there anything special about them? Project 35 was also outsourced, but in this case, the actual effort was known. The most important factor was that the same team had already developed earlier releases, so that is probably why they were more effective. Project 51 was not outsourced. It was an enhancement project. The basic structure and database were already in use. It was not very integrated with the core banking systems.

What about the low productivity projects? Project 21 was an infrastructure for one core banking system. This project had to resolve lots of architectural issues. Project 8 was related to Project 21 and their schedules were dependent. Project 20 was one of the first projects to implement a three-tier architecture. Many message transfers had to be redone. This breakthrough project often had to wait for architectural decisions to be made. Finally, the scope of the project had to be restricted to get something implemented.

Although all projects were special in some way, Project 1 was the only exceptional project that did not belong in the database. You may be interested to know that if I did not drop Project 1, but left it in and continued with the rest of the analysis, I would have found out in the end that Project 1 exerted a very high influence on the results. I would then have had to drop it and redo everything. It is a better use of your time to detect and remove outliers during the preliminary analyses.

As the removal of Project 1 modified the summary data, I printed it out again for the numerical variables in the model (Example 2.10). The database now contained 62 projects. Although the average values were modified, the minimum and maximum values of size, effort, and duration did not change. The biggest difference concerned the maximum value of productivity (*prod*), which dropped to 0.26 function points per hour.

Example 2.10

```
.  summarize
```

Variable	Obs	Mean	Std. Dev.	Min	Max
prod	62	.1012435	.0579057	.0264517	.2592593
size	62	673.1613	783.5263	48	3634
effort	62	8223.21	10499.9	583	63694
duration	62	17.20968	10.65116	4	54
t01	62	3.048387	.9988094	1	5
t02	62	3.048387	.7112081	1	5
t03	62	3.032258	.8864692	2	5
t04	62	3.193548	.6975063	2	5
t05	62	3.048387	.7112081	1	5
t06	62	2.903226	.6944671	1	4
t07	62	3.241935	.8996444	1	5
t08	62	3.806452	.9553767	2	5
t09	62	4.064516	.7437382	2	5
t10	62	3.612903	.8935991	2	5
t11	62	3.419355	.9842762	2	5
t12	62	3.822581	.6900747	2	5
t13	62	3.064516	.95593	1	5
t14	62	3.258065	1.007114	1	5
t15	62	3.33871	.7453363	1	5
nlan	62	2.548387	1.019119	1	4
time	62	5.580645	2.131331	1	9

Tables

What is the average productivity for each categorical variable?

Example 2.11

```
. table app, c(n prod mean prod)
```

Application Type	N(prod)	mean(prod)
CustServ	18	0.0987
MIS	4	0.0988
TransPro	29	0.0926
ProdCont	1	0.1352
InfServ	10	0.1283

Example 2.11 shows that on average, information/on-line service applications (*InfServ*) had the highest productivity. Customer service (*CustServ*), management information system (*MIS*), and transaction processing (*TransPro*) applications had the lowest productivity. As there is only one production control (*ProdCont*) application, we don't have enough information to make any generalizations about this type of application. However, I still print out its productivity as it might be of interest to the project manager (ditto for the *PC* and *Mini* hardware types, which are shown in Example 2.12.

Example 2.12

```
. table har, c(n prod mean prod)
```

Hardware Type	N(prod)	mean(prod)
Network	7	0.1160
Mainfrm	37	0.0909
PC	1	0.1200
Mini	1	0.0992
Multi	16	0.1176

On average, mainframe (*Mainfrm*) applications had the lowest productivity; Networked (*Network*) and multi-platform (*Multi*) applications had the highest productivity (Example 2.12).

Example 2.13

```
. table ifc, c(n prod mean prod)
```

User Interface	N(prod)	mean(prod)
GUI	4	0.2016
TextUI	58	0.0943

From Example 2.13, graphical user interface (*GUI*) applications seem to have been a lot more productive than text user interface (*TextUI*) applications.

Example 2.14

```
. table source, c(n prod mean prod)
```

Where Developed	N(prod)	mean(prod)
Inhouse	54	0.0960
Outsrced	8	0.1367

And in Example 2.14, we see that, on average, outsourced projects (*Outsrced*) had a higher productivity than projects developed in-house (*Inhouse*).

Example 2.15

```
. table telonuse, c(n prod mean prod)
```

Telon Use	N(prod)	mean(prod)
No	47	0.0990
Yes	15	0.1082

Telon use does not seem to have led to any large gain in productivity (Example 2.15).

Correlation Analysis

In Chapter 1, I explained why I look at the correlation of the independent variables and showed you how to interpret the correlation analysis output. In this study, I have 20 numerical variables, which result in 190 Spearman's correlation output tables (using my statistical analysis tool). I will not show all of the output from the correlation analysis as it would take far too many pages. (The total number of correlation combinations between n variables is $n(n-1)/2$.) Instead, I searched the correlation output for any significant correlation coefficients greater than |0.5|. The summary is presented in Table 2.3.

Tools use (*t06*) increased over time. Projects with higher logical complexity (*t07*) often required more effort and were bigger in size. The more development languages used in a project (*nlan*), the higher its installation requirements (*t11*). Staff analysis skills (*t12*) and staff team skills (*t15*) are positively correlated; project staff with good analysis skills generally have good team skills, too. Quality (*t09*) and efficiency requirements (*t10*) are also positively correlated; projects with high quality requirements often have high efficiency requirements too. Size, effort, and duration are all positively correlated with

TABLE 2.3
Summary of Correlation Coefficients

Variables	Num Obs	Correlation
t06 and *time*	62	0.54
t07 and *effort*	62	0.59
t07 and *size*	62	0.57
t11 and *nlan*	62	0.58
t12 and *t15*	62	0.53
t09 and *t10*	62	0.60
size and *duration*	62	0.54
effort and *size*	62	0.75
effort and *duration*	62	0.75

each other; bigger projects usually take longer and require more effort. The correlations between effort and size, and effort and duration are so strong that these pairs of variables should not be in the final model together (risk of multi-collinearity).

I also thought it would be interesting to see how time was related to the different factors. Table 2.4 summarizes all significant correlations involving time. I discussed the correlation analysis results with the data provider to see if they made sense in the context of his company. He agreed with the results and was able to provide some explanations.

The increased level and use of methods (*t05*) over time indicate some process improvement in the company. The level and use of tools (*t06*) also increased over time. Requirements volatility (*t08*) decreased over time as well. This could be because the company learned better requirements management. Staff tool skills (*t14*) and team skills (*t15*) increased over time. This is because staff turnover was low, another factor that increased organizational learning.

TABLE 2.4
Variables Correlated with *time*

Variable	Num Obs	Correlation
t05	62	0.30
t06	62	0.54
t08	62	−0.43
t14	62	0.28
t15	62	0.27
duration	62	−0.35
nlan	62	0.32

Project duration decreased over time. This could be the result of process improvement in the company. The number of languages (*nlan*) increased over time. This was due to the development of more three-tier architecture projects at the end of the time period.

Stepwise Regression Analysis

As productivity is defined as size divided by effort, any stepwise regression procedure run with both size and effort as independent variables will find that size and effort perfectly explain the variation in productivity (R-squared = 1.0)! Forward and backward stepwise regressions need to be carried out twice: once for all numerical variables excluding effort, and once for all numerical variables excluding size. An *l* in front of a variable in the statistical output (*lprod, lsize, ldur*[4], and *leffort*) means a natural log transformation was used.

Forward Stepwise Regression Excluding *leffort*   The forward stepwise regression procedure found five variables that explained 58% of the variance in productivity (Example 2.16). All 62 observations were used. The procedure shows that productivity (*lprod*) increased with increasing project size (*lsize*) and staff tool skills (*t14*); productivity decreased with increasing quality requirements (*t09*), efficiency requirements (*t10*), and project duration (*ldur*). These relationships make sense to me.

Example 2.16

```
. sw regress lprod lsize ldur time nlan t01 t02 t03 t04 t05 t06 t07
t08 t09 t10 t11 t12 t13 t14 t15, pe(.05)
                              begin with empty model
p = 0.0017 <  0.0500  adding   ldur
p = 0.0000 <  0.0500  adding   lsize
p = 0.0001 <  0.0500  adding   t09
p = 0.0103 <  0.0500  adding   t14
p = 0.0480 <  0.0500  adding   t10
```

Source	SS	df	MS
Model	13.6939918	5	2.73879836
Residual	8.61777376	56	.153888817
Total	22.3117655	61	.365766648

Number of obs	= 62
$F_{(5, 56)}$	= 17.80
Prob > F	= 0.0000
R-squared	= 0.6138
Adj R-squared	= 0.5793
Root MSE	= .39229

---

4. *ln(duration)* is abbreviated *ldur* because variable names can be no more than eight characters.

lprod	Coef.	Std. Err.	t	P > |t|	[95% Conf. Interval]	
ldur	-.7223637	.1020141	-7.081	0.000	-.9267224	-.518005
lsize	.4475299	.0633893	7.060	0.000	.3205459	.574514
t09	-.190931	.0855067	-2.233	0.030	-.3622215	-.0196405
t14	.144847	.0518125	2.796	0.007	.0410541	.2486399
t10	-.1437862	.0711115	-2.022	0.048	-.2862396	-.0013328
_cons	-2.406596	.478281	-5.032	0.000	-3.364708	-1.448484

Backward Stepwise Regression Excluding *leffort*   The backward stepwise regression procedure found a different model (Example 2.17). Seven variables explained 61% of the variation in productivity. All 62 projects were used. In this procedure, productivity (*lprod*) increased with increasing size (*lsize*), time (*time*), and staff application knowledge (*t13*); productivity decreased with increasing duration (*ldur*), quality requirements (*t09*), tools use (*t06*), and staff availability (*t03*).

Example 2.17

```
. sw regress lprod lsize ldur time nlan t01 t02 t03 t04
    t05 t06 t07 t08 t09 t10 t11 t12 t13 t14 t15, pr(.05)
                    begin with full model

p = 0.9856 >= 0.0500    removing t08
p = 0.8291 >= 0.0500    removing t01
p = 0.7310 >= 0.0500    removing t02
p = 0.7019 >= 0.0500    removing t11
p = 0.6877 >= 0.0500    removing t07
p = 0.7006 >= 0.0500    removing t12
p = 0.4567 >= 0.0500    removing t04
p = 0.3497 >= 0.0500    removing t15
p = 0.1998 >= 0.0500    removing t05
p = 0.1864 >= 0.0500    removing nlan
p = 0.1015 >= 0.0500    removing t14
p = 0.0834 >= 0.0500    removing t10
```

Source	SS	df	MS		Number of obs = 62
Model	14.6916604	7	2.09880863		F(7, 54) = 14.87
Residual	7.62010512	54	.141113058		Prob > F = 0.0000
					R-squared = 0.6585
Total	22.3117655	61	.365766648		Adj R-squared = 0.6142
					Root MSE = .37565

lprod	Coef.	Std. Err.	t	P > |t|	[95% Conf. Interval]	
lsize	.4539171	.0640334	7.089	0.000	.325538	.5822963
ldur	-.7491616	.1098508	-6.820	0.000	-.9693992	-.528924
time	.0929364	.0298588	3.113	0.003	.0330731	.1527996
t06	-.2866383	.0868354	-3.301	0.002	-.4607328	-.1125438
t09	-.3292682	.0685175	-4.806	0.000	-.4666374	-.1918989
t13	.1217216	.0556766	2.186	0.033	.0100967	.2333465
t03	-.1576981	.0624409	-2.526	0.015	-.2828845	-.0325117
_cons	-1.440158	.4814565	-2.991	0.004	-2.40542	-.4748955

I find these last two results perplexing. Why would productivity decrease with the use of higher level tools? Why would having more staff available and involved almost full-time on a project decrease its productivity? I decided to go back and look at the two-dimensional graphs showing the relationships between productivity and these two variables (Figures 2.33 and 2.36). Neither of these graphs shows a very clear relationship. It looks to me like the staff availability result could be influenced by the fact that four projects where the staff availability was very high had lower than average productivities. It is possible that this was because highly qualified personnel were allocated full-time to projects expected to be difficult, not that people allocated full-time to projects tended to waste time! In Figure 2.36, I do not see a negative relationship between use of tools (*t06*) and productivity. If anything, the relationship is positive, especially if you ignore the one project with minimal tool use, which has a high productivity (*id* = 12). It is for this reason that I do not trust the above model. It does not make sense and I will not use it.

Forward and Backward Stepwise Regressions Excluding *lsize*

The forward and backward stepwise regression procedures excluding *lsize* found the same model (Example 2.18). Four variables explained 32% of the variance in productivity. This model is not as good as the forward stepwise regression model excluding *leffort* (Example 2.16).

Example 2.18

Source	SS	df	MS		Number of obs	=	62
Model	8.15760394	4	2.03940099		F(4, 57)	=	8.21
Residual	14.1541616	57	.248318624		Prob > F	=	0.0000
					R-squared	=	0.3656
Total	22.3117655	61	.365766648		Adj R-squared	=	0.3211
					Root MSE	=	.49832

lprod	Coef.	Std. Err.	t	P >|t|	[95% Conf.	Interval]
leffort	-.19433	.0721994	-2.692	0.009	-.3389068	-.0497532
t15	.2753912	.0996376	2.764	0.008	.0758703	.4749122
t09	-.2860773	.0978822	-2.923	0.005	-.482083	-.0900715
time	.0729533	.0334308	2.182	0.033	.0060094	.1398973
_cons	-.9727094	.619623	-1.570	0.122	-2.213483	.2680643

Building the Multi-Variable Model

The best model with numerical variables alone explained 58% of the variation in productivity (Example 2-16). Do any of the categorical variables, *subapp* (application type subset), *subhar* (hardware platform subset), *ifc* (user interface), *source* (where developed), and/or *telonuse* (Telon use), explain more of the variation in productivity? I used the stepwise ANOVA procedure explained in Chapter 1 to see if an improvement in the R-squared value could be made. The results are shown in Sidebar 2.1.

SIDEBAR 2.1
STATISTICAL OUTPUT SUMMARY SHEET

Date: 29/03/2001

Directory: C:\my documents\data analysis book\productivity\
Data File: bankdata63.dta
Procedure Files: *var.do (* = one, two, three, etc..)
Output Files: *var.log

Dependent Variable: lprod

Variables	Num Obs	Effect	Adj R²	Significance of Added Variable	Comments
1-variable models					
t05	62	+	0.04	.078	
t08	62	−	0.13		
t09	62	−	0.06		
t10	62	−	0.04	.058	
t14	62	+	0.08		
leffort	62	−	0.14		constant not sign.
* ldur	**62**	**−**	**0.14**		
time	62	+	0.11		
ifc	62		0.12		
2–variable models with ldur					
t04	62	−	0.18	.053	constant not sign.
t08	62	−	0.20		
t09	62	−	0.20		constant not sign.
t10	62	−	0.18		constant not sign.
* lsize	**62**	**+**	**0.38**		
ifc	62		0.20		
source	62		0.18		
3–variable models with ldur, lsize					
t03	62	−	0.41		
t04	62	−	0.40	.067	

(Continued)

SIDEBAR 2.1 (Continued)

Variables	Num Obs	Effect	Adj R^2	Significance of Added Variable	Comments
t07	62	–	0.40		
t08	62	–	0.40	.085	
* t09	62	–	0.51		
t10	62	–	0.49		
t11	62	–	0.40	.06	
t14	62	+	0.43		
4-variable models with *ldur, lsize, t09*					
t10	62	–	0.53	.075	
* t14	62	+	0.56		
time	62	+	0.53	.068	
ifc	62		0.53	.079	
5-variable models with *ldur, lsize,* t09, t14					
t10	62	–	0.58		best model, sign. = 0.0000
6-variable models with *ldur, lsize,* t09, t14, t10					
none significant					no further improvement possible

From the summary of one-variable models, I see that there are significant relationships between productivity (*lprod*) and each of the following variables: t05 (methods use), t08 (requirements volatility), t09 (quality requirements), t10 (efficiency requirements), t14 (staff tool skills), *leffort, ldur,* and *time,* and one of the categorical variables, *ifc* (user interface). Productivity increases with the use of methods (t05), staff tool skills (t14), and time, and decreases with the other significant numerical variables. Productivity depends on the type of user interface (*ifc*). The best one-variable model is based on duration and explains 14% of the variation in productivity.

Next, I add duration (*ldur*) to the RHS of the model and begin the search for the best two-variable model. The best two-variable model includes size (*lsize*) along with duration (*ldur*) and explains 38% of the variation in productivity. 51% of the variation in productivity is explained by the best three-variable model: requirements volatility (*t09*), *lsize*, and *ldur*. The best four-variable model explains 56% of the variation and includes staff tool skills (*t14*) along with *ldur*, *lsize*, and *t09*. The best five-variable model explains 58% of the variation in productivity and also includes efficiency requirements (*t10*). No further improvement can be made. As no categorical variables were found to be important in the final model, this model is the same as the best model found in the stepwise regression analysis step (Example 2.19).

The Final Model
Example 2.19

```
. fit lprod ldur lsize t09 t14 t10
```

Source	SS	df	MS
Model	13.6939918	5	2.73879836
Residual	8.61777376	56	.153888817
Total	22.3117655	61	.365766648

Number of obs = 62
F(5, 56) = 17.80
Prob > F = 0.0000
R-squared = 0.6138
Adj R-squared = 0.5793
Root MSE = .39229

lprod	Coef.	Std. Err.	t	P >|t|	[95% Conf.	Interval]
ldur	-.7223637	.1020141	-7.081	0.000	-.9267224	-.518005
lsize	.4475299	.0633893	7.060	0.000	.3205459	.574514
t09	-.190931	.0855067	-2.233	0.030	-.3622215	-.0196405
t14	.144847	.0518125	2.796	0.007	.0410541	.2486399
t10	-.1437862	.0711115	-2.022	0.048	-.2862396	-.0013328
_cons	-2.406596	.478281	-5.032	0.000	-3.364708	-1.448484

Checking the Model

Before we can accept the final model, we must check that the assumptions underlying the statistical tests have not been violated.

Numerical Variable Checks

None of the numerical independent variables in the final model are so highly correlated with each other that they cause multicollinearity problems. Referring to Table 2.3 in the preliminary analyses, I see that the highest correlation, 0.60 between *t09* and *t10*, is still below my |0.75| threshold.

Categorical Variable Checks

No categorical variables were found to be important, so nothing needs to be checked.

Testing the Residuals

Figure 2.46 shows no pattern in the residuals of our final model.

We can see in Figure 2.47 that the residuals are approximately normally distributed.

Detecting Influential Observations

As there are 62 projects in the database, the four projects with Cook's distances greater than $4/62 = 0.065$ (Example 2.20) should be examined closely.

Example 2.20

```
. list id size effort cooksd if cooksd>4/62

              id      size     effort       cooksd
    11.       12       739       4150     .1078585
    33.       34        71       1233     .0774779
    44.       45       299       5279      .101717
    50.       51      1526       5931      .069229
```

No project has an enormous influence as none of these values is extremely large compared to the cut-off value. The data provider saw no reason to

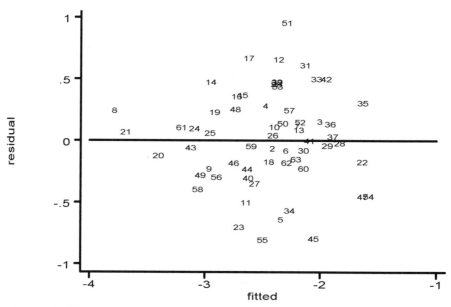

FIGURE 2.46
Residuals vs. fitted values

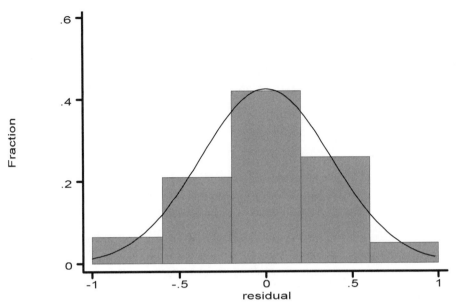

FIGURE 2.47
Distribution of residuals.

remove any of these projects from the database. Nonetheless, I decided to try to understand why these four projects were influencing the results. First, all four have large errors (see Figure 2.46). The productivity of Projects 12 and 51 is underestimated, while the productivity of Projects 34 and 45 is overestimated. Table 2.5 summarizes the values of the key variables for each project. Projects 12 and 51 are high-productivity (*prod*) projects; Projects 34 and 45 are low-productivity projects.

TABLE 2.5
Influential Projects' Key Variable Values

id	12	34	45	51	**Mean (62 projects)**
prod	0.178	0.058	0.057	0.257	0.101
duration	21	6	6	28	17.2
size	739	71	299	1526	673
t09	3	4	4	4	4.06
t10	2	2	3	3	3.61
t14	1	4	2	3	3.26
residual	0.640	−0.589	−0.816	0.936	0

I also went back and calculated the Cook's distance at each step of the ANOVA method to discover when each project became influential. I found that Project 51 became influential when duration (*ldur*) was added; this leads me to believe that Project 51's influence on the results is mainly due to its being a very high-productivity project with a longer than average duration. All other projects with the same or longer duration had much lower productivities. This explains why Project 51's productivity was underestimated by the model.

Project 45 became influential with the addition of size (*lsize*) to the model. Project 45 has a very low productivity for its small size and short duration. This explains why the model overestimated its productivity.

Project 12 became influential with the addition of staff tool skills (*t14*) to the model. Project 12 was one of only two projects with very low staff tool skills. Even though high staff tool skills are associated with high productivity for most projects, Project 12 had a high productivity even though it had very low staff tool skills (see Figure 2.44).

Project 34 became influential with the addition of efficiency requirements (*t10*) to the model. Project 34 has low efficiency requirements and a low productivity (see Figure 2.40). Since the model found that most low productivities were associated with high efficiency requirements, it underestimated the productivity of Project 34.

Extracting the Equation

The equation as read from the final model's output is:

$$ln(prod) = -2.406596 - 0.7223637 \times ln(duration) + 0.4475299 \times ln(size)$$
$$- 0.190931 \times t09 + 0.144847 \times t14 - 0.1437862 \times t10$$

This can be transformed into the following equation for productivity (*prod*):

$$prod = 0.0901 \times duration^{-0.7224} \times size^{0.4475}$$
$$\times e^{-0.1909 \times t09} \times e^{-0.1448 \times t14} \times e^{-0.1438 \times t10}$$

Interpreting the Equation

How can I interpret this equation? Let's look at the influence of the productivity factors on the value of productivity (*prod*). First, I calculate the value of each productivity factor multiplier (Table 2.6); that is, what is *e* to the power $-0.190931 \times t09$ when *t09* is 1, when it is 2, etc.?

TABLE 2.6
Productivity Factor Multipliers

Defn.	Value	t09 Multiplier	t14 Multiplier	t10 Multiplier
very low	1	*0.826190	1.155863	*0.866073
low	2	0.682589	1.336019	0.750082
average	3	0.563948	1.544254	0.649626
high	4	0.465928	1.784946	0.562623
very high	5	0.384945	2.063152	0.487273

It is easier to think of an effect on productivity as being more or less than average. To do this, I calculate the normalized productivity factor multipliers by dividing each variable's multiplier by its average value (Table 2.7).

From Table 2.7, I can easily see that if all other variables remain constant, the effect on productivity (*prod*) of low quality requirements (*t09*) as opposed to average quality requirements is to increase productivity by 21%. On the other hand, if quality requirements are very high, I can expect productivity to be about 32% lower (1-.683) than for an identical project with average quality requirements. Staff tool skills (*t14*) and efficiency requirements (*t10*) can be interpreted in the same manner. The quality requirements (*t09*) multiplier has the largest spread, from 0.683 to 1.465, thus quality requirement differences have a stronger impact on productivity than staff tool skills (*t14*) or efficiency requirements (*t10*). You can also deduce this from the equations because *t09*'s coefficient has the largest absolute value.

You should also keep in mind that no project in the database actually had very low quality requirements or efficiency requirements (denoted by * in Tables 2.6 and 2.7). So although the model says that very low quality requirements would increase productivity by 46.5% compared with average quality

TABLE 2.7
Normalized Productivity Factor Multipliers

Defn.	Value	t09 Multiplier	t14 Multiplier	t10 Multiplier
very low	1	*1.465	0.748	*1.333
low	2	1.210	0.865	1.155
average	3	1	1	1
high	4	0.826	1.156	0.866
very high	5	0.683	1.336	0.750

requirements, we cannot be completely sure about this. However, within the bank, this should not pose a problem because the bank is unlikely to ever undertake a project with either very low quality requirements or very low efficiency requirements.

What about the effects of duration and size on productivity? What can I learn from the equations? The coefficient of duration is approximately –0.72. This means that for every 1% increase in duration, productivity is expected to decrease by 0.72%, all other variables remaining constant. For example, if duration is increased by 5%, productivity should decrease by 3.6%. The coefficient of size is approximately 0.45. Assuming that all other variables remain constant, this means that for every 1% increase in size, productivity should increase by 0.45%.

Management Implications

The data provider was surprised to learn that bigger projects had higher productivities. As past research had indicated that there were large diseconomies of scale, the trend in the bank was to break large software development projects into smaller projects. However, these smaller projects' proportionally larger overhead probably made them less productive.

Of the three significant productivity factors, quality requirements, efficiency requirements, and staff tool skills, only the level of staff tool skills is controllable. The quality and efficiency requirements of the projects were fixed. Tool skills are very important in the banking sector. It is important for a project team to be fully trained in all development and documentation tools. The bank could improve this by carefully selecting a small portfolio of development and documentation tools to use in their projects, sticking to their choice for a number of years, fully training their staff to use these tools, and reducing staff turnover. The implications of changing tools should be considered very carefully. Even if a better tool becomes available, the cost of retraining everyone may not make the change worthwhile.

Project duration had an impact on productivity in this bank. Can the bank do anything to reduce the duration of their projects? I will look closely at this question in the next case study (Chapter 3).

It is also worth noting that many of the variables considered did not have a significant impact on productivity. None of the categorical variables, application type, hardware platform, user interface, number of languages used, Telon use, or whether or not the project was outsourced, explained any additional variation in productivity once size, duration, quality and efficiency requirements, and staff tool skills were taken into consideration. In addition, only 3 of the 15 productivity factors explained any variation in productivity. Does that mean that collecting the other 12 was a waste of time? Only 58% of the variation in productivity was explained by the variables collected. This means that 42% of the variation is still unexplained. Are there other variables that should have been collected? Before deciding what to collect or not collect in the future, we should first determine if any of the collected variables influenced project duration and cost. You must also keep in mind that a variable that is not important today might be important in the future, so you may want to collect it anyway.

Case Study: Time to Market

3

The complexity and criticality of software within industry is high and continues to grow significantly every year as software becomes an increasingly important component in many consumer goods such as home appliances, cameras, cars, and mobile phones. The effective management of embedded software development in consumer goods poses difficult challenges for managers. Many factors contribute to this challenge; however, the driving force is cost: the cost of hardware components, the cost of software development, and most importantly, the cost of being late to market.

In efforts to meet time-to-market requirements, companies have succeeded in decreasing hardware development time through applying just-in-time and total quality management techniques, or simply by buying off-the-shelf solutions. However, this means that software often lies on the critical path for product introduction. In the telecommunications industry, for example, developing high-quality software quicker is probably more important to a company than accurately estimating its cost or knowing its productivity.

Even if your company doesn't develop embedded software, or there is no window of opportunity to miss in your industry, chances are that someone up there cares about how long it takes to develop your software applications.

In this chapter, I will show you how to determine which variables affect software development duration. This case study builds on the two previous chapters. Because the focus in these case studies is on interpreting the output results, you need to be familiar with my data analysis methodology, which was explained in Chapter 1. This case study uses the bank database (Appendix B) we validated and analyzed in Chapter 2. Thus, the data validation, variable selection, histogram, and correlation analysis steps do not need to be repeated. As you can see, if the data has been analyzed once, subsequent analyses are less time-consuming. This is mainly due to the amount of time saved using a database that has already been validated.

Data Validation, and Variable and Model Selection _____

The validation of the data, creation of new variables, modifications to the data, and identification of subsets of categorical variables were already undertaken in Chapter 2. Unfortunately, we do not have any data for team size in this database. It is a good idea to collect the maximum team size during a project, that is, the maximum number of people working on a project at its peak, whether they are full- or part-time.[1] If I had had this variable, I could have studied the relationship between duration and team size. Is there an optimal team size for a project? Often, it is in analyzing the data that you realize what should have been collected. However, there is always something to be learned from what you already have. The bank, for instance, can learn about the relationships between the available variables and duration now, and collect team size in the future.

Model Selection

My goal in this study is to determine which variables explain the differences in the durations of software development projects in this bank.

duration = f(size, effort, subapp, subhar, ifc, source, t01-t15, nlan, telonuse, time)

What are the relationships between the duration and size of an application, the amount of effort spent, the type of application (*subapp*), the type of hardware (*subhar*), the user interface (*ifc*), whether or not the development

---

1. It would be even better to collect the maximum team size during each phase of a project.

was outsourced (*source*), the 15 different productivity factors (*t01-t15*), the number of languages used (*nlan*), whether or not Telon was used (*telonuse*), and time?

Preliminary Analyses _____

The following analyses should be undertaken before building the multi-variable model. See Chapter 1 for more explanation.

Graphs

I always look at two types of graphs: histograms and two-dimensional graphs.

Histograms   See the section by this same name in Chapter 2.

Two-Dimensional Graphs   I plotted the relationships between *ln(duration)* and each independent numerical variable to see if there were any obvious relationships.

Figure 3.1 shows a linear relationship between *ln(duration)* and *ln(effort)*. It is clear that duration increases with an increasing amount of effort.

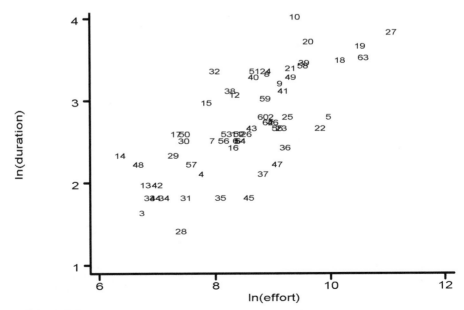

FIGURE 3.1
ln(duration) vs. *ln(effort)*

Figure 3.2 suggests that duration increases with increasing application size. There are no obvious outliers in these two graphs.

In Figure 3.3, it appears that project duration decreases over time (*syear*).

Figure 3.4 shows that there is no clear relationship between duration and the number of languages used (*nlan*).

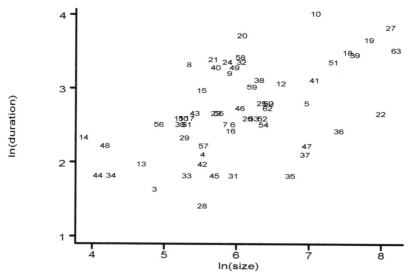

FIGURE 3.2
ln(duration) vs. *ln(size)*

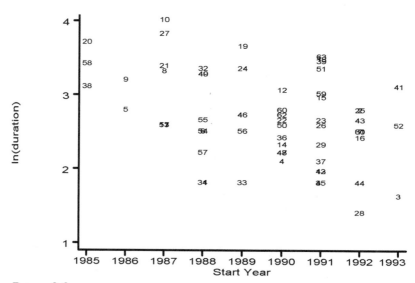

FIGURE 3.3
ln(duration) vs. *syear*

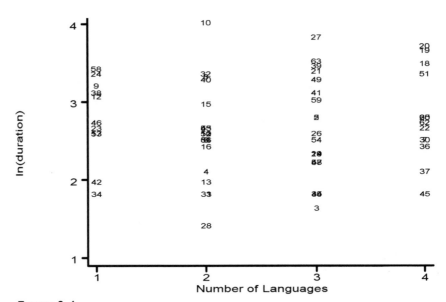

FIGURE 3.4

ln(duration) vs. *nlan*

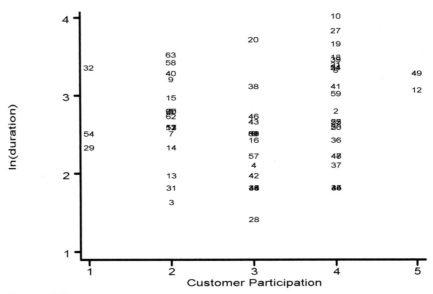

FIGURE 3.5

ln(duration) vs. *t01*

In Figures 3.5 and 3.6, there are no clear relationships between customer participation (*t01*) and duration or between duration and development environment adequacy (*t02*).

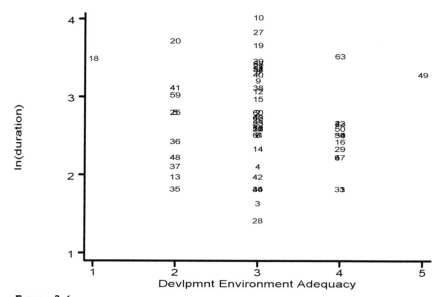

FIGURE 3.6
ln(duration) vs. *t02*

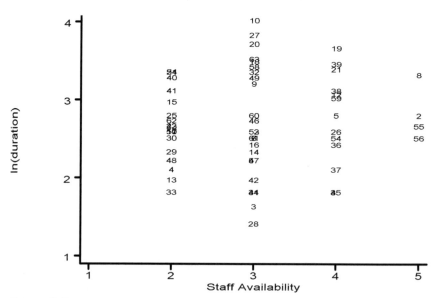

FIGURE 3.7
ln(duration) vs. *t03*

I don't see any clear relationship in Figure 3.7 between duration and staff availability (*t03*), or in Figure 3.8 between duration and use of standards (*t04*).

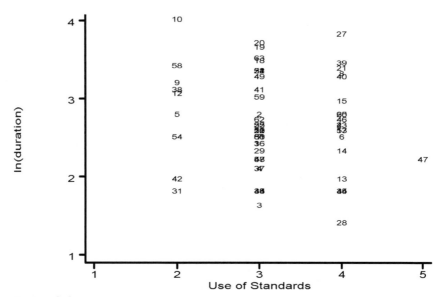

FIGURE 3.8
ln(duration) vs. *t04*

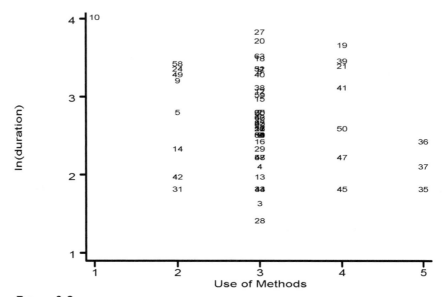

FIGURE 3.9
ln(duration) vs. *t05*

Figure 3.9 shows that there is no clear relationship between duration and use of methods (*t05*). Figure 3.10 indicates what appears to be a negative relationship between duration and use of tools (*t06*).

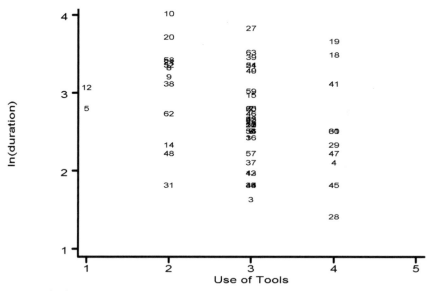

FIGURE 3.10

ln(duration) vs. *t06*

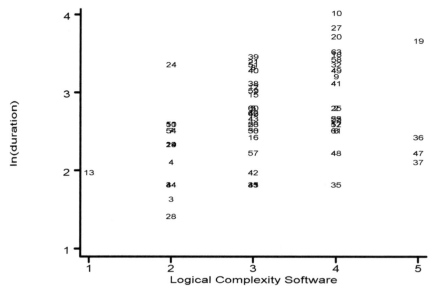

FIGURE 3.11

ln(duration) vs. *t07*

If you examine Figure 3.11, there appears to be a positive relationship between project duration and the logical complexity of the software (*t07*). On average, it looks like more complex software takes longer to develop. In Figure 3.12, there

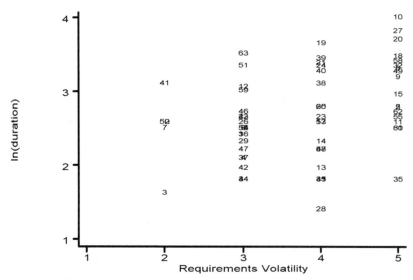

FIGURE 3.12
In(duration) vs. *t08*

also appears to be a positive relationship between duration and requirements volatility (*t08*); the more volatile the requirements, the longer the duration.

Figure 3.13 shows no clear relationship between duration and quality requirements (*t09*), and Figure 3.14 shows no relationship between duration and efficiency requirements (*t10*).

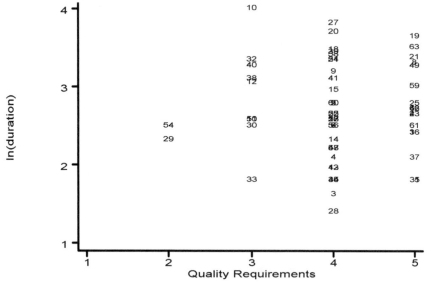

FIGURE 3.13
In(duration) vs. *t09*

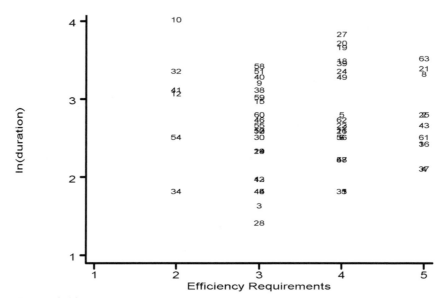

FIGURE 3.14
ln(duration) vs. *t10*

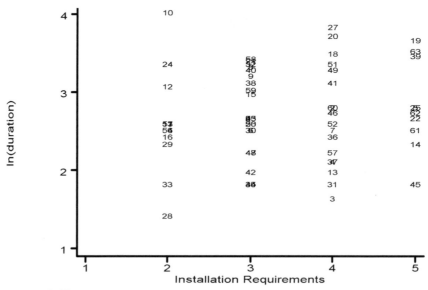

FIGURE 3.15
ln(duration) vs. *t11*

In Figure 3.15, there is no obvious relationship between duration and installation requirements (*t11*); in Figure 3.16, there is no obvious relationship between duration and staff analysis skills (*t12*).

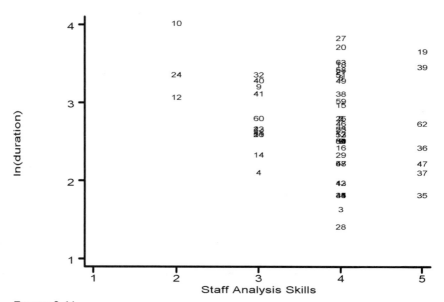

FIGURE 3.16

ln(duration) vs. *t12*

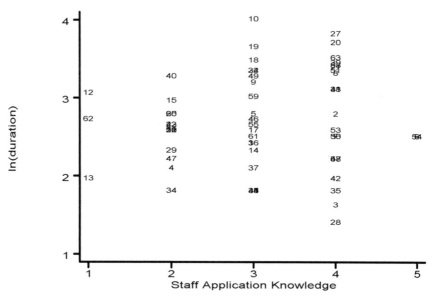

FIGURE 3.17

ln(duration) vs. *t13*

Staff application knowledge (*t13*) and staff tool skills (*t14*) do not appear to be related to project duration (Figures 3.17 and 3.18). However, in Figure 3.19, there appears to be a negative relationship between staff team skills

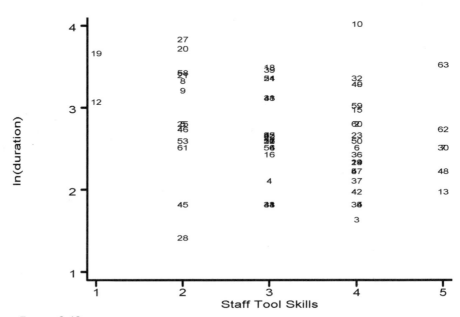

FIGURE 3.18
ln(duration) vs. *t14*

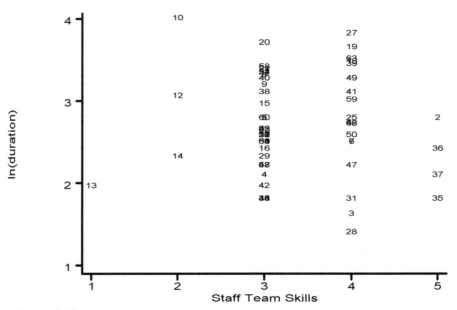

FIGURE 3.19
ln(duration) vs. *t15*

(*t15*) and duration. This could lead us to conclude that the better the team skills, the shorter the project duration.

Tables

What is the average duration for each categorical variable?

Example 3.1

```
. table app, c(n duration mean duration)
```

Application Type	N(duration)	mean(duration)
CustServ	18	17.6
MIS	4	21.5
TransPro	29	18.4
ProdCont	1	10.0
InfServ	10	12.0

Example 3.1 shows that the single production control (*ProdCont*) application had the shortest duration (10 months). For categories with at least three observations, we find that on average, information/on-line service applications (*InfServ*) had the shortest duration (12 months). The durations of customer service (*CustServ*) and transaction processing (*TransPro*) applications were longer and similar. Management information systems (*MIS*) applications had the longest average duration (21.5 months).

Example 3.2

```
. table har, c(n duration mean duration)
```

Hardware Type	N(duration)	mean(duration)
Network	7	14.9
Mainfrm	37	16.8
PC	1	7.0
Mini	1	54.0
Multi	16	17.5

In Example 3.2, we see that the shortest and longest durations were in the personal computer (*PC*) and mini computer (*Mini*) categories, but there were not enough projects to make any generalizations about them. Networked (*Network*), mainframe (*Mainfrm*), and multi-platform (*Multi*) applications had similar durations.

Example 3.3

```
. table ifc, c(n duration mean duration)

User Interface     N(duration)     mean(duration)
GUI                      4              8.0
TextUI                  58             17.8
```

Graphical user interface (*GUI*) applications had much shorter durations than text user interface (*TextUI*) applications (Example 3.3).

Example 3.4

```
. table source, c(n duration mean duration)

Where Developed    N(duration)     mean(duration)
Inhouse                 54             16.9
Outsrced                 8             19.6
```

And in Example 3.4, we can see that outsourced projects (*Outsrced*) took longer to develop than in-house (*Inhouse*) projects.

Example 3.5

```
. table telonuse, c(n duration mean duration)

Telon Use         N(duration)     mean(duration)
No                     47             17.0
Yes                    15             17.9
```

Telon use does not appear to have affected project duration (Example 3.5).

Correlation Analysis

See the section with this same name in Chapter 2.

Stepwise Regression Analysis

The final step of the preliminary analysis is to run forward and backward stepwise regression procedures to see how good of a model can be built with the non-categorical variables. The natural log transformations of the variables *duration, effort,* and *size* are called *ldur, leffort,* and *lsize* in the statistical output.

Forward Stepwise Regression   The forward stepwise regression procedure found three variables that explained 66% of the variation in project duration (Example 3.6). All 62 observations were used. We can see that duration (*ldur*) increased with increasing effort (*leffort*). In addition, duration increased with decreasing staff analysis skills (*t12*), and it decreased over time. Unfortunately, there is a problem with this model. Note that the coefficient of the constant (*_cons*) has a $P > |t|$ of 0.404. This means that there is a 40% probability that the constant term in the equation is due to chance. As the constant term is the number to which all adjustments are made, its significance is very important. I cannot accept a model where I am not sure about the starting point of duration.

Example 3.6

```
. sw regress ldur leffort lsize time nlan t01 t02 t03 t04
     t05 t06 t07 t08 t09 t10 t11 t12 t13 t14 t15, pe(.05)
begin with empty model
p = 0.0000 < 0.0500 adding leffort
p = 0.0003 < 0.0500 adding t12
p = 0.0136 < 0.0500 adding time
```

Source	SS	df	MS		Number of obs =	62
Model	14.6593636	3	4.88645453		F(3,58) =	39.60
Residual	7.15667412	58	.123390933		Prob > F =	0.0000
					R-squared =	0.6720
Total	21.8160377	61	.357639963		Adj R-squared =	0.6550
					Root MSE =	.35127

ldur	Coef.	Std. Err.	t	P>|t|	[95% Conf. Interval]	
leffort	.4136638	.0452761	9.136	0.000	.3230338	.5042938
t12	-.2422332	.0660675	-3.666	0.001	-.3744816	-.1099848
time	-.0558882	.021946	-2.547	0.014	-.0998179	-.0119585
_cons	.3954862	.4699868	0.841	0.404	-.5452947	1.336267

Backward Stepwise Regression The backward stepwise regression procedure found four variables that explained 67% of the variation in project duration (Example 3.7). All 62 observations were used. Here, we can see that duration (*ldur*) increased with increasing effort (*leffort*) and staff application experience (*t13*). Additionally, duration increased with decreasing staff team skills (*t15*) and staff analysis skills (*t12*). It is interesting to note that all of the productivity factors that influenced project duration had to do with people skills. But why would staff with more application experience be found on longer projects? Perhaps they were assigned to the most difficult projects?

Unfortunately, this model has the same problem as the forward stepwise regression model: the coefficient of the constant (*_cons*) has a $P > |t|$ of 0.483. This means that there is a 48% probability that the constant term in the equation is due to chance. If we compare the two models, we can see that the constant term is very different. In the first model, it is a positive 0.3955, and in the second, it is a negative 0.3049. This is a sign that we cannot trust the models. The coefficients of *leffort* and *t12* are more believable as they are somewhat similar in both models.

Example 3.7

```
. sw regress ldur leffort lsize time nlan t01 t02 t03 t04
      t05 t06 t07 t08 t09 t10 t11 t12 t13 t14 t15, pr(.05)
begin with full model
p = 0.9218 >= 0.0500   removing t02
p = 0.9101 >= 0.0500   removing t11
p = 0.7903 >= 0.0500   removing t05
p = 0.7210 >= 0.0500   removing nlan
p = 0.8028 >= 0.0500   removing time
p = 0.6561 >= 0.0500   removing t07
p = 0.5582 >= 0.0500   removing lsize
p = 0.3911 >= 0.0500   removing t04
p = 0.4657 >= 0.0500   removing t09
p = 0.3954 >= 0.0500   removing t01
p = 0.1867 >= 0.0500   removing t08
p = 0.1746 >= 0.0500   removing t10
p = 0.1602 >= 0.0500   removing t14
p = 0.0638 >= 0.0500   removing t03
p = 0.0596 >= 0.0500   removing t06
```

Source	SS	df	MS			
Model	15.0332909	4	3.75832274	Number of obs	=	62
Residual	6.78274677	57	.118995557	F(4, 57)	=	31.58
				Prob > F	=	0.0000
Total	21.8160377	61	.357639963	R-squared	=	0.6891
				Adj R-squared	=	0.6673
				Root MSE	=	.34496

ldur	Coef.	Std. Err.	t	P>|t|	[95% Conf.	Interval]
leffort	.4766454	.0455497	10.464	0.000	.3854336	.5678571
t13	.108993	.048757	2.235	0.029	.0113588	.2066272
t15	-.1933105	.0753016	-2.567	0.013	-.3440993	-.0425217
t12	-.1990815	.0767957	-2.592	0.012	-.3528622	-.0453009
_cons	-.3048544	.4320763	-0.706	0.483	-1.170072	.5603635

Building the Multi-Variable Model _____

The models found by the stepwise regression procedures cannot be used because the constant term was not significant. We will have to build our stepwise ANOVA models taking special care to find models where the constant is significant.

From the summary (see Sidebar 3.1) of one-variable models, I learn that there are significant relationships between duration (*ldur*) and each of the following variables: *t06* (tools use), *t07* (software's logical complexity), *t08* (requirements volatility), *t12* (staff analysis skills), *t14* (staff tool skills), *leffort*, *lsize*, *time*, and *ifc* (user interface). Project duration becomes longer with increasing logical complexity (*t07*), requirements volatility (*t08*), effort, and size; project duration becomes shorter with increasing tools use (*t06*), staff analysis skills (*t12*), staff tool skills (*t14*), and time. Project duration depends on the type of user interface (*ifc*). All of these relationships make sense to me.

The best one-variable model by far is based on effort and explains 53% of the variation in duration. Effort (*leffort*) is added to the RHS of the model and the search for the best two-variable model begins. Note that many of the two-variable models do not have significant constant terms—the same problem that was found in the stepwise regression step. I will not build on these models as they do not make sense. The best two-variable model is therefore based on effort and user interface type (*ifc*) and explains 58% of the variation in duration.

The choice of the best three-variable model poses more of a problem. The model based on efficiency requirements (*t10*) has the highest R-squared value. However, the relationship between duration (*ldur*) and *t10* is strange. The model says that duration increases with decreasing efficiency goals of the software. I would expect the opposite to be true. Referring back to Figure 3.14, I had initially concluded in the preliminary analyses that there was no obvious relationship between efficiency requirements (*t10*) and duration. Now I look at the graph more closely and I see that if we remove Project 10 from the database, the graph would appear to show that, if anything, duration slightly increases with increasing efficiency requirements— not decreases. This leads me to believe that Project 10 is over-influencing these results. In fact, if I remove Project 10 from the database and rerun the same model, *t10* is no longer significant. I decide to reject this model because it does not make sense.

The next best choice is the model based on installation requirements (*t11*). However, once again, the relationship between duration (*ldur*) and *t11* is strange. The model says that duration increases with decreasing installation/training requirements. I would expect the opposite to be true. Referring back to Figure 3.15, I had initially concluded in the preliminary analyses that there was no obvious relationship between installation/training requirements (*t11*) and duration. Now I look at the graph more closely and I see that if we remove Project 10 from the database, the graph would appear to show that duration increases with increasing installation requirements—not decreases. This leads me to believe that Project 10 is over-influencing these results. In fact, if I remove Project 10 from the database and rerun the same

Sidebar 3.1
Statistical Output Summary Sheet

Date: 18/04/2001

Directory: C:\my documents\data analysis book\duration\
Data File: bankdata63.dta (id=1 is dropped)
Procedure Files: *var.do (* = one, two, three, etc..)
Output Files: *var.log

Dependent Variable: *ldur*

Variables	Num Obs	Effect	Adj R^2	Significance of Added Variable	Comments
1-variable models					
t06	62	–	.06		
t07	62	+	.12		
t08	62	+	.11		
t12	62	–	.04	.058	
t14	62	–	.05	.053	
* *leffort*	**62**	+	**.53**		
lsize	62	+	.28		constant not sign.
time	62	–	.15		
ifc	62		.06		
2-variable models with *leffort*					
t05	62	–	.60		constant not sign.
t06	62	–	.59		constant not sign.
t08	62	+	.55	.065	
t09	62	–	.59		constant not sign.
t10	62	–	.58	.082	constant .082
t11	62	–	.55	.057	
t12	62	–	.62		constant not sign.
t15	62	–	.62		constant not sign.
time	62	–	.58		constant not sign.
nlan	62	–	.55	.071	
* *ifc*	**62**		**.58**		
3-variable models with *leffort*, *ifc*					
t04	62	–	.60	.093	constant not sign.
t06	62	–	.64		constant not sign.

Variables	Num Obs	Effect	Adj R²	Significance of Added Variable	Comments
t08	62	+	.60	.081	**best model, sign. = 0.0000**
t09	62	–	.61		constant not sign.
t10	62	–	.61		constant .089; t10 relationship strange
t11	62	–	.60	.059	constant .051; t11 relationship strange
time	62	–	.62		constant not sign.
4-variable models with *leffort*, *ifc*, *t08*					
t10	62	–	.63		t08 0.056; t10 relationship does not make sense; no further improvement possible

model, *t11* is no longer significant either. I decide to reject this model too because it does not make sense.

The next best choice is the model based on requirements volatility (*t08*). Here, duration increases with increasing requirements volatility. This makes sense; therefore, this is the best model to build on. This model explains 60% of the variation in duration. Requirements volatility has a significance level of 0.081. While I would prefer all variables in the model to be significant at the 0.05 level or less, I am willing to accept variables with significance levels up to 0.10 in my model, especially if they add something to our knowledge.

I find one four-variable model based on *leffort*, *ifc*, *t08*, and *t10*; however, the relationship between duration (*ldur*) and *t10* does not make sense again. Thus, the best model is the three-variable model shown in Example 3.8 based on effort (*leffort*), user interface (*ifc*), and requirements volatility (*t08*). No further improvement is possible.

The Final Model
Example 3.8

```
        . anova ldur leffort ifc t08, category(ifc) regress

Source        SS         df       MS          Number of obs =      62
Model     13.4625337     3    4.48751122      F(3, 58)      = 31.16
Residual  8.35350406    58    .144025932      Prob > F      = 0.0000
                                              R-squared     = 0.6171
Total     21.8160377    61    .357639963      Adj R-squared = 0.5973
                                              Root MSE      = .37951
```

ldur	Coef.	Std. Err.	t	P >|t|	[95% Conf. Interval]	
_cons	-1.027968	.4159735	-2.471	0.016	-1.86063	-.1953068
leffort	.3975376	.0489184	8.127	0.000	.2996167	.4954585
ifc						
1	-.5385765	.1970109	-2.734	0.008	-.9329368	-.1442163
2	(dropped)					
t08	.0938698	.0528447	1.776	0.081	-.0119102	.1996499

Checking the Model

Before we can accept the final model, we must check that the assumptions underlying the statistical tests have not been violated.

Numerical Variable Checks

None of the numerical variables in the final model are so highly correlated with each other that they cause multicollinearity problems.

Categorical Variable Checks

Is *ifc* confounded with *leffort* or *t08*? No, neither of the models below is significant (Example 3.9).

Example 3.9

```
                    . anova leffort ifc
```

Number of obs = 62			R-squared	= 0.0030	
Root MSE = 1.03686			Adj R-squared	= -0.0136	

Source	Partial SS	df	MS	F	Prob > F
Model	.193128718	1	.193128718	0.18	0.6732
ifc	.193128718	1	.193128718	0.18	0.6732
Residual	64.5048602	60	1.075081		
Total	64.6979889	61	1.06062277		

```
                    . anova t08 ifc
```

Number of obs = 62			R-squared	= 0.0072	
Root MSE ' = .959825			Adj R-squared	= -0.0093	

Source	Partial SS	df	MS	F	Prob > F
Model	.401557286	1	.401557286	0.44	0.5116
ifc	.401557286	1	.401557286	0.44	0.5116
Residual	55.2758621	60	.921264368		
Total	55.6774194	61	.91274458		

Testing the Residuals

Figure 3.20 shows no pattern in the residuals of our final model.

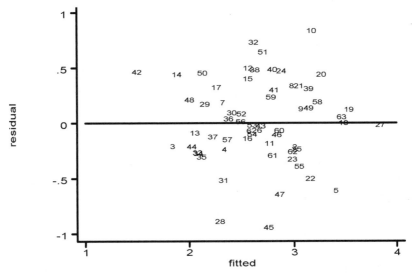

FIGURE 3.20
Residuals vs. fitted values

We can see in Figure 3.21 that the residuals are normally distributed.

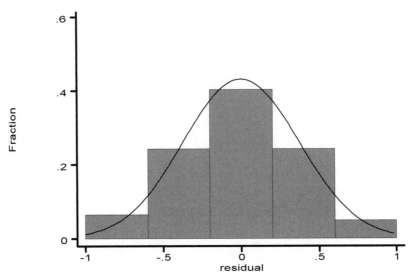

FIGURE 3.21
Distribution of residuals

Detecting Influential Observations

As there are 62 projects in the database, the two projects with a Cook's distance greater than $4/62 = 0.065$ should be examined closely (Example 3.10).

Example 3.10

```
. list id duration effort cooksd if cooksd>4/62

          id    duration   effort    cooksd
34.       35        6        3240    .1098356
41.       42        7        1100    .1825333
```

Projects 35 and 42 are both influential. Table 3.1 summarizes the values of the key variables for each project. I went back and calculated Cook's distance at each step of the ANOVA method to discover when a project became influential. Project 35 became influential when *t08* was added to the model. If I look at Figure 3.12, I can see that Project 35 had a much shorter duration than other projects with very high requirements volatility. This might explain why Project 35's duration is overestimated by the model.

Project 42 in particular has a very large influence on the results. I found that Project 42 became influential when *ifc* was added, this leads me to believe that Project 42's influence on the results is mainly due to it being one of only four *GUI* applications. It is no surprise that the two projects with a high influence are *GUI* applications. The category is represented by only four applications, so those four projects had quite a lot of influence. Because the Cook's distance of Project 42 is so high, I decided to drop Project 42 from the database and rerun the final model to see what would happen (Example 3.11).

TABLE 3.1
Influential Projects' Key Variable Values

id	35	42	Mean (62 projects)
duration	6	7	17.2
effort	3240	1100	8223
ifc	*GUI*	*GUI*	mostly *TextUI*
t08	5	3	3.8
residual	−0.324	0.447	0

Example 3.11

```
. anova ldur leffort ifc t08, category(ifc) regress
```

Source	SS	df	MS		Number of obs	=	61
Model	13.2042216	3	4.4014072		F(3, 57)	=	31.06
Residual	8.07768521	57	.141713776		Prob > F	=	0.0000
					R-squared	=	0.6204
Total	21.2819068	60	.354698447		Adj R-squared	=	0.6005
					Root MSE	=	.37645

ldur	Coef.	Std. Err.	t	P >|t|	[95% Conf.	Interval]
_cons	-1.136105	.4198382	-2.706	0.009	-1.976816	-.295393
leffort	.4092035	.0492394	8.310	0.000	.3106032	.5078037
ifc						
1	-.6894738	.2233591	-3.087	0.003	-1.136743	-.242205
2	(dropped)					
t08	.0961922	.0524452	1.834	0.072	-.0088275	.2012119

I found that all of the variables were still significant even when Project 42 was dropped, although the coefficients of *ifc* and the constant (*_cons*) differed quite a bit. So, dropping Project 42 does not change which variables are important in explaining project duration. Effort (*leffort*), user interface (*ifc*), and requirements volatility (*t08*) explain 60% of the variation in the duration (*ldur*) of 61 projects.

No project has a high influence in the 61-project model. Now you must make an important decision. Should you use the 62-project model or the 61-project model? My decision is to go ahead and use the 62-project model because there are only four *GUI* projects and I don't want to lose one.

Extracting the Equation

The equation as read from the final model's output[2] (Example 3.8) is:

$$ln(duration) = -1.027968 + ifc\_coef + 0.3975376 \times ln(effort) + 0.0938698 \times t08$$

where *ifc_coef* = –0.5385765 for a graphical user interface (*GUI*) and *ifc_coef* = 0 for a text user interface (*TextUI*).

---

2. Stata automatically assigns numbers less than 100 to the categories of *ifc*. Referring to Table 2.1, graphical user interface, coded as 2001, is represented by 1 and text user interface, coded as 2002, is represented by 2 in the statistical output.

This can be transformed into the following equation for duration:

$$duration = 0.3577 \times ifc\_mult \times effort^{0.3975} \times e^{0.0939 \times t08}$$

where $ifc\_mult = 0.5836$ for a graphical user interface (*GUI*) and $ifc\_mult = 1$ for a text user interface (*TextUI*). Note that $ifc\_mult = e^{ifc\_coef}$.

Interpreting the Equation

How can I interpret this equation? Let's look first at the influence of the productivity factors on duration. There is only one, requirements volatility (*t08*). I calculate the value of the *t08* multipliers (Table 3.2); that is, what is *e* to the power $0.0938698 \times t08$ when *t08* is 1, when it is 2, etc.?

It is easier to think of an effect on duration as being more or less than average. To do this, I calculate the normalized requirements volatility multipliers by dividing each value in Table 3.2 by the average value (1.325261).

From Table 3.3, I can easily see that if all other variables remain constant, the effect on duration of low requirements volatility as opposed to average requirements volatility is to decrease duration by 9% (1–.91). On the other hand, if requirements volatility is very high, I can expect a project's duration to be about 21% longer than for an identical project with average requirements volatility. You should also keep in mind that no project in the database actually had very low requirements volatility (denoted by * in Tables 3.2 and 3.3). So although the model says that very low requirements volatility would decrease duration by 17% compared with average requirements volatility, we cannot be completely sure about this.

What about the effects of effort and user interface (*ifc*) on duration? What can I learn from the equation? The coefficient of effort is approximately 0.40. This means that for every 1% increase in effort, duration should increase by

TABLE 3.2
Requirements Volatility Multipliers

Defn.	Value	*t08* Multiplier
very low	1	*1.098417
low	2	1.206519
average	3	1.325261
high	4	1.455689
very high	5	1.598953

TABLE 3.3
Normalized Requirements Volatility Multipliers

Defn.	Value	*t08* Multiplier
very low	1	*0.829
low	2	0.910
average	3	1.000
high	4	1.098
very high	5	1.207

0.40%, all other variables remaining constant. For example, if effort is increased by 5%, duration should increase by 2%. The user interface multiplier (*ifc_mult*) is 0.58 when the *ifc* is a graphical user interface (*GUI*), and 1 when it is a text user interface (*TextUI*). This means that, assuming all other variables remain constant, using a graphical user interface instead of a text user interface can decrease duration by 42%. (The duration when using a *GUI* is 58% of the *TextUI*'s duration.)

Management Implications

The most important variable affecting a project's duration was determined to be effort. Thus, it follows that reducing the effort will reduce the duration. Unfortunately, this variable is not really controllable, and its very definition is related to duration. What is more interesting is the influence of the controllable variables: user interface and requirements volatility. The ease of use of the *GUI* development tool appears to have helped programmers develop applications quicker. The bank should keep in mind that this result was based on only four *GUI*-type projects; data is needed on more *GUI* projects to confirm this. Controlling requirements volatility is very important. Although this result seems obvious, it is interesting that it is the only productivity factor that was linked to duration once effort and user interface were taken into account. The bank now has proof that wisely managing customer requirements is critical to reducing project duration.

In addition, four other productivity factors, the use of tools, software's logical complexity, staff analysis skills, and staff tool skills, plus time all explained some variation in duration before effort was added to the model. Project duration became longer with increasing logical complexity and shorter with increasing tools use, staff analysis skills, and staff tool skills. The bank should also pay attention to these factors.

Finally, project duration decreased over time. From the correlation analysis in Chapter 2, we learned that over the time period studied, the level and use of methods, the level and use of tools, staff tool skills, and staff team skills increased and requirements volatility decreased. Therefore, time represents these factors, as well as other unmeasured managerial and contextual factors. The relationship between duration and time may be the result of process improvement in the company; however, the bank should reflect on what else changed during the nine years studied. Are there other factors that can and should be measured?

Case Study: Developing a Software Development Cost Model

How much will it cost to develop your software application? Whether you are bidding for a fixed-price contract, looking to outsource some of your software development, or developing in-house, accurate effort estimation of software applications is critical. Even though there are many commercial estimation tools available to help you, don't forget that they have been developed using data from companies that may be quite different from your own. To improve their accuracy, you need to calibrate these tools with your company's data. Since you have to collect data anyway, why not analyze it yourself? What factors influence the cost of projects in your company? How accurately can your model predict total effort? Your company-specific model may give you the most reliable estimate.

In this chapter, I will show you how to develop and measure the accuracy of software development effort estimation models. This case study builds on Chapters 1 and 2. As in the previous chapter, this case study uses the bank database we already validated and analyzed in Chapter 2.

Example A: 1993 Effort Estimation Model_____

Data Validation, and Variable and Model Selection_____

The validation of the data, creation of new variables, modifications to the data, and identification of subsets of categorical variables were done in Chapter 2.

Choice of Data

What data should you use to build your effort estimation model? It depends on why you are building it. In practice, I believe software managers should use all available data. If a company has a very large database, it should use only the most up-to-date data and develop, for example, a new model each year based on the last 5-10 years of data. Researchers who want to compare different estimation techniques will want to test their theories on one or several holdout samples.

In this example, I will build a model based on all available data. In Example B, I will look at what would happen if the bank developed an effort estimation model and then used it for two years without re-analyzing the data. It will be interesting to see what differences there are in the two models. Does the importance of certain factors evolve over time?

Model Selection

My goal in this study is to develop a predictive model with the variables that significantly explain the effort differences among software development projects in this bank. All independent variables in a predictive model must be able to be estimated before the project begins.

$$effort = f(size, subapp, subhar, ifc, source,$$
$$t01\text{-}t15, nlan, telonuse, time)$$

What are the relationships between the effort (*effort*) and size of an application (*size*), the type of application (*subapp*), the type of hardware (*subhar*), the user interface (*ifc*), whether or not the development was out-sourced (*source*), the 15 different productivity factors (*t01-t15*), the number of languages used (*nlan*), whether or not Telon was used (*telonuse*), and time (*time*)?

Preliminary Analyses _____

The following analyses should be undertaken before building the multi-variable model. See Chapter 1 for more explanation.

Graphs

I always look at two types of graphs: histograms and two-dimensional graphs.

Histograms   See the section by this same name in Chapter 2.

Two-Dimensional Graphs   I plotted the relationships between the transformed effort variable, *ln(effort)*, and each independent numerical variable.

Figure 4.1 shows a linear relationship between *ln(effort)* and *ln(size)*; the bigger a project's size, the more effort that is needed.

In Figure 4.2, effort appears to be decreasing over time (*syear*). There does not seem to be any relationship between the number of languages used (*nlan*) and effort (Figure 4.3).

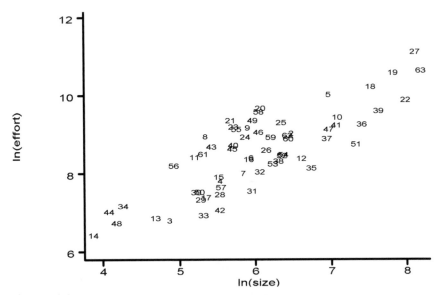

FIGURE 4.1
ln(effort) vs. *ln(size)*

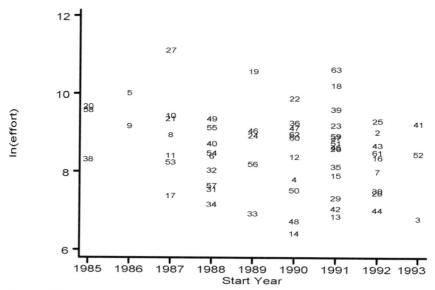

FIGURE 4.2

ln(effort) vs. *syear*

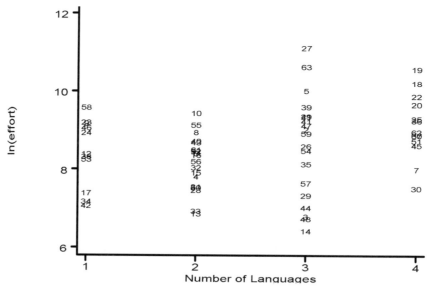

FIGURE 4.3

ln(effort) vs. *nlan*

It looks to me (Figure 4.4) like effort increases slightly with increasing customer participation (*t01*). In Figure 4.5, if I ignore Project 49, it looks like effort decreases with increasing development environment adequacy (*t02*).

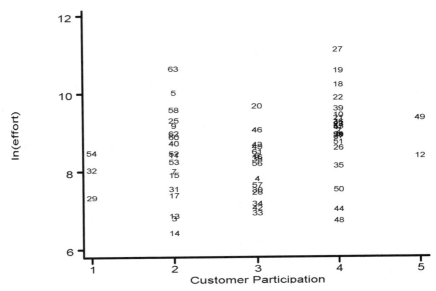

FIGURE 4.4

In(effort) vs. *t01*

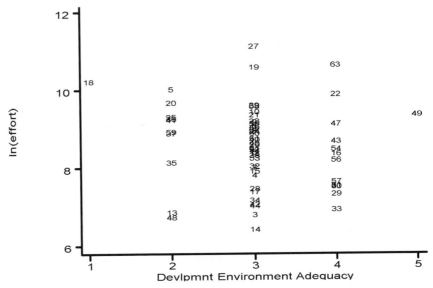

FIGURE 4.5

In(effort) vs. *t02*

Figure 4.6 does not show any relationship between effort and staff availability (*t03*). In Figure 4.7, there appears to be no relationship between effort and use of standards (*t04*).

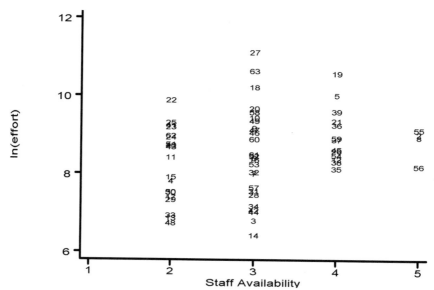

FIGURE 4.6
ln(effort) vs. *t03*

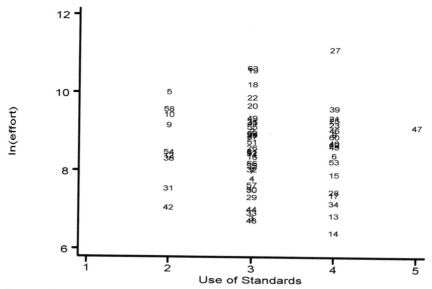

FIGURE 4.7
ln(effort) vs. *t04*

There are no obvious relationships (Figures 4.8 and 4.9) between effort and the use of methods (*t05*) or the use of tools (*t06*), respectively.

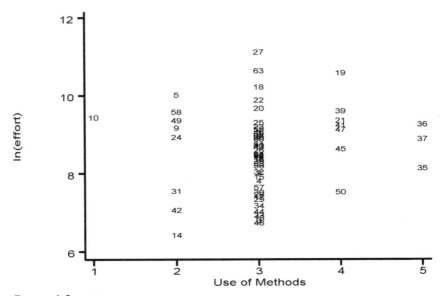

FIGURE 4.8
ln(effort) vs. *t05*

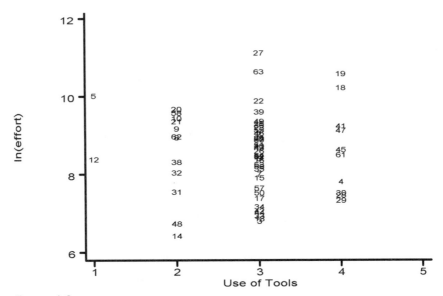

FIGURE 4.9
ln(effort) vs. *t06*

In Figure 4.10, effort appears to increase when software's logical complexity increases (*t07*). The relationship between effort and requirements volatility (*t08*) is not clear in Figure 4.11.

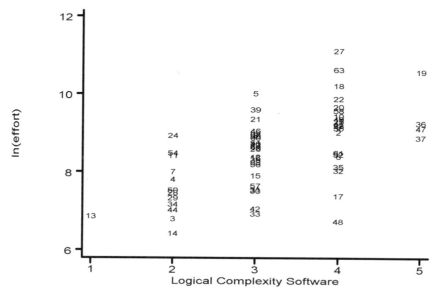

FIGURE 4.10
ln(effort) vs. *t07*

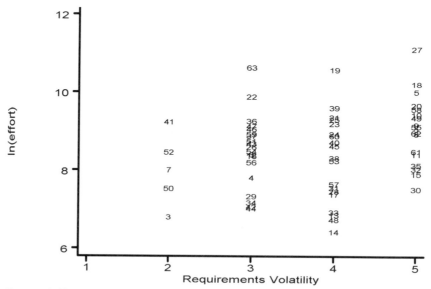

FIGURE 4.11
ln(effort) vs. *t08*

In Figures 4.12 and 4.13, the relationships between effort and quality requirements (*t09*) and effort and efficiency requirements (*t10*) are not obvious.

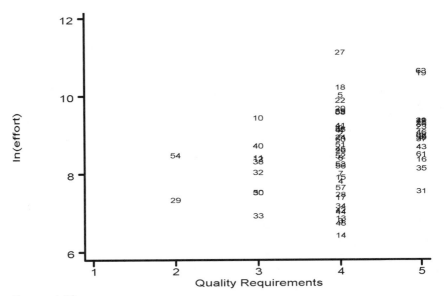

FIGURE 4.12
ln(effort) vs. *t09*

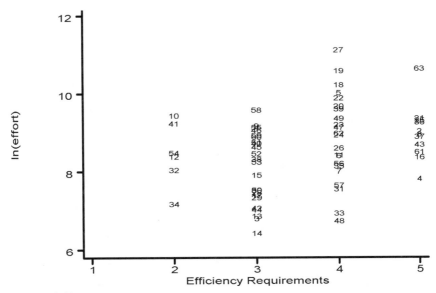

FIGURE 4.13
ln(effort) vs. *t10*

Figure 4.14 shows no obvious relationship between effort and installation requirements (*t11*). In Figure 4.15, I do not see any relationship between effort and staff analysis skills (*t12*).

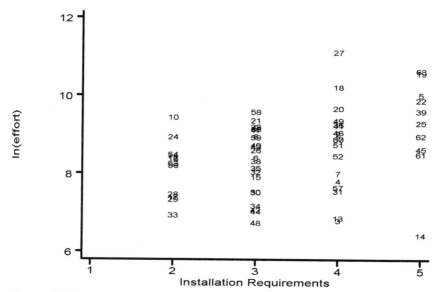

FIGURE 4.14
ln(effort) vs. *t11*

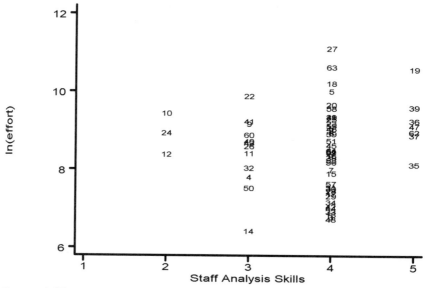

FIGURE 4.15
ln(effort) vs. *t12*

Figure 4.16 shows that the relationship between effort and staff application knowledge (*t13*) is not clear. With the exception of Project 63, effort appears to decrease with increasing staff tool skills (*t14*) in Figure 4.17.

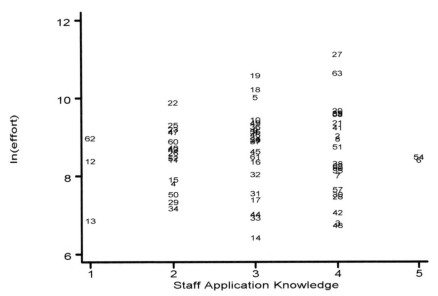

FIGURE 4.16

ln(effort) vs. *t13*

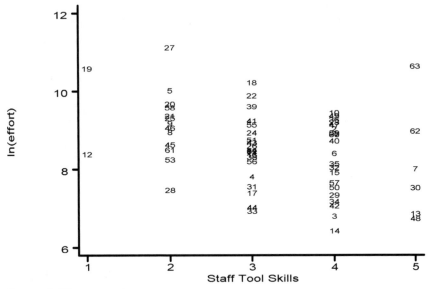

FIGURE 4.17

ln(effort) vs. *t14*

There is no obvious relationship between effort and staff team skills (Figure 4.18).

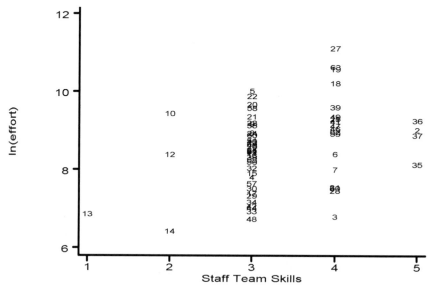

FIGURE 4.18
ln(effort) vs. *t15*

Tables

What is the average effort for each categorical variable? Remember, we learned in Chapter 2 that there is a very strong relationship between effort and size (Spearman's correlation = 0.75), so the explanation behind many of the relationships in the tables and two-dimensional graphs is that the size is different.

Example 4.1

```
. table app, c(n effort mean effort)
```

Application Type	N(effort)	mean(effort)
CustServ	18	9824.4
MIS	4	5101.5
TransPro	29	9628.9
ProdCont	1	1450.0
InfServ	10	3190.6

Referring to Example 4.1, we can see that on average, customer service (*CustServ*) and transaction processing (*TransPro*) applications required the most effort, more than 9500 person-hours. The one production control (*ProdCont*) application required the least effort; however, because there is only one application of this type, we don't have enough information to make any generalizations about production control applications.

Example 4.2

```
. table har, c(n effort mean effort)

Hardware Type    N(effort)    mean(effort)
Network              7            4232.6
Mainfrm             37            8250.5
PC                   1             900.0
Mini                 1           11900.0
Multi               16           10133.9
```

Multi-platform (*Multi*) applications and the one mini computer (*Mini*) application required the most effort (Example 4.2). The one personal computer (*PC*) application required the least effort.

Example 4.3

```
. table ifc, c(n effort mean effort)

User Interface    N(effort)    mean(effort)
GUI                   4            5285.0
TextUI               58            8425.8
```

On average, graphical user interface (*GUI*) applications required less effort than text user interface (*TextUI*) applications (Example 4.3).

Example 4.4

```
. table source, c(n effort mean effort)

Where Developed    N(effort)    mean(effort)
Inhouse               54           8347.2
Outsrced               8           7386.1
```

Outsourced (*Outsrced*) applications required a little less effort than in-house (*Inhouse*) applications (Example 4.4).

Example 4.5

```
. table telonuse, c(n effort mean effort)

Telon Use    N(effort)    mean(effort)
No              47           7806.7
Yes             15           9528.2
```

Applications developed with Telon required more effort than those not developed with Telon (Example 4.5).

Correlation Analysis

See the section with this same name in Chapter 2.

Stepwise Regression Analysis

The final step of the preliminary analysis is to run forward and backward stepwise regression procedures to see how good of a model can be built with the numerical variables.

Forward Stepwise Regression   The forward stepwise regression procedure (Example 4.6) found four variables that explained 76% of the variance in effort. All 62 observations were used. Effort (*leffort*) increased with increasing application size (*lsize*), requirements volatility (*t08*), and quality requirements (*t09*); effort decreased with increasing staff tool skills (*t14*). These relationships make sense to me.

Example 4.6

```
            . sw regress leffort lsize nlan time t01 t02 t03 t04 t05
                t06 t07 t08 t09 t10 t11 t12 t13 t14 t15, pe(.05)
begin with empty model
p = 0.0000 <  0.0500   adding    lsize
p = 0.0014 <  0.0500   adding    t08
p = 0.0099 <  0.0500   adding    t14
p = 0.0110 <  0.0500   adding    t09
```

Source	SS	df	MS		
Model	50.4469966	4	12.6117492		Number of obs = 62
Residual	14.2509923	57	.250017408		$F(4,57)$ = 50.44
Total	64.6979889	61	1.06062277		Prob > F = 0.0000

Number of obs = 62
$F(4,57)$ = 50.44
Prob > F = 0.0000
R-squared = 0.7797
Adj R-squared = 0.7643
Root MSE = .50002

lprod	Coef.	Std. Err.	t	P>|t|	[95% Conf.	Interval]
lsize	.797413	.0682888	11.677	0.000	.660667	.934159
t08	.2155296	.067823	3.178	0.002	.0797164	.3513427
t14	-.1744292	.0656657	-2.656	0.010	-.3059225	-.0429359
t09	.2298329	.0874515	2.628	0.011	.0547143	.4049516
_cons	2.495378	.6472703	3.855	0.000	1.199242	3.791514

Backward Stepwise Regression   The backward stepwise regression procedure (Example 4.7) found five variables that explained 78% of the variance in effort. All 62 observations were used. In this procedure, effort (*leffort*) increased with increasing application size (*lsize*), requirements volatility (*t08*), and quality requirements (*t09*); effort decreased with increasing staff analysis skills (*t12*). It also decreased over time (*time*). These relationships make sense to me.

Example 4.7

```
. sw regress leffort lsize nlan time t01 t02 t03 t04 t05
       t06 t07 t08 t09 t10 t11 t12 t13 t14 t15, pr(.05)
begin with full model

p = 0.8422 >= 0.0500   removing t15
p = 0.7869 >= 0.0500   removing t11
p = 0.7929 >= 0.0500   removing t01
p = 0.6107 >= 0.0500   removing t02
p = 0.3519 >= 0.0500   removing t07
p = 0.3587 >= 0.0500   removing t13
p = 0.3052 >= 0.0500   removing t10
p = 0.2864 >= 0.0500   removing t05
p = 0.2581 >= 0.0500   removing t04
p = 0.2788 >= 0.0500   removing t03
p = 0.0894 >= 0.0500   removing t14
p = 0.1490 >= 0.0500   removing nlan
p = 0.0662 >= 0.0500   removing t06
```

Source	SS	df	MS		
Model	51.3483219	5	10.2696644	Number of obs =	62
Residual	13.3496671	56	.238386912	F(5,56) =	43.08
				Prob > F =	0.0000
Total	64.6979889	61	1.06062277	R-squared =	0.7937
				Adj R-squared =	0.7752
				Root MSE =	.48825

lprod	Coef.	Std. Err.	t	P>|t|	[95% Conf. Interval]	
lsize	.8346822	.0660518	12.637	0.000	.7023645	.9669999
t08	.1529148	.0754093	2.028	0.047	.0018519	.3039777
time	-.0861892	.0345163	-2.497	0.015	-.1553337	-.0170447
t09	.3703023	.0945451	3.917	0.000	.1809057	.5596988
t12	-.2034259	.0999903	-2.034	0.047	-.4037306	-.0031212
_cons	2.628214	.6206441	4.235	0.000	1.384915	3.871514

Building the Multi-Variable Model _____

The best model with numerical variables alone explained 78% of the variation in effort (Example 4.7). Do any of the categorical variables, *subapp* (application type subset), *subhar* (hardware platform subset), *ifc* (user interface), *source* (where developed), and/or *telonuse* (Telon use), explain more of the variation in effort? I use the stepwise ANOVA procedure described in Chapter 1 to see if the R-squared value can be improved. The results are shown in Sidebar 4.1.

SIDEBAR 4.1
STATISTICAL OUTPUT SUMMARY SHEET

Date: 25/05/2001

Directory: C:\my documents\data analysis book\cost estimation\
Data File: bankdata63.dta (id=1 is dropped)
Procedure Files: *var.do (* = one, two, three, etc..)
Output Files: *var.log

Dependent Variable: leffort

Variables	Num Obs	Effect	Adj R^2	Significance of Added Variable	Comments
1-variable models					
t01	62	+	.07		
t03	62	+	.05		
t07	62	+	.33		
t08	62	+	.05		
t09	62	+	.08		
t10	62	+	.08		
t11	62	+	.11		
t14	62	–	.12		
t15	62	+	.09		
* lsize	**62**	**+**	**.66**		
time	62	–	.04	.062	
nlan	62	+	.06		
subhar	60		.05	.080	
2-variable models with lsize					
t07	62	+	.68	.062	
* t08	**62**	**+**	**.71**		
t09	62	+	.69		
t10	62	+	.69		
t14	62	–	.70		

Variables	Num Obs	Effect	Adj R²	Significance of Added Variable	Comments
time	62	−	.70		
ifc	62		.70		
3-variable models with *lsize, t08*					
* *t09*	62	+	.740		follow Path D
t10	62	+	.73		
* *t14*	62	−	.740		follow Path C
time	62	−	.72	.099	
* *ifc*	62		.741		continue on this path
4-variable models with *lsize, t08, ifc*					
t01	62		.75	.057	
t03	62		.75	.059	
t07	62		.76		
* *t09*	62		.79		
t10	62		.77		
t14	62		.76		
5-variable models with *lsize, t08, ifc, t09*					
t03	62		.80	.086	
B- *t14*	62		.80	.052	best Model B: sign. = 0.0000
A- *time*	62		.81		t08 = .070, best Model A: sign. = 0.0000
A: 6-variable models with *lsize, t08, ifc, t09, time*					
none significant					no further improvement possible

(Continued)

SIDEBAR 4.1 (*Continued*)

Variables	Num Obs	Effect	Adj R²	Significance of added Variable	Comments
B: 6-variable models with *lsize, t08, ifc, t09, t14*					
none significant					no further improve-ment possible
Path C:					
4-variable models with *lsize, t08, t14*					Result: This path leads to Model B
Path D:					
4-variable models with *lsize, t08, t09*					Result: This path leads to Models A and B

From the summary of one-variable models, I learn that there are significant relationships between effort (*leffort*) and each of the following variables: *t01* (customer participation), *t03* (staff availability), *t07* (software's logical complexity), *t08* (requirements volatility), *t09* (quality requirements), *t10* (efficiency requirements), *t11* (installation requirements), *t14* (staff tool skills), *t15* (staff team skills), *lsize*, *time*, *nlan* (number of languages), and *subhar* (hardware platform). Effort increases with increasing customer participation (*t01*), staff availability (*t03*), logical complexity (*t07*), requirements volatility (*t08*), quality requirements (*t09*), efficiency requirements (*t10*), installation requirements (*t11*), staff team skills (*t15*), size (*lsize*), and number of languages (*nlan*); effort decreases with increasing staff tool skills (*t14*) and time (*time*). Effort depends on the hardware platform (*subhar*). All of these relationships do not make sense to me. For example, why would effort increase with increasing staff availability and staff team skills? I will not spend too much time wondering about this as size is clearly the most important factor (66% of variation explained). In fact, once size (*lsize*) is added to the model, these two variables are no longer important.

The best two-variable model is based on size (*lsize*) and requirements volatility (*t08*) and explains 71% of the variation in effort (*leffort*). Choosing the best three-variable model is difficult. Three of the models explain 74% of the variation in effort. The model which includes user interface (*ifc*) is the best choice by only 0.1%. I decide to continue for the moment with *ifc*, but will return to build the four-variable models with *t14* (Path C) and *t09* (Path D) to see where they lead. 79% of the variation in effort (*leffort*) is explained by the best four-variable model: *lsize, t08, ifc,* and *t09*.

Choosing the best five-variable model is more difficult. Two models explain nearly the same amount of variation in *leffort*. Model A, with *time*, explains slightly more variation (81%), but the significance of *t08* (0.070) is worse than the significance of *t14* (0.052) in Model B, which explains 80% of the variation. Which model is better? Time (*time*) is an interesting variable to have in a model because it represents many things evolving over time that we haven't measured or can't measure. Staff tool skills (*t14*) is also an interesting variable to have in a model. People factors are important, a fact that doesn't emerge in Model A. The two models are so close that I really can't choose one over the other, so I will check the accuracy of both of them. No further improvement can be made. I also find that building the best Path C and Path D models leads again to Models A and B.

Final Model A
Example 4.8

```
. anova leffort ifc t09 lsize t08 time, category(ifc) regress
```

Source	SS	df	MS		Number of obs =	62
Model	53.1986067	5	10.6397213		F(5,56) =	51.81
Residual	11.4993822	56	.205346111		Prob > F =	0.0000
					R-squared =	0.8223
Total	64.6979889	61	1.06062277		Adj R-squared =	0.8064
					Root MSE =	.45315

ldur	Coef.	Std. Err.	t	P>|t|	[95% Conf.	Interval]
_cons	1.89815	.5646683	3.362	0.001	.7669836	3.029317
ifc						
1	−.9135228	.2457736	−3.717	0.000	−1.405866	−.4211791
2	(dropped)					
t09	.3632764	.0834529	4.353	0.000	.1961002	.5304526
lsize	.8530214	.0615819	13.852	0.000	.7296581	.9763847
t08	.1291866	.0699594	1.847	0.070	−.010959	.2693322
time	−.0826743	.0320336	−2.581	0.013	−.1468455	−.0185032

In the final Model A (Example 4.8), five variables explained 81% of the variance in effort. All 62 observations were used. Effort (*leffort*) increased with increasing application size (*lsize*), requirements volatility (*t08*), and quality requirements (*t09*). Effort decreased over time (*time*). Effort was dependent on the type of user interface (*ifc*).

Final Model B
Example 4.9

```
. anova leffort ifc t09 lsize t08 t14, category(ifc) regress
```

Source	SS	df	MS		Number of obs =	62
Model	52.6791989	5	10.5358398		F(5,56) =	49.09
Residual	12.01879	56	.21462125		Prob > F =	0.0000
					R-squared =	0.8142
Total	64.6979889	61	1.06062277		Adj R-squared =	0.7976
					Root MSE =	.46327

leffort		Coef.	Std. Err.	t	P >|t|	[95% Conf.	Interval]
_cons		1.938946	.6240303	3.107	0.003	.6888634	3.189029
ifc							
	1	-.8336486	.2584952	-3.225	0.002	-1.351477	-.3158203
	2	(dropped)					
t09		.2959509	.0835785	3.541	0.001	.1285232	.4633787
lsize		.8360667	.0643957	12.983	0.000	.7070666	.9650667
t08		.2014694	.0629899	3.198	0.002	.0752855	.3276533
t14		-.1247745	.0627581	-1.988	0.052	-.250494	.0009451

In Model B (Example 4.9), five variables explained 80% of the variance in effort. All 62 observations were used. Effort (*leffort*) increased with increasing application size (*lsize*), requirements volatility (*t08*), and quality requirements (*t09*). Effort decreased with increasing staff tool skills (*t14*). Effort was dependent on the type of user interface (*ifc*).

Checking the Models

I will present the checks for both models simultaneously as they are not very different. In practice, I checked them individually.

Numerical Variable Checks

None of the numerical variables in the final models are so highly correlated with each other that they cause multicollinearity problems (see the section titled "Correlation Analysis" in Chapter 2). The highest correlation (−0.48) is between time (*time*) and requirements volatility (*t08*).

Categorical Variable Checks

Is *ifc* confounded with *lsize*, *t08*, *t09*, *time*, or *t14*? As can be seen in the ANOVA tables in Example 4.10, there are no strong relationships between *ifc* and *lsize, t08, time,* or *t14.* The user interface (*ifc*) explains 4.4% of the variation in quality requirements (*t09*), which is not enough to cause any problems.

Example 4.10

```
. anova lsize ifc
```

```
             Number of obs =      62     R-squared     =  0.0288
             Root MSE      = .961568     Adj R-squared = -0.0126
```

Source	Partial SS	df	MS	F	Prob > F
Model	1.64632592	1	1.64632592	1.78	0.1871
ifc	1.64632592	1	1.64632592	1.78	0.1871
Residual	55.476742	60	.924612366		
Total	57.1230679	61	.936443736		

```
. anova t08 ifc
```

```
             Number of obs =      62     R-squared     =  0.0072
             Root MSE      = .959825     Adj R-squared = -0.0093
```

Source	Partial SS	df	MS	F	Prob > F
Model	.401557286	1	.401557286	0.44	0.5116
ifc	.401557286	1	.401557286	0.44	0.5116
Residual	55.2758621	60	.921264368		
Total	55.6774194	61	.91274458		

```
. anova t09 ifc
```

```
             Number of obs =      62     R-squared     =  0.0595
             Root MSE      = .727241     Adj R-squared =  0.0439
```

Source	Partial SS	df	MS	F	Prob > F
Model	2.00917686	1	2.00917686	3.80	0.0560
ifc	2.00917686	1	2.00917686	3.80	0.0560
Residual	31.7327586	60	.52887931		
Total	33.7419355	61	.553146483		

```
. anova time ifc
```

```
             Number of obs =      62     R-squared     =  0.0211
             Root MSE      = 2.12623     Adj R-squared =  0.0048
```

Source	Partial SS	df	MS	F	Prob > F
Model	5.84677419	1	5.84677419	1.29	0.2600
ifc	5.84677419	1	5.84677419	1.29	0.2600
Residual	271.25	60	4.52083333		
Total	277.096774	61	4.54257007		

```
                                   . anova t14 ifc
                    Number of obs =        62     R-squared     = 0.0380
                    Root MSE       = .995969     Adj R-squared = 0.0220

Source      Partial SS        df          MS            F       Prob > F
Model       2.35372636        1      2.35372636       2.37      0.1287
ifc         2.35372636        1      2.35372636       2.37      0.1287
Residual    59.5172414       60       .991954023
Total       61.8709677       61      1.01427816
```

Testing the Residuals

Figures 4.19 and Figure 4.20 show no pattern in the residuals of either final model.

We can see in Figures 4.21 and 4.22 that the residuals of both models are approximately normally distributed.

Detecting Influential Observations

Because there are 62 projects in the database, the projects with a Cook's distance greater than $4/62 = 0.065$ should be examined closely in both models (Examples 4.11 and 4.12).

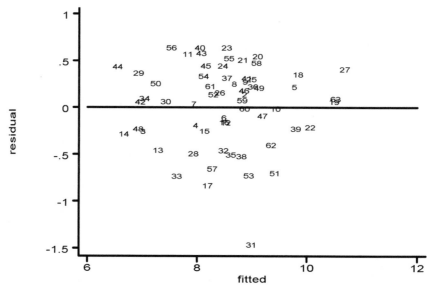

FIGURE 4.19

Model A residuals vs. fitted values

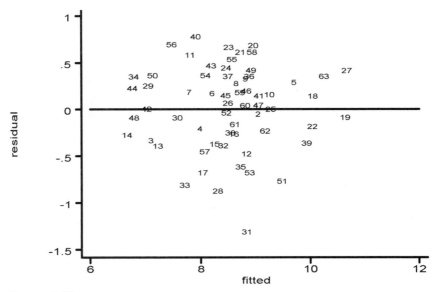

FIGURE 4.20
Model B residuals vs. fitted values

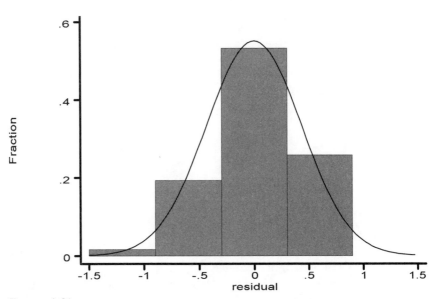

FIGURE 4.21
Distribution of Model A residuals

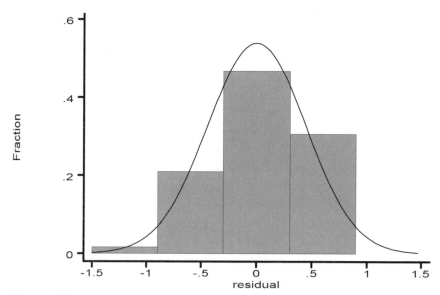

FIGURE 4.22
Distribution of Model B residuals

Model A
Example 4.11

```
. list id size effort cooksd if cooksd>4/62

           id     size    effort      cooksd
    30.    31      387      1798    .1378167
    34.    35      840      3240    .1443154
```

Model B
Example 4.12

```
. list id size effort cooksd if cooksd>4/62

           id     size    effort      cooksd
    30.    31      387      1798    .0746465
    34.    35      840      3240    .1859343
```

Projects 31 and 35 are influential in both models. Table 4.1 summarizes the values of the key variables for each project. I went back and calculated Cook's distance at each step of the ANOVA method to discover when a project became influential. Project 35 became influential when requirements volatility (*t08*) was added to the model. Because size is such an important factor in the calculation of effort (size alone explains 66% of the

TABLE 4.1
Influential Projects' Key Variable Values

id	31	35	Mean (62 projects)
effort	1798	3240	8223
size	387	840	673
t08	4	5	3.8
ifc	TextUI	GUI	mostly TextUI
t09	5	5	3.8
time	4 (1988)	7 (1991)	5.58
t14	3	4	3.3
residual	−1.3313	−0.6696	0

variation), it is necessary to adjust effort for size to see the effects of the other variables.

Effort divided by size is the project delivery rate, that is, the inverse of the definition of productivity (*prod*), so I will refer to the productivity graphs we made in Chapter 2 to see the relationships. If I look at Figure 2.38, I can see that Project 35 had a much higher productivity rating than other projects with very high requirements volatility. Project 35's team was probably more effective because they had already developed earlier releases of the software. This might explain why Project 35's effort is overestimated by the models. Perhaps it would be a good idea for the bank to collect this information for all projects!

Project 31 became influential when the quality requirements (*t09*) variable was added. Referring back to Figure 2.39, we can see that Project 31 had a high productivity rating (along with Project 35) for an application with very high quality requirements. In addition, Project 31 used a text user interface (*TextUI*), which is supposed to be less productive than a *GUI*, but wasn't in this case. Project 31 was developed to run in a separate transaction processing system than the ordinary core banking applications. This might explain why Project 31 was more productive than expected, resulting in an effort overestimation of nearly 350%.

I removed Projects 31 and 35 from each model and ran them again to see what would happen (Examples 4.13 and 4.14). In Model A, the key variables remained significant. In fact, the significance of *t08* improved to 0.031. Five variables explained 85% of the variation of 60 projects. No project has too much influence.

Model A with Two Projects Removed
Example 4.13

```
. anova leffort ifc t09 lsize t08 time, category(ifc) regress
```

Source	SS	df	MS			
Model	54.7644612	5	10.9528922			
Residual	8.73585543	54	.161775101			
Total	63.5003166	59	1.07627655			

Number of obs = 60
F(5,54) = 67.70
Prob > F = 0.0000
R-squared = 0.8624
Adj R-squared = 0.8497
Root MSE = .40221

leffort	Coef.	Std. Err.	t	P >|t|	[95% Conf.	Interval]
_cons	1.728021	.5096088	3.391	0.001	.7063173	2.749725
ifc						
1	-.7769672	.2497854	-3.111	0.003	-1.277757	-.2761776
2	(dropped)					
t09	.4227937	.0756665	5.588	0.000	.2710915	.574496
lsize	.8453856	.0547011	15.455	0.000	.7357166	.9550546
t08	.1428785	.0645738	2.213	0.031	.0134159	.2723411
time	-.0914392	.029005	-3.153	0.003	-.1495907	-.0332877

In Model B, the key variables also remained significant. In fact, the significance of *t14* improved to 0.037. Five variables explain 84% of the variation of 60 projects. No project has too much influence.

Model B with Two Projects Removed
Example 4.14

```
. anova leffort ifc t09 lsize t08 t14, category(ifc) regress
```

Source	SS	df	MS			
Model	53.9660826	5	10.7932165			
Residual	9.53423398	54	.176559889			
Total	63.5003166	59	1.07627655			

Number of obs= 60
F(5,54) = 61.13
Prob > F = 0.0000
R-squared = 0.8499
Adj R-squared= 0.8360
Root MSE = .42019

leffort	Coef.	Std. Err.	t	P >|t|	[95% Conf.	Interval]
_cons	1.677677	.5720869	2.933	0.005	.5307117	2.824642
ifc						
1	-.6534076	.2661614	-2.455	0.017	-1.187029	-.1197862
2	(dropped)					
t09	.346181	.0770707	4.492	0.000	.1916635	.5006984
lsize	.8308308	.0584324	14.219	0.000	.7136808	.9479807
t08	.2292321	.0587611	3.901	0.000	.1114232	.347041
t14	-.1219702	.0569658	-2.141	0.037	-.2361796	-.0077607

Now I have to make an important decision. Should I use the 62-project models, the 61-project models, or the 60-project models? My decision is to go ahead and use the 62-project models. Why? I have already validated the data and removed the projects that don't belong. Although they decrease the accuracy of the model on the underlying data, there may be other projects like 31 and 35 in the future. I do not want to drop Project 35 because it is one of only four *GUI* applications and thus I expect it to have a high influence. The influence of Project 31 is just due to its having a very large error. Just because I can't estimate it accurately does not mean I should get rid of it.

You may decide to do something else. This is where the "art" of statistical analysis comes in. Just be sure to write down **why** you made certain decisions. If you don't and you return to your analysis later, you may wonder why you did something and then spend a few extra hours reaching the same conclusion again.

Measuring Estimation Accuracy

The accuracy of cost estimation models is commonly measured with two or three indicators. The fact that these accuracy indicators are based on only two terms, the actual and estimated effort, allows you to easily compare the estimation accuracy of different methods. For example, the accuracy of an expert can be compared with the accuracy of an ANOVA model. The fact that these indicators are expressed in terms of percentages allows the comparison of models based on different measurement units. For example, the accuracy of a model where effort is measured in person-hours can be directly compared to a model where effort is measured in person-months.

Common Accuracy Statistics

- MMRE (mean magnitude of relative error)—The relative error, RE, is relative to the actual effort: *[(actual effort − estimated effort) / actual effort]* × *100*. The magnitude of relative error, MRE, is the absolute value of the RE. The mean magnitude of relative error, MMRE, is the average of all MREs. Researchers consider a model to perform well when its MMRE is 25% or less.
- Pred(.25)—This is the percentage of projects with an MRE of 25% or less. Researchers consider a model to perform well when at least 75% of the projects have an MRE of 25% or less.
- MedMRE (median magnitude of relative error)—If you sort projects by their MREs, the median value is at the midpoint: 50% of projects have

a larger error and 50% have a smaller error. This has the advantage of being less influenced by extremely large MREs. Like the MMRE, 25% is considered an acceptable value.

There are some problems with these measures. First, a project can only be underestimated between 0% and 100%, but it can be overestimated to infinity. Thus, overestimates influence accuracy measures more than underestimates, while the reality is that it is probably worse to underestimate a project's effort. You also don't have any idea from these measures if they are over- or underestimating big or small sized projects. Inaccurately estimating a large project may have worse consequences than a similar error in a small project. For example, a 25% underestimation error in a small project may correspond to 100 extra hours, whereas the same percentage of error in a large project could mean 10,000 extra hours. In addition, what is considered an acceptable model by researchers may be completely unacceptable for your company. You might only find that a 10% error is acceptable in 90% of your projects. Thus, in practice, I don't think these measures are extremely useful **within** a company, except as a general indicator of accuracy.

Because I used a log transformation on the raw data, I must transform each model's effort predictions back into hours before calculating their accuracy. The *estimate* is thus the inverse natural log of the effort predicted by the model. The *actual* is the actual effort in hours.

In Table 4.2, we can see that Model A performs better than Model B on the underlying data. The medMREs of both models are less influenced by the large error of Project 31 and are close to 25%. However, the Pred(.25) values are not very good for either model. Only 45% of Model A's projects have an MRE of 25% or less.

As MMRE, MedMRE, and Pred(.25) are just three characteristics that describe the accuracy distribution, they can sometimes give contradictory results. It is not unheard of to find that one model has the best MMRE and a second model the best Pred(.25). To decide which is better, we need more information about the accuracy distribution. It is for this reason that researchers

TABLE 4.2
Comparison of Model A and Model B Accuracy

	Model A	Model B
MMRE	40%	40%
MedMRE	28%	29%
Pred(.25)	45%	39%

present boxplots of the estimation errors of competing prediction systems in their papers in addition to the more commonly used accuracy statistics.

Boxplots of Estimation Error

The estimation error is calculated by subtracting the *estimate* from the *actual*, that is, *estimation error = actual – estimate*. Thus, positive numbers mean underestimates and negative numbers mean overestimates.

A boxplot (Figure 4.23) is just another way of looking at a distribution. It has the advantage of containing more information than a simple histogram, and the disadvantage of being a little more difficult to understand when you have never seen one before. The line in the middle of each box represents the median, or 50th percentile of the estimation error. In both cases, the median estimation error is slightly above zero. Thus, there is a slight tendency to underestimate in both models. The box extends from the 25th percentile to the 75th percentile. (The xth percentile means that x% of the observations have values lower than x.) A narrow symmetrical box centered close to zero is good. In a perfect model, all the estimation errors would be zero, so it is better to have a large number of projects with estimation errors close to zero.

The lines going up and down from each box (called whiskers) represent the theoretical range within which each model's estimation errors should lie if their distribution is normal. The smaller the range, the better. It is better if a

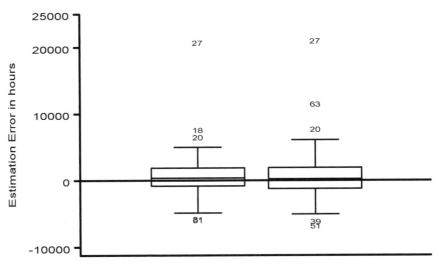

For 1993 Model A and Model B

FIGURE 4.23
Boxplots of Model A and Model B estimation errors

model's upper and lower whiskers have the same length. The values outside the lower and upper whiskers are called outliers. Each model has five outliers. I conclude from comparing these boxplots that one model is not clearly better than the other. Although the box and whiskers of Model B are wider and the outliers are farther away from zero, its median value is closer to zero.

Wilcoxon Signed-Rank Test

You can check if either model has consistently smaller errors by applying the Wilcoxon signed-rank test to matched pairs. This test compares the magnitude of each model's estimation error for each project. The magnitude is the absolute value of the estimation error ($|actual - estimate|$). In the statistical output (Example 4.15), *aModel_A* refers to Model A's absolute estimation errors and *aModel_B* refers to Model B's absolute estimation errors. We are interested in the value of *Prob > |z|* in bold. If this value is greater than 0.05, it means there is no significant difference between the two models. In our case, it is 0.2108, so we conclude that there is no significant difference. You will learn more about this test in Chapter 6.

Example 4.15

```
          . signrank aModel_A=aModel_B
Wilcoxon signed-rank test

sign                    obs      sum ranks       expected
positive                 26           798          976.5
negative                 36          1155          976.5
zero                      0             0              0
all                      62          1953           1953

unadjusted variance     20343.75
adjustment for ties         0.00
adjustment for zeros        0.00
adjusted variance       20343.75

Ho: aModel_A = aModel_B
         z =  -1.251
  Prob > |z|  =  0.2108
```

Accuracy Segmentation

In your company, you probably want to know which projects have large errors and why. That way, you will know in the future not to expect the model to perform well on those types of projects. I recommend that you look at the relative errors (REs) of each project with a graph like Figure 4.24

or Figure 4.25. These figures show you a snapshot of the RE in relation to the size of a project, as well as which projects are over- or underestimated. I used size instead of effort because I am developing a predictive model and the

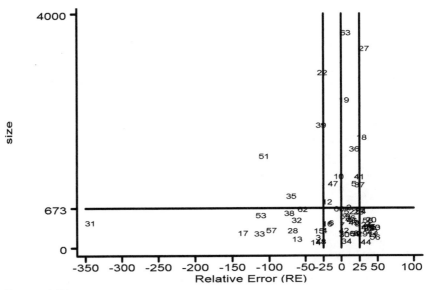

FIGURE 4.24
size vs. Model A's relative error (RE)

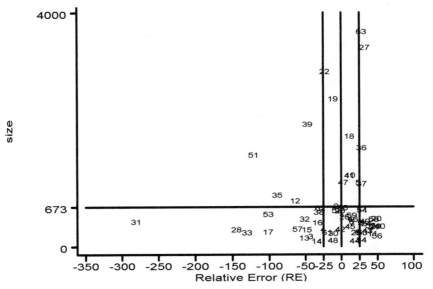

FIGURE 4.25
size vs. Model B's relative error (RE)

size of a new project can be estimated, whereas the actual effort of a project is not known until it is completed. Obviously, sometimes you also need to print out the values of RE and size to correctly categorize projects.

Draw one line where y = either the average size of projects in your company or the cut-off value above which projects are considered to be large in your company. I chose the average project size, 673 function points, in Figures 4.24 and 4.25.

Draw two lines where x = the RE you are willing to accept, say + or -25% for this case. This divides the graph into eight sections. The two sections on the extreme left-hand side contain the overestimated projects. (If the *estimate* is bigger than the *actual*, the RE is negative.) The two sections on the extreme right-hand side contain the underestimated projects. The upper sections contain the above average sized projects, and the lower sections contain the below average sized projects. I can then identify the problem projects and categorize the accuracy by size and error type (Tables 4.3 and 4.4).

TABLE 4.3
Model A Accuracy Segmentation

Model A	Overestimate Error Not Acceptable	Underestimate Error Not Acceptable
Large projects, above average size (15 projects)	27% (4 projects)	13% (2 projects)
Small projects, below average size (47 projects)	30% (14 projects)	30% (14 projects)

TABLE 4.4
Model B Accuracy Segmentation

Model B	Overestimate Error Not Acceptable	Underestimate Error Not Acceptable
Large projects, above average size (15 projects)	27% (4 projects)	27% (4 projects)
Small projects, below average size (47 projects)	30% (14 projects)	32% (15 projects)

In Tables 4.3 and 4.4, we can see that most projects, 47, were below average in size. Models A and B are equally likely to overestimate or underestimate below average sized projects. They will overestimate small projects 30% of the time, underestimate approximately 30% of the time, and have an acceptable error 40% of the time. Model A is least likely to underestimate above average sized projects, which is probably the most critical situation in the bank. Model A also has no underestimates larger than 50% (Figure 4.24). In addition, five projects were overestimated by more than 100%, of which Project 31 was overestimated by nearly 350%.

For Model B (Figure 4.25), one project, Project 40, was underestimated by more than 50% and six projects were overestimated by more than 100%. Future projects similar to these projects will probably be overestimated too. Knowing this, the bank can use the models wisely rather than blindly. As a result of my close look at the two models' performances, I now have a preference for Model A. However, as we will see in the next example, a model that performs better on the underlying data does not necessarily estimate the effort of future projects more accurately.

Although overestimating effort by 350% sounds terrible in theory, in practice it might not be that bad. Project 31 was a small project (387 function points) that actually had a very low effort (1798 hours). The bank probably cares more about estimating large projects more accurately. The one-million-dollar question is: If the bank overestimates the effort needed for a project, will the bank complete it with less effort, or will the overestimated effort become a self-fulfilling prophecy? If this was not a bank, but a company bidding for a project, this overestimate could have two consequences. The good consequence would be that the company wins a fixed-price contract, completes it with much less effort than planned, and makes a lot of money. The bad consequence would be that the company's bid looks way too big compared to other bids and it does not get the contract.

The 95% Confidence Interval

When I first started studying software cost estimation models, I was surprised to learn how large the 95% confidence intervals (CIs) were in the databases I was analyzing. Even a model that explains a large amount of the variation in the data can be lousy when it comes to estimating with high confidence. For example, if I told you that I had developed a model that explained 80% of the cost variation in your company and based on this model, your project should take 7000 person-hours, you'd probably feel pretty confident in the estimate. But what if I told you that I was 95% confident that the actual effort would be somewhere between 2700 and 18000 hours. Would you still be happy? Be sure to check your 95% confidence intervals.

The 95% confidence interval is approximately equal to the estimated value plus or minus 1.96 multiplied by the standard error of the forecast (*stdf*). You will learn more about confidence interval theory in Chapter 6. Applied to effort prediction, it means that we are approximately 95% confident that the actual value of effort will be between the lower and upper limits given by the following equation. Thus, there is still a 5% chance that the true value of effort will be outside this range.

Upper and lower 95% CI limits of estimate
$$= estimate \pm 1.96 \times stdf$$

The calculation of our models' confidence intervals (CIs) is slightly complicated because we took log transformations of the raw data. Thus, our estimates, errors, and 95% confidence intervals have units of *ln*(hours), not hours. The equation needed to calculate the upper and lower 95% confidence limits of Models A and B is:

Upper and lower 95% CI limits of *ln(estimate)*
$$= ln(estimate) \pm 1.96 \times ln(stdf)$$

The estimates and stdfs of our models, *ln(estimate)* and *ln(stdf)*, are automatically calculated by my statistical tool. I can use them to calculate the upper and lower 95% CI limits for *ln(estimate)*. Then I transform these limits (by taking their inverse natural logs) into CI limits in units of hours, which is easier for people to understand. Due to the properties of logs, this results in the upper confidence limit being much farther away from each project's effort estimate than the lower confidence limit.

The 95% confidence intervals for Model A are shown in Example 4.16. We can see that the effort estimate for Project 2 is 7022 hours (*estimate*). I am 95% confident that the actual value for effort will be between 2745 hours (*lower95*) and 17966 hours (*upper95*). The actual effort is 7871 hours (*effort*), which is very close to my estimate, and also falls within this range. For Project 31, the worst case, my estimate is 7968 hours (*estimate*). I am 95% confident that the actual effort will be between 3184 hours (*lower95*) and 19942 hours (*upper95*). The actual effort is 1798 hours (*effort*). This is outside my 95% confidence interval. Remember that there is an approximately 5% chance that the actual effort will be outside the 95% confidence interval. We actually experience a 2% chance in our sample as only one effort out of 62 lies outside these limits.

Example 4.16

```
.  list id estimate lower95 upper95 effort

id      estimate     lower95     upper95      effort
 2         7022         2745       17966        7871
 3         1116          438        2842         845
 4         2882         1168        7110        2330
 5        17514         6959       44084       21272
 6         4827         1936       12033        4224
 7         2788         1108        7014        2826
 8         5823         2292       14791        7320
 9         7093         2833       17762        9125
10        12336         4847       31396       11900
11         2491          985        6295        4300
12         4984         1986       12505        4150
13         1456          583        3634         900
14          792          312        2011         583
15         3378         1340        8514        2565
16         4853         1937       12156        4047
17         3588         1441        8929        1520
18        18681         7278       47950       25910
19        35804        14104       90892       37286
20         8910         3518       22565       15052
21         6807         2687       17245       11039
22        23370         9182       59479       18500
23         5061         2031       12613        9369
24         4717         1925       11560        7184
25         7930         3162       19885       10447
26         4461         1809       10999        5100
27        43368        16897      111306       63694
28         2770         1112        6902        1651
29         1029          394        2688        1450
30         1678          641        4398        1745
31         7968         3184       19942        1798
32         4797         1906       12073        2957
33         2055          825        5118         963
34         1146          449        2929        1233
35         5497         1992       15170        3240
36         8194         3005       22343       10000
37         5073         1873       13742        6800
38         6644         2593       17025        3850
39        17957         7119       45295       14000
40         3119         1253        7762        5787
41         7284         2848       18626        9700
42         1061          387        2907        1100
43         3192         1270        8020        5578
44          703          277        1788        1060
45         3470         1407        8558        5279
46         6941         2756       17485        8117
47         9733         3919       24172        8710
48         1025          407        2580         796
```

id	estimate	lower95	upper95	effort
49	9127	3636	22912	11023
50	1393	546	3557	1755
51	12248	4891	30668	5931
52	3968	1567	10049	4456
53	7604	3067	18848	3600
54	3340	1278	8730	4557
55	5290	2134	13110	8752
56	1860	745	4643	3440
57	3908	1586	9629	1981
58	8717	3442	22078	13700
59	6741	2698	16843	7105
60	7040	2866	17296	6816
61	3773	1467	9702	4620
62	11425	4544	28726	7451
63	36920	14285	95421	39479

As you can see, the 95% confidence intervals are very wide. Although the predictive capability of the bank's model is nothing to get excited about, the bank has learned which factors explain differences in project costs in their company.[1] Let's look at the impact of these factors.

Extracting the Equations

Model A

The equation as read from final Model A's output (Example 4.8) is:

$$ln(effort) = 1.89815 + ifc\_coef + 0.8530214 \times ln(size) +$$
$$0.3632764 \times t09 + 0.1291866 \times t08 - 0.0826743 \times time$$

where $ifc\_coef^{2} = -0.9135228$ for a graphical user interface (GUI) and $ifc\_coef = 0$ for a text user interface (TextUI).

This can be transformed into the following equation for effort:

$$effort = 6.6735 \times ifc\_mult \times size^{0.8530} \times e^{0.3633 \times t09} \times$$
$$e^{0.1297 \times t08} \times e^{-0.0827 \times time}$$

where $ifc\_mult = 0.4011$ for a graphical user interface (GUI) and $ifc\_mult = 1$ for a text user interface (TextUI).

---

1. It is of interest to note that these same factors explain the productivity differences among applications if we remove project duration from the productivity model developed in Chapter 2.
2. Stata automatically assigns numbers less than 100 to the categories for *ifc*. Referring to Table 2.1, graphical user interface, coded as 2001, is represented by 1 and text user interface, coded as 2002, is represented by 2 in the statistical output.

Model B

The equation as read from final Model B's output (Example 4.9) is:

$$ln(effort) = 1.938946 + ifc\_coef + 0.8360667 \times ln(size) + \\ 0.2959509 \times t09 + 0.2014694 \times t08 - 0.1247745 \times t14$$

where $ifc\_coef = -0.8336484$ for a graphical user interface (GUI) and $ifc\_coef = 0$ for a text user interface (TextUI).

This can be transformed into the following equation for effort:

$$effort = 6.9514 \times ifc\_mult \times size^{0.8361} \times e^{0.2960 \times t09} \times \\ e^{0.2015 \times t08} \times e^{-0.1248 \times t14}$$

where $ifc\_mult = 0.4345$ for a graphical user interface (GUI) and $ifc\_mult = 1$ for a text user interface (TextUI).

Interpreting the Equations

We have two different models that explain the effort differences of projects in the bank. The explanatory variables and their coefficients are not the same in both models. Nonetheless, they both explain nearly the same amount of variation in the data and we cannot say that one is clearly better than the other. We cannot ignore Model B just because it explains 0.9% less variation than Model A. If the interpretation is that in Model A, using a GUI can decrease effort by 60%, and in Model B, using a GUI can decrease effort by 57%, what is the true value? My conclusion is that the truth is somewhere near these two values. Using a GUI in the bank is likely to reduce effort by 57-60%, all other variables remaining constant. The fact that 57% is close to 60% gives me more confidence that the GUI effect is real. I have found nearly the same effect in two models. The coefficient of size is also nearly the same in both models: 0.8530 in Model A and 0.8361 in Model B. This means that for every 1% increase in size, effort is expected to increase by approximately 0.84-0.85%, all other variables remaining constant.

Now let's look at the influence of the three productivity factors on effort. First, I calculate the value of the productivity factor multipliers for both models (Tables 4.5 and 4.6). For Model A's t08 multiplier, I calculate e to the power $0.1291866 \times t08$ when t08 is 1, when it is 2, etc.

It is easier to think of an effect on effort as being more or less than average. To do this, I calculate the each normalized productivity factor's multiplier by dividing by its average value.

Requirements volatility has a more noticeably different effect in both models. From Tables 4.7 and 4.8, I can see that if all other variables remain constant, the effect of low requirements volatility, as opposed to average requirements volatility, is to decrease effort by approximately 12-18%. On the other hand, if requirements volatility is very high, I can expect a project's effort to be about 30-50% higher than for an identical project with average

TABLE 4.5
Model A Productivity Factor Multipliers

Defn.	Value	*t08* Multiplier	*t09* Multiplier
very low	1	*1.137902	*1.438033
low	2	1.294822	2.067940
average	3	1.473381	2.973766
high	4	1.676564	4.276375
very high	5	1.907766	6.149569

TABLE 4.6
Model B Productivity Factor Multipliers

Defn.	Value	*t08* Multiplier	*t09* Multiplier	*t14* Multiplier
very low	1	*1.223199	*1.344404	0.882696
low	2	1.496215	1.807423	0.779152
average	3	1.830169	2.429906	0.687754
high	4	2.238660	3.266776	0.607078
very high	5	2.738327	4.391867	0.535865

TABLE 4.7
Model A Normalized Productivity Factor Multipliers

Defn.	Value	*t08* Multiplier	*t09* Multiplier
very low	1	*0.772	*0.484
low	2	0.879	0.695
average	3	1.000	1.000
high	4	1.138	1.438
very high	5	1.295	2.068

TABLE 4.8
Model B Normalized Productivity Factor Multipliers

Defn.	Value	t08 Multiplier	t09 Multiplier	t14 Multiplier
very low	1	*0.668	*0.553	1.283
low	2	0.818	0.744	1.133
average	3	1.000	1.000	1.000
high	4	1.223	1.344	0.883
very high	5	1.496	1.807	0.779

requirements volatility. You should also keep in mind that no project in the database actually had very low requirements volatility (denoted by *). So although the models say that very low requirements volatility would decrease effort 23-33% compared with average requirements volatility, we cannot be completely sure about this.

The effect of changes in quality requirements ($t09$) is very strong. A project with very high quality requirements is expected to require up to twice the effort of a project with average quality requirements. No project actually had very low quality requirements. Effort is expected to be 22% less for projects where staff tool skills ($t14$) are very high instead of average.

The effect of time on effort can be calculated in the following way: The time multiplier from Model A, $e^{-.0826743 \times time}$, can also be written as $(0.920651)^{time}$. This means that for each year between 1985 and 1993, a project's effort is 92% of the effort the same project would have taken in the previous year. Thus, all other variables remaining constant, effort is decreasing at the rate of approximately 8% per year.

Example B: 1991 Effort Estimation Model

What would happen if the bank developed an effort estimation model and then used it for two years without re-analyzing the data? How accurate would it estimate any new project's effort? To answer this question, I will develop a predictive effort model with the variables that significantly explain the productivity differences among software development projects in this bank through 1991 and then test the model on 1992 and 1993 data. The database contained 50 valid projects at the end of 1991. The 1992/1993 holdout sample had 12 projects.

Variable and Model Selection _____

The variable definitions are the same as in Chapter 2. However, everything else must be redone as I am now working with a smaller 50-project data set. I first use the summary function (Example 4.17) to see how the average values of the data available in 1991 compare with the full data set (Chapter 2). The average values of the project's sizes and efforts were approximately 10% bigger in 1991. Average project duration was approximately one month longer in 1991. The average values of the productivity factors (*t01-t15*) did not change much. The biggest differences were in average tools use (*t06*), about 3% lower in 1991, and average requirements volatility (*t08*), about 3% higher in 1991. Average productivity remained the same.

Example 4.17

```
                            . summarize
```

Variable	Obs	Mean	Std. Dev.	Min	Max
size	50	740.02	848.1621	48	3634
effort	50	9099.86	11435.53	583	63694
duration	50	18.48	11.26352	6	54
syear	50	1988.94	1.856154	1985	1991
nlan	50	2.48	1.054437	1	4
t01	50	3.08	1.046666	1	5
t02	50	3.04	.7273098	1	5
t03	50	3.08	.8998866	2	5
t04	50	3.18	.7475129	2	5
t05	50	3.04	.7814168	1	5
t06	50	2.8	.6998542	1	4
t07	50	3.28	.904411	1	5
t08	50	3.92	.8533248	2	5
t09	50	4.02	.7690439	2	5
t10	50	3.56	.8369039	2	5
t11	50	3.38	.9874726	2	5
t12	50	3.82	.7475129	2	5
t13	50	3.02	.9791708	1	5
t14	50	3.26	1.006307	1	5
t15	50	3.28	.7570081	1	5
time	50	4.94	1.856154	1	7
prod	50	.1024677	.0615639	.0264517	.2592593

Identifying Subsets of Categorical Variables

Because I am analyzing a subset of the initial data, I also need to check the breakdown of the categorical variables again. I may have to create new subsets of categorical variables if there are new categories with less than three observations. I am particularly concerned about user interface. In our previous analyses we found that *GUI* applications were more productive; however, we only had four of them. We may not have enough observations in this subset to analyze this factor. So while we know now that in 1993 this factor was important, in 1991, we may not have been able to see this yet. I printed out the average productivity (*prod*) for each categorical variable type (Examples 4.18 through 4.23).

Example 4.18

```
. table app, c(n prod mean prod)
```

Application Type	N(prod)	mean(prod)
CustServ	15	0.0916
MIS	4	0.0988
TransPro	22	0.0948
ProdCont	1	0.1352
InfServ	8	0.1416

Example 4.18 shows that there are not enough observations to analyze the influence of production control (*ProdCont*) applications. On average, information/on-line service (*InfServ*) applications had the highest productivity. Customer service (*CustServ*), Management Information System (*MIS*), and transaction processing (*TransPro*) applications had the lowest productivity.

Example 4.19

```
. table har, c(n prod mean prod)
```

Hardware Type	N(prod)	mean(prod)
Network	7	0.1160
Mainfrm	28	0.0922
PC	1	0.1200
Mini	1	0.0992
Multi	13	0.1162

In Example 4.19, we see that there are not enough observations to analyze the influence of the personal computer (*PC*) or mini computer (*Mini*) categories. On average, mainframe (*Mainfrm*) applications had the lowest productivity. Networked (*Network*) and multi-platform (*Multi*) applications had the highest productivity.

Example 4.20

```
. table dbms, c(n prod mean prod)

DBMS Architecture   N(prod)     mean(prod)
None                      2         0.1012
Relatnl                  46         0.1030
Other                     1         0.0817
Sequentl                  1         0.0992
```

There are not enough observations in the different categories to analyze the influence of differences in DBMS architecture (Example 4.20).

Example 4.21

```
. table ifc, c(n prod mean prod)

User Interface   N(prod)     mean(prod)
GUI                    4         0.2016
TextUI                46         0.0939
```

Example 4.21 shows that the four *GUI* applications were already in the database in 1991, so we will be able to analyze the influence of this variable. Applications that used a graphical user interface (*GUI*) seemed to be a lot more productive than those that used a text user interface (*TextUI*).

Example 4.22

```
. table source, c(n prod mean prod)

Where Developed   N(prod)     mean(prod)
Inhouse               42         0.0959
Outsrced               8         0.1367
```

The influence of outsourcing projects can be analyzed. Example 4.22 shows that on average, outsourced (*Outsrced*) projects had a higher productivity than projects developed inhouse (*Inhouse*).

Example 4.23

```
. table telonuse, c(n prod mean prod)

Telon Use   N(prod)     mean(prod)
No               41         0.1006
Yes               9         0.1110
```

The influence of Telon use can be analyzed. In Example 4.23, we see that Telon use (*telonuse*) does not seem to lead to any large difference in productivity. Thus, in 1991, the subsets of categorical variables were the same as in 1993.

Model Selection

There is no change in the model we used in Example A. We are able to analyze the influence of the same variables.

$$effort = f(size, subapp, subhar, ifc, source, t01\text{-}t15,$$
$$nlan, telonuse, time)$$

What are the relationships between the effort (*effort*) and size of an application (*size*), the type of application (*subapp*), the type of hardware (*subhar*), the user interface (*ifc*), whether or not the development was outsourced (*source*), the 15 different productivity factors (*t01-t15*), the number of languages used (*nlan*), whether or not Telon was used (*telonuse*), and time (*time*)?

Preliminary Analyses _____

The following analyses should be undertaken before building the multivariable model. See Chapter 1 for more explanation.

Graphs

I always look at two types of graphs: histograms and two-dimensional graphs.

Histograms   I reran all the histograms to check for normality. There was not much difference between the histograms of the 1993 data set (see Chapter 2) and the 1991 data set. The only histogram with a very different shape was the one concerned with efficiency requirements (*t10*). In 1991, most projects had high efficiency requirements (Figure 4.26). By 1993, the majority of projects had average efficiency requirements (see Figure 2.20).

Two-Dimensional Graphs   I plotted the relationship between the transformed effort variable, *leffort*, and *lsize*. In Figure 4.27, we can see that there is a very strong relationship between *leffort* and *lsize*. As we learned in the previous example, many variables' apparent relationships with effort are in fact due to differences in size. This has also been the case in every software project database I have ever analyzed. It is for this reason that I plotted the

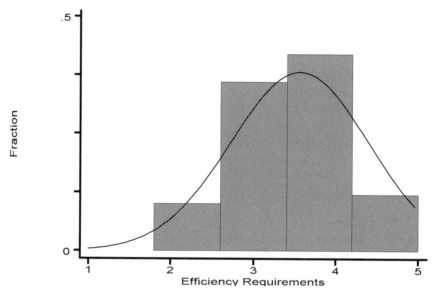

FIGURE 4.26
Distribution of *t10*

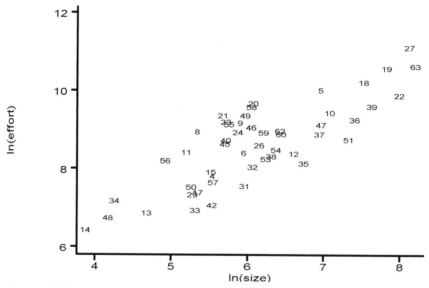

FIGURE 4.27
ln(effort) vs. *ln(size)*

relationships between *lprod* and each independent variable. As size explains so much variation, I wanted to see the effect of a variable on effort once size had been taken into consideration.

Again, there was not much difference in the two-dimensional graphs between the 1993 data set (Chapter 2) and the 1991 data set. None of my interpretations changed with the exception of number of languages (*nlan*). In 1991, applications developed with more languages appeared to have a higher productivity on average. By 1993, it didn't seem to make much difference how many languages were used.

Tables

I saved some time in this analysis by printing out the average productivity of each categorical variable in the "Identifying Subsets of Categorical Variables" step. Thus, I do not need to redo this here. The conclusions I reached concerning the average productivities of each categorical variable for 1991 do not differ from those I made for 1993.

Correlation Analysis

As I did in Chapter 2, I searched the correlation output for any significant correlation coefficients greater than |0.5|. My summary is presented in Table 4.9.

As of 1991, the use of methods (*t05*) was positively correlated with staff analysis skills (*t12*). This correlation was weaker (<0.5) in 1993. In 1991, tools use (*t06*) had been increasinged over time. Projects with higher logical complexity (*t07*) often required more effort and were bigger in size. The more

TABLE 4.9
Summary of Correlation Coefficients

Variables	Num Obs	Correlation
t05 and *t12*	50	0.51
t06 and *time*	50	0.51
t07 and *effort*	50	0.53
t07 and *size*	50	0.54
t11 and *nlan*	50	0.61
t12 and *t15*	50	0.61
t09 and *t10*	50	0.57
t09 and *t12*	50	0.53
t09 and *t15*	50	0.55
effort and *size*	50	0.73
effort and *duration*	50	0.72

development languages used in a project (*nlan*), the greater its installation requirements (*t11*). Staff analysis skills (*t12*) and staff team skills (*t15*) were positively correlated. Project staffs with good analysis skills generally had good team skills, too. Quality requirements (*t09*) were positively correlated with efficiency requirements (*t10*), staff analysis skills (*t12*), and team skills (*t15*). Projects with high quality requirements often had high efficiency requirements, too, and required staff with better analysis and team skills. Size and effort were positively correlated with each other; projects bigger in size usually required more effort. None of the correlations were high enough to cause multicollinearity problems. By 1993, these relationships were mainly unchanged with the exception of the correlations between quality requirements (*t09*), staff analysis skills (*t12*), and staff team skills (*t15*), which were weaker, and the correlation between size and duration, which was stronger (see Table 2.3).

I also thought it would be interesting to see how time was related to the different factors. Table 4.10 summarizes all significant correlations involving time.

As of 1991, the use of methods (*t05*), the use of tools (*t06*), staff tool skills (*t14*), and number of development languages (*nlan*) had been increasing over time. Requirements volatility (*t08*), staff application experience (*t13*), and project duration (*duration*) had been decreasing over time.

There are three main differences between 1991 and 1993 (see Table 2.4). The positive correlation between time and staff tool skills (*t14*) was stronger in 1991 than 1993. Staff team skills (*t15*) were not correlated with time in 1991. And, in 1993, staff application experience (*t13*) was not correlated with time. Thus, the measured variables that made up the variable *time* differed in 1991 and 1993, staff tool skills and staff application experience lost importance, and staff team skills gained importance.

TABLE 4.10
Variables Correlated with *time*

Variable	Num Obs	Correlation
t05	50	0.36
t06	50	0.51
t08	50	− 0.44
t13	50	− 0.30
t14	50	0.46
duration	50	− 0.30
nlan	50	0.35

Stepwise Regression Analysis

Both the forward and backward stepwise regression procedures (Example 4.24) found the same model. Three variables explained 75% of the variation in effort. All 50 projects were used. Effort (*leffort*) increased with increasing application size (*lsize*) and quality requirements (*t09*), and decreased over time (*time*). This model makes sense to me.

Example 4.24

Source	SS	df	MS		Number of obs =	50
Model	42.008953	3	14.0029843		F(3,46) =	49.35
Residual	13.0535739	46	.283773346		Prob > F =	0.0000
					R-squared =	0.7629
Total	55.0625269	49	1.12372504		Adj R-squared =	0.7475
					Root MSE =	.5327

leffort	Coef.	Std. Err.	t	P>|t|	[95% Conf.	Interval]
lsize	.8447128	.0783079	10.787	0.000	.6870872	1.002338
t09	.2934205	.1023111	2.868	0.006	.087479	.499362
time	-.1637923	.0416727	-3.930	0.000	-.2476752	-.0799095
_cons	3.043039	.5788253	5.257	0.000	1.877924	4.208154

Building the Multi-Variable Model

The best model with numerical variables alone explained 75% of the variation in effort. Do any of the categorical variables, *subapp* (application type subset), *subhar* (hardware platform subset), *ifc* (user interface), *source* (where developed) and/or *telonuse* (Telon use), explain more variation in effort? I use the stepwise ANOVA procedure described in Chapter 1 to see if an improvement in the R-squared value can be made. The results are shown in Sidebar 4.2.

SIDEBAR 4.2
STATISTICAL OUTPUT SUMMARY SHEET

Date: 07/06/2001

Directory: C:\my documents\data analysis book\cost estimation\1991 model
Data File: bankdata63.dta   (id=1 is dropped, syear=1992,1993 is dropped)
Procedure Files: *var.do (* = one, two, three, etc..)
Output Files: *var.log
Dependent Variable: *leffort*

(Continued)

SIDEBAR 4.2 (*Continued*)

Variables	Num Obs	Effect	Adj R²	Significance of Added Variable	Comments
1-variable models					
t01	50	+	.08		
t03	50	+	.07		
t07	50	+	.27		
t08	50	+	.05	.064	
t09	50	+	.09		
t10	50	+	.08		
t11	50	+	.12		
t14	50	−	.13		
t15	50	+	.12		
* *lsize*	**50**	**+**	**.65**		
nlan	50	+	.11		
subhar	48		.07	.079	
2-variable models with *lsize*					
* *t08*	**50**	**+**	**.705**		**follow Path B**
t09	50	+	.67	.053	
t14	50	−	.69		
* *time*	**50**	**−**	**.709**		**follow Path A**
ifc	50		.69		
Path A:					
3-variable models with *lsize, time*					
t01	50	+	.72	.071	
t04	50	+	.73		
t08	50	+	.72	.062	
* *t09*	**50**	**+**	**.75**		
t10	50	+	.73		
ifc	50		.73		
4-variable models with *lsize, time, t09*					
ifc	50		.79		**best Model A: sign. = 0.000**

Variables	Num Obs	Effect	Adj R²	Significance of Added Variable	Comments
5-variable models with lsize, time, t09, ifc,					
none significant					no further improvement possible
Path B:					
3-variable models with lsize, t08					
t03	50	+	.72		
t09	50	+	.72		
t10	50	+	.72		
t14	50	−	.729		
time	50	−	.72		
* ifc	50		.734		
4-variable models with lsize, t08, ifc					
t01	50		.75		
t03	50		.76		
* t09	50		.77		
t10	50		.76		
t14	50		.75	.081	
5-variable models with size, t08, ifc, t09					
t03	50	+	.789		constant not sign.
* t14	50		.786	.053	best Model B: sign. = 0.000
6-variable models with lsize, t08, ifc, t09, t14					
none significant					no further improvement possible

From the summary of one-variable models, I learn that effort (*leffort*) increases with increasing customer participation (*t01*), staff availability (*t03*), logical complexity (*t07*), requirements volatility (*t08*), quality requirements (*t09*), efficiency requirements (*t10*), installation requirements (*t11*), staff team skills (*t15*), size (*lsize*), and number of languages (*nlan*). Effort decreases with increasing staff tool skills (*t14*). In addition, effort depends on the hardware platform (*subhar*). As in the previous example, all of these relationships do not make sense to me; however, size is clearly the most important factor (65% of variation explained).

The choice of the best two-variable model is not easy. In addition to *lsize*, two variables, *t08* and *time*, explain 71% of the variation in *leffort*. The best two-variable model is based on *lsize* and *time*; however, it is only best by 0.4%. I decide to continue down this path with *time* (Path A). I will redo the analysis later using *t08* (Path B). Time is an interesting variable to have in a model because it represents many things evolving over time that we haven't measured or can't measure. The best three-variable model for Path A (with *time*) includes quality requirements (*t09*) and explains 75% of the variation in effort. 79% of the variation in effort is explained by the best four-variable model for Path A: *lsize, time, t09,* and *ifc*. No further improvement can be made.

Now I return to the point where I chose *time* and choose *t08* instead. I call this Path B. The best three-variable model for Path B is based on *lsize, t08,* and *ifc*, and explains 73% of the variation in *leffort*. The best four-variable model for Path B also includes quality requirements (*t09*) and explains 77% of the variation in *leffort*. The best five-variable model for Path B also includes staff tool skills (*t14*) and explains 79% of the variation in *leffort*. No further improvement can be made.

Final 1991 Model A   In our final Model A (Example 4.25), four variables explained 79% of the variance in effort. All 50 observations were used. Effort (*leffort*) increased with increasing application size (*lsize*) and quality requirements (*t09*). Effort decreased over time (*time*). Effort was lower for projects that used a graphical user interface (*ifc=1*). The variables in this model are similar to the 1993 Model A; only requirements volatility (*t08*) was not yet significant in 1991.

Example 4.25

```
. anova leffort ifc t09 lsize time, category(ifc) regress
```

Source	SS	df	MS		
Model	44.3144968	4	11.0786242	Number of obs =	50
Residual	10.74803	45	.238845112	F(4,45) =	46.38
				Prob > F =	0.0000
Total	55.0625269	49	1.12372504	R-squared =	0.8048
				Adj R-squared =	0.7875
				Root MSE =	.48872

leffort		Coef.	Std. Err.	t	P >|t|	[95% Conf.	Interval]
_cons		2.545036	.5546949	4.588	0.000	1.427824	3.662249
ifc							
	1	-.8582148	.2762279	-3.107	0.003	-1.414566	-.3018633
	2	(dropped)					
t09		.3610081	.096351	3.747	0.001	.1669471	.555069
lsize		.8679457	.07223	12.016	0.000	.7224669	1.013424
time		-.1328334	.039509	-3.362	0.002	-.2124086	-.0532582

Final 1991 Model B   The 1991 Model B (Example 4.26) contained the same variables that were significant for Model B in 1993. There were some changes in the value of the coefficients. Five variables explained 79% of the variance in effort. All 50 observations were used. Effort (*leffort*) increased with increasing application size (*lsize*), requirements volatility (*t08*), and quality requirements (*t09*). Effort decreased with increasing staff tool skills (*t14*). Effort was lower for projects that used a graphical user interface (*ifc*=1).

Example 4.26

`. anova leffort ifc t09 lsize t08 t14, category(ifc) regress`

Source	SS	df	MS			
Model	44.4543797	5	8.89087595	Number of obs =	50	
Residual	10.6081471	44	.241094253	F(5,44) =	36.88	
				Prob > F =	0.0000	
Total	55.0625269	49	1.12372504	R-squared =	0.8073	
				Adj R-squared =	0.7855	
				Root MSE =	.49101	

leffort		Coef.	Std. Err.	t	P >|t|	[95% Conf.	Interval]
_cons		2.105346	.7212479	2.919	0.006	.6517663	3.558925
ifc							
	1	-.821658	.2809596	-2.924	0.005	-1.387895	-.2554212
	2	(dropped)					
t09		.2961956	.0973356	3.043	0.004	.1000286	.4923626
lsize		.8178686	.0752952	10.862	0.000	.6661211	.969616
t08		.2126006	.0847423	2.509	0.016	.0418138	.3833874
t14		-.1491295	.07486	-1.992	0.053	-.3	.001741

Checking the Models _____

All checks were carried out and no problems were found with the models. Model A was slightly less influenced by individual observations.

Measuring Estimation Accuracy

I judged the accuracy of the models using four different methods: common accuracy statistics, boxplots, the Wilcoxon signed-rank test, and accuracy segmentation tables. These are all explained in detail in the Example A section of this chapter.

Common Accuracy Statistics

As in Example A, the 95% confidence intervals were very wide. Table 4.11 shows the performance of the two models on the underlying data measured with the commonly used accuracy statistics. Table 4.12 shows the performance of the two models on the holdout sample. It is of interest to note that while in 1991 we would have concluded, based on these indicators, that Model A was the more accurate model (42% of the estimates were within 25% of the actuals), Model B actually estimated more accurately the 1992 and 1993 projects. MedMRE was a very respectable 16%, and 58% of the estimates were within 25% of the actuals.

The fact is, you never really know how well a model is going to estimate in the future until it is too late. If you can't clearly choose one model over another in a specific case, then one option is to take the average of your models' estimates to estimate new projects. You can see in Tables 4.11 and 4.12 that

TABLE 4.11
Accuracy on Underlying Data

	1991 Model A	1991 Model B	Ave. A and B
MMRE	42%	43%	42%
MedMRE	29%	31%	28%
Pred(.25)	42%	34%	44%

TABLE 4.12
Accuracy on 1992/93 Holdout Sample

	1991 Model A	1991 Model B	Ave. A and B
MMRE	29%	32%	25%
MedMRE	33%	16%	16%
Pred(.25)	33%	58%	67%

averaging the estimates of Models A and B appears to be not only more accurate on the underlying data, but also more accurate on the holdout sample for the bank.

Wilcoxon Signed-Rank Test

No significant differences were found between the models.

Boxplots of Estimation Error

The boxplots of the estimation errors on the underlying data do not show any notable difference in the different models (Figure 4.28). The spread of the estimation errors is very wide for all three models, with one project (*id* = 27) always being underestimated by approximately 20,000 hours. All models show a small tendency to underestimate (the medians are all above zero). The boxplots of the estimation errors on the holdout sample show quite a big difference among the three models (Figure 4.29). Model A is more likely to underestimate and Model B is more likely to overestimate. Taking the average is also more likely to result in an underestimate. The spread of the estimation errors is much smaller on the holdout sample than on the underlying data. There are no outliers. Based on these boxplots, I conclude that Model A appears to be less stable than Model B. Its behavior on the underlying data and the holdout sample is very different.

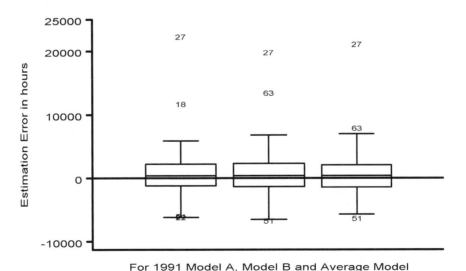

For 1991 Model A, Model B and Average Model

FIGURE 4.28

Boxplots of 1991 Model A and Model B estimation errors on underlying data

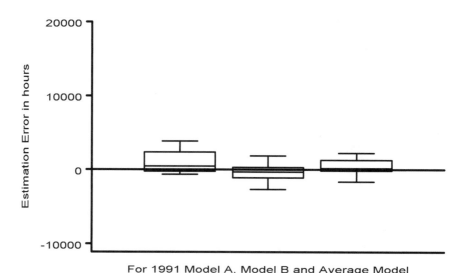

FIGURE 4.29
Boxplots of 1991 Model A and Model B estimation errors on 1992/93 holdout
sample

Accuracy Segmentation

Another way to judge accuracy is to see how well each model estimates
small and large projects. If you find, for example, that one model is much
better at estimating large projects, then use only that model to estimate large
projects.

If we go by the performance of the models on the underlying data (Tables
4.13 and 4.14), we should conclude that Model B is more likely than Model
A to underestimate above average sized projects, and is more likely to overestimate below average sized projects. Model A's greatest weakness is to
underestimate small projects, although no more than Model B. Is this true?
Do the same strengths and weaknesses show up in estimations of the
1992/93 holdout sample?

The holdout sample had one big project and 11 small projects. Looking at
Tables 4.15 and 4.16, we find that Model B does tend to overestimate more
below average sized projects. Both Models A and B got the one big project
right; however, Model A underestimated many more small projects than
Model B. So although looking at the performance on the underlying data can
give you an idea about how the model will perform in the future, it does not
get it exactly right.

TABLE 4.13
1991 Model A Accuracy Segmentation (underlying data)

1991 Model A	Overestimate Error Not Acceptable	Underestimate Error Not Acceptable
Large projects, above average size (13 projects)	23% (3 projects)	15% (2 projects)
Small projects, below average size (37 projects)	30% (11 projects)	35% (13 projects)

TABLE 4.14
1991 Model B Accuracy Segmentation (underlying data)

1991 Model B	Overestimate Error Not Acceptable	Underestimate Error Not Acceptable
Large projects, above average size (13 projects)	23% (3 projects)	31% (4 projects)
Small projects, below average size (37 projects)	35% (13 projects)	35% (13 projects)

TABLE 4.15
1991 Model A Accuracy Segmentation (1992/93 holdout sample)

Model A	Overestimate Error Not Acceptable	Underestimate Error Not Acceptable
Large projects, above average size (1 project)	0% (0 projects)	0% (0 projects)
Small projects, below average size (11 projects)	18% (2 projects)	55% (6 projects)

TABLE 4.16
1991 Model B Accuracy Segmentation (1992/93 holdout sample)

Model B	Overestimate Error Not Acceptable	Underestimate Error Not Acceptable
Large projects, above average size (1 project)	0% (0 projects)	0% (0 projects)
Small projects, below average size (11 projects)	36% (4 projects)	9% (1 project)

TABLE 4.17
Effect on Effort of Increase in Variable

Significant Variables from Models A and B	In 1991	In 1993
size: a 1% increase in size	0.82% - 0.87% increase	0.84% - 0.85% increase
t08: if very high instead of average	53% increase	30% - 50% increase
t09: if very high instead of average	81% - 106% increase	81% - 107% increase
t14: if very high instead of average	26% decrease	22% decrease
time	Decreasing at rate of 13%/year	Decreasing at rate of 8%/year
ifc: if *GUI*	56% - 58% decrease	57% - 60% decrease

Comparison of 1991 and 1993 Models

The 1991 equations were extracted and interpreted in the same manner as the 1993 equations. Table 4.17 shows the effect of an increase in each significant variable on effort for 1991 and for 1993.

There are many similarities between the models for 1991 and for 1993. Overall, the same six variables were significant, although *t08* was not a significant factor in Model A in 1991. The effects of size, quality requirements (*t09*), and user interface type (*ifc*) on effort remained nearly the same. There are also several notable differences. By 1993, the effect on effort of an increase from average to very high staff tool skills (*t14*) was approximately 15% less than in 1991. In 1991, we concluded that a change from average to very high requirements volatility (*t08*) would increase effort by 53%, all other factors remaining constant. By 1993, we learned that this increase was more likely to be somewhere between 30-50%. There is also a big difference in the importance of time. Remember that the variable *time* is more than time, it represents many things evolving over time that we haven't measured or can't measure. In 1991, effort was decreasing at the rate of 13% per year. By 1993, effort was decreasing at a rate of 8% per year. Thus, the influence of time had decreased by approximately 38% during a two-year period. What could have changed in the bank that we did not measure? This explains why Model A, with *time*, was worse than Model B at predicting future projects' efforts.

Management Implications

The models and relationships found in this case study are only true for similar projects in this bank during a specific period of time. By following the same steps using your company's data, you can identify the key factors that contribute to project effort in your company and develop your company-specific model. The analysis of the bank's data in this chapter illustrated several important issues that you may face in your effort estimation model development:

- Application size is the most important factor in effort estimation. To estimate effort accurately, you must first estimate size accurately. Don't neglect this key step.
- It is okay to use more than one model; do not feel you have to select only one. Consider averaging different models' results.
- The importance of variables can change over time. Use your most up-to-date data and analyze it regularly.
- Use a model that includes time as a variable with caution.
- Use boxplots, the Wilcoxon signed-rank test, and accuracy segmentation, in addition to general indicators, to obtain more detailed information about the strengths and weaknesses of your model(s).
- Look at your 95% confidence intervals.

Many companies find estimating the cost of software development difficult. Nothing seems to stay the same in the software industry for long. There are always new languages, new tools, and new methods to learn, and new employees to train—not to mention the impact on requirements volatility when customers do not know what is possible or what they want until they see it. On the other hand, if your company always does the same type of project, for example, tailoring SAP packages, you can get pretty good at estimating. The key is in reaching a steady state—stable requirements, materials, and people. If the software you are developing and the materials you are using to develop it are constantly being modified, it will be more difficult. In the meantime, learn as much as you can from your data, and see how accurate of an effort estimation model you can build with it.

In addition to developing your own equations, I recommend using two or three additional methods to estimate the cost of your projects:

- Use one or two cost estimation tools calibrated to your company. These tools are also useful for sizing a project and tracking its progress.
- Look at the most similar projects in your company's database (analogy method).
- Rely on your memory and your colleagues' (expert opinion).

Different methods or combinations of methods will be more accurate in different contexts. It is up to you to determine what works best in your company.

Case Study: Software Maintenance Cost Drivers

5

It's the Results That Matter

There are two reasons why I decided to begin this chapter with an example of how to present data analysis results. First, it is very important to remember that no one really wants to know how you analyzed the data. You may have spent months looking at the data from many different angles, but please, spare us the details. The reason you analyzed the data was to find something interesting—hopefully, some breakthrough insight that will forever change how software is developed or maintained in your company. If you are unable to summarize the thousands of pages of computer output you generated into a short list of management implications, no one will ever bother to read your report or listen to your presentation.

Second, I would like to point out that although analyzing data is a solitary activity, interpreting the results usually is not. If you do not have an in-depth knowledge of the context in which the data was collected, you need to talk to those who do. Good interviewing skills are essential. The following case study is a good example of how value can be added to data through teamwork. It is the result of a close collaboration between a data analyst with software development experience, me, and a domain expert, Pekka Forselius, who had worked in the bank for many years, collected the data, and amassed a great deal of expert knowledge. If I had just analyzed the data without discussing the results at different stages with Pekka, the story would not be nearly as interesting. After all, I had never maintained large software applications, I had never worked in a bank, and I knew nothing about this bank in particular. What else was going on in the bank at the time of data collection? What was the economic climate in Finland? I needed to interview Pekka to understand the context, to validate the data, and to find out what he thought was interesting. Did he have any questions that he would like my help to answer? Why did he think something came out in the analysis as being important or not important? My opinion about what could be interesting or important to this bank could be off the mark. On the other hand, I had absolutely no pre-conceived ideas about what I should find or look for in the bank's data. As an outsider, I could bring new insights and question the bank's way of doing things.

Pekka and I decided to write up our results in a format suitable for publication in a journal aimed at software managers. I think you will find it useful to first read the results, and then to see how we got there. The section "From Data to Knowledge" immediately following the article below contains the data this case study was based on and explains how it was analyzed.

Cost Drivers of Annual Corrective Maintenance: One Commercial Bank's Experience

Katrina D. Maxwell and Pekka Forselius

Abstract

Over an application's lifecycle, more money is spent on software maintenance than on software development; however, not much is known about the factors that influence annual software maintenance cost. In this article, the authors present the results of an analysis performed on one commercial bank's software maintenance database to determine their key cost drivers.

1. Introduction

If you don't measure and control maintenance effort, it will grow more than necessary. One great risk is that work not allocated during more strictly controlled new development projects will be hidden in maintenance endeavors.

That is why one of the biggest commercial banks in Finland began to collect development and maintenance effort data as early as 1985. Every employee, from managers to secretaries, reported time spent on all types of projects into an effort accounting system every week.

The bank's knowledge of new software development projects was already very good because of systematic project portfolio management. Between 1987 and 1995, 250 new IBM applications were developed during a big migration project that moved applications from a Bull mainframe environment to a three-tier architecture system constructed of PCs, local servers, and IBM mainframes. Running and maintaining two separate mainframe environments was very expensive. Migration projects could not be cancelled, and all available resources needed to be allocated to them to finish the migration program as soon as possible. In parallel, the amount of maintenance effort was growing and becoming more important each year. This, combined with a pressing need to minimize personnel costs due to a recession and banking crisis in Finland, made controlling maintenance costs a priority.

To improve the annual budgeting of maintenance effort, both for in-house maintenance suppliers and application owners, Pekka Forselius and his team collected a large amount of data, including actual effort, size, age, defects, classification variables, and risk factors, to better understand the qualitative differences among applications. This data was simply used to help organize maintenance and manage risks; it was not statistically analyzed at the time.

What lessons could the bank have learned through the statistical analysis of this rich data set? Statistical analysis would have been useful to determine which of the factors collected had a real impact on maintenance cost. In addition, other interesting relationships could have been studied, for example: What effect did an application's age have on maintenance effort? Did any development tools prove to be more productive than others? For example, did applications built with Telon require less maintenance than traditional COBOL applications? What impact did the number of defects have? In this paper, we present the results of our statistical analysis of this data set to answer these questions. We conclude with Pekka's response to a very important question: Would he have recommended that anything be done differently had he known the answers to these questions at the time?

Although this study looks in detail at the software maintenance database of one bank, it should be of interest to a wider audience because nearly all of the applications were programmed with the most widely used maintenance language, COBOL. COBOL applications and mainframe computing dominate a large segment of the business community in which conventional data and transaction processing requirements drive major applications [1]. COBOL mainframes process more than 83% of transactions worldwide [2].

The maintenance of COBOL applications is especially critical in the banking sector where large customer databases (1-2 million customers), large account databases, and advanced online services typify banking projects. In a recent merger of two banks, the COBOL-based assets of one bank were cited as one of the key reasons for the merger [2].

2. Presentation of Data

250 applications in one business environment is a large number; unfortunately, not all of them were controlled equally. Data was collected with varying accuracy and completeness by the different departments responsible for each application's maintenance. Based on Pekka's knowledge, we used only applications that had the most complete and valid data for our study. Thus, of the 250 IBM mainframe applications, a subset of 67 applications that were being maintained during 1993 and that had effort, size, and defect data were analyzed. Risk factor data was available for 56 of these applications. All applications studied were developed in-house and all but two used the DB2 database management system. The applications used combinations of four different programming languages. All but five used COBOL. Most also used JCL, a job control language used for programming and controlling batch processing in an IBM mainframe environment. In addition, some applications used Easytrieve+, a language for generating reports, and/or Telon, which is a higher level tool for generating COBOL code.

Table 5.1 presents the 26 variables used in our analysis. These are broken down into three groups: classification variables, quantitative project data, and risk factors. Additional background about how the data was used to manage risks in the bank and definitions of the 10 risk factors can be found in

TABLE 5.1
List of Variables

Variable Name	Type[1]	Values (or levels)	Definition
			Classification Variables
borg	Nominal	6	Business organization type (retail, company, big corporation, etc.)
morg	Nominal	17	Internal business unit (deposit, treasury, accounting, payment, securities trading, etc.)

1. An explanation of variable types can be found in Chapter 6.

Variable Name	Type[1]	Values (or levels)	Definition
			Classification Variables
apptype	Nominal	4	Application type (information service/decision support, operative backoffice, operative core banking, interconnection service)
tpms	Nominal	5	Transaction processing management system (IMS, batch, etc.)
avetlev	Ordinal	3	Level of average number of transactions per 24 hours, in thousands
dsplev	Ordinal	4	Level of disk space, in MB
cpulev	Ordinal	4	Level of CPU (seconds/24 hours)
telonuse	Nominal	2	Telon used? (yes, no)
easyuse	Nominal	2	Easytrieve+ used? (yes, no)
			Quantitative Project Data
acorreff	Ratio	25-3031	Annual corrective maintenance effort in 1993, in hours
totalfp	Ratio	18-2328	Total number of function points in 1993
pcobol	Ratio	0-100	Percentage of COBOL code
pjcl	Ratio	0-100	Percentage of JCL code
ageend	Ratio	8-85	Total number of months maintained at end of 1993
appdef	Ratio	0-163	Number of application program defects found during 1993
ptelon	Ratio	6-87	Percentage of Telon code (in Telon applications)

(Continued)

TABLE 5.1 (Continued)

Variable Name	Type[1]	Values (or levels)	Definition / Risk Factors
r1	Ordinal	1-5	Number of users
r2	Ordinal	1-5	Flexibility of configuration management
r3	Ordinal	1-5	Flexibility of change management
r4	Ordinal	1-5	Structural flexibility/ maintainability
r5	Ordinal	1-5	Quality of documentation
r6	Ordinal	1-5	Dependence on people
r7	Ordinal	1-5	Shutdown time constraints
r8	Ordinal	1-5	Integration of online transaction processing
r9	Ordinal	1-5	Integration of batch processing
r10	Ordinal	1-5	Capacity flexibility

Appendix A at the end of this paper. Table 5.2 shows the average and total size, effort, and defects for the observations in our subset and for the original database. The 67 applications studied were similar in size and effort to the portfolio of all 250 IBM applications, but had a higher number of average defects.

TABLE 5.2
Comparison of Several Descriptive Variables

	Subset of 67 Applications Maintained in 1993	Portfolio of 250 IBM Applications
average size (function points)	471	425
total size (function points)	31531	106200
average annual corrective effort (hours)	521	495
total corrective effort (hours)	34907	123750
average number of defects	9.4	6.9
total number of defects	632	1725

Size was initially measured in source statements of code. The number of source statements of COBOL, Telon, Easytrieve+, and JCL were counted individually. The equivalent number of function points was backfired for each language using Capers Jones' table [3]. Capers Jones' conversions were used because, at that time, he had the most statistical evidence for applications developed with COBOL and Telon. Pekka also counted some applications' function points, compared the results with the backfired number, and found them acceptable. In addition, all applications in our data set were developed by one supplier during a reasonably short period, so there should not have been any large differences in lines of code due to style and cultural differences. The number of function points for each language was then combined to give the total number of function points. The size of each application was determined in the summer of each year, and was thus an indication of the average size of the application during the year.

Corrective effort was defined as changes that were necessary to keep the application running. This included fixing bugs, making very easy technical improvements such as implementing and testing improved features of new versions of development tools to improve layouts, and testing the application when the environment changed. (For example, if the system level software, source libraries, DBMS version, or operating system version changed, some parameters or interfaces may have required modification.) Corrective effort did not include the day-to-day effort needed to run the application (parameter changes, repairing inputs, controlling data transfer interfaces), nor did it include the effort needed to enhance or redo the application for the customer. Corrective effort was aggregated on an annual basis in January for the previous year.

Defect statistics were collected very carefully in the bank. Defects were mainly failures detected automatically by the operating system or middleware during the running of the application programs. In addition, some faults detected either by the end-user/customer representatives or maintainers were recorded manually into the defect accounting system. All defects were then classified by systems managers and maintainers into nine different types (application program, hardware/electricity, parameter data, operator, telecommunication, and so on) and five levels of criticality (insignificant to critical). Table 5.3 and Figure 5.1 show a snapshot of the entire defect database in May 1993.

In our study, we concentrated on all kinds of failures and faults caused by the application program as this is an important indicator of application quality. Approximately 8% of all registered defects were due to the application program. Application program defects included requirements, design, and programming defects. We did not use the criticality breakdown because of

TABLE 5.3
Defect Breakdown in May 1993

Category	% Total Defects
Process control/parameters	23
Operating system/middleware	19
Other reason	12
Hardware/electricity	9
Application Program	8
Telecommunications	8
Operator	4
Customer/interface	4
Unidentified	0
Not yet classified	13

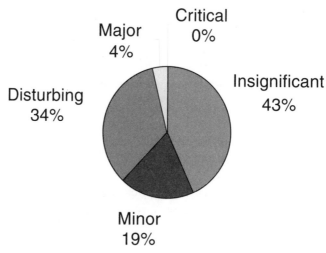

FIGURE 5.1
Criticality levels in May 1993

the small total number of defects and applicable applications. Defect data was compiled on an annual basis in January for the previous year. According to the users, the quality of the individual applications was between very good and satisfying. Overall application quality was considered to be good.

21 applications had zero defects, 10 had one defect, and 6 had two defects. Only 7 applications had more than 21 defects.

3. Results of Analysis

The data was statistically analyzed using a stepwise analysis of variance method to determine which combination of variables explained the most variance in annual corrective maintenance effort.[2] The analysis was first performed on the entire data set. In addition, to evaluate the strategic decision to use the Telon development tool, the same analysis was undertaken for the 11 applications that used Telon.

3.1. Annual Corrective Maintenance Effort Each autumn, representatives from both the independent software development and maintenance business unit and the banking business unit(s) that owned the application met to negotiate next year's costs. The amount of maintenance effort was one of the most important cost drivers. It is widely believed that maintenance costs represent as much as 50-80% of total software lifecycle costs [4,5,6]. In the 1990s, approximately 180 of the bank's 320 software developers were maintaining software. Maintenance effort was divided into two main categories in the bank: corrective maintenance and independent enhancements. Our study looks in detail at corrective maintenance because it is more related to defects, and because it is a more sensible value to compare among applications. In addition, most of the bank's software personnel resources were allocated to corrective maintenance. Of the bank's 180 software maintainers, 100 were doing corrective maintenance, and 80 were making enhancements.

3.1.1. The Model The corrective effort model is presented in Table 5.4. Five variables explained 61.9% of the variance in annual corrective maintenance effort. The variables are listed in order of importance. The single most important variable was the application size, which explained 27% of the variation in effort. Annual corrective maintenance effort was found to increase with increasing application size. Once size had been taken into consideration, the next most important variable was the integration of batch processing. Annual corrective maintenance effort was found to increase with a higher integration of batch processing. The next variable to enter the model was the organizational team that planned the maintenance. This variable also represented the internal business sectors of the bank.

---

2. Note that this is **all** we mention about how the data was analyzed.

TABLE 5.4
Annual Corrective Maintenance Effort Model

Dependent Variable	Significant Variables	Effect on Dependent Variable	Total Variance Explained
corrective effort	Size in function points	Positive	61.9%
	Batch processing integration	Positive	
	Internal business sector	Depends on type	
	Change management flexibility	Negative	
	Number of months maintained	Negative	

All variables were significant at the 5% level.

Figure 5.2 shows the annual corrective maintenance delivery rate by internal business sector for sectors with four or more observations. After adjustment for application size, securities trading systems and deposit applications required the most annual corrective effort; accounting, payment, treasury, and common banking service applications had lower corrective efforts.

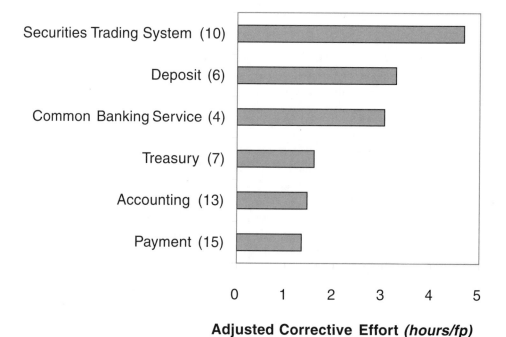

Adjusted Corrective Effort *(hours/fp)*

FIGURE 5.2
Annual corrective maintenance delivery rate by internal business sector

Some differences in effort among sectors can be attributed to application structures; for example, deposit applications were all very big and independent. Also, there were remarkable differences by user interface architecture. Most deposit applications were actually server parts of cooperative client/server systems. Banking products such as payment, accounting, and common banking service systems were probably less complex than the others. Common banking services included common services that other applications used: customer management services, customer database services (over 2 million customers), product management systems, product management databases, and an organization management system (which included information about who was responsible for each customer and contract). Some of these used online processing and some used batch processing. The amount of effort required by treasury applications was actually greater in practice than appears in this data set. The treasury market in Finland and resulting business instruments were changing so fast that the most complex applications were not in the mainframe environment we studied. They were in lighter PC applications and we didn't have any reliable effort data for them. Although very important in banking, loan applications do not appear in this analysis because they did not have enough detailed data.

Securities trading systems required the highest annual corrective maintenance effort per function point. These systems were very integrated, big batch processing applications. The rules for securities instruments were complicated and included lots of exceptions. In addition, the rules changed frequently as there were often new series of shares and new types of issues. Hence, lots of testing was needed. Standardization was very low as companies were always inventing new ways of getting funding. As a result, it was difficult for software staff to predict and plan for the next financial innovation.

What is important here is that we found significant differences in effort and productivity for "internal business sectors" within the bank. The actual levels of average effort by sector would be different in other banks. In this bank, for example, payment systems required the lowest annual corrective maintenance effort per function point. This is because payment system maintenance was very well standardized. In the 1990s in Finland, there was a very high level of automation between companies and banks, and between banking groups. Everything was processed electronically. In the UK, however, all banks sent material to a clearing center. These differences had a strong influence on the way payment system applications were developed in various countries, as well as on their resulting maintenance needs.

The fourth most important variable was the flexibility of change management. Less corrective effort was required by applications that were dependent on other applications, had more owners, and for which no quick decisions could be made. Meetings between several parties were required before deciding on modifications to these types of applications, and it is likely that only very necessary modifications would be agreed on.

Finally, the number of months an application had been maintained had an impact on annual corrective maintenance effort; less corrective effort was required for older applications. Equation 1 and Figure 5.3 show the relationship between annual corrective maintenance effort and the age of an application.[3] If we hold the other four variables (size, batch processing integration, internal business sector, and change management flexibility) constant, effort equals a constant (represented by k) multiplied by an "age multiplier," that is, an exponential function dependent on age. The age multiplier is 1 when the application enters the maintenance phase (*ageend* = 0) and decreases thereafter.

$$acorreff = ke^{-0.0159 \times ageend} \tag{1}$$

It is of interest to note that we found that age had an exponential effect on effort in our analysis. Exponential functions are commonly used in business,

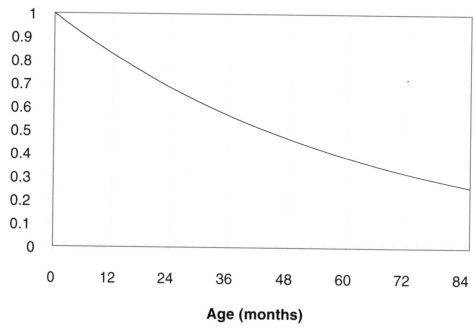

Age (months)

FIGURE 5.3

Corrective maintenance decay rate as a function of maintenance age

---

3. Note that there is only one equation on this article.

economics, and the sciences to express rates of growth and decay. Interest compounding is generally expressed in terms of exponential functions dependent on time. In this case, the relationship we found between age and effort bears a close resemblance to equations used to calculate the decay rate of elements, such as Carbon 14. Similarly, we can think of our age multiplier as a "corrective maintenance decay rate."

In this bank, annual corrective maintenance effort was found to decrease at the rate of approximately 17.4% per year. Thus, we would expect an application that required 100 hours of annual maintenance effort for its first entire year of maintenance to require 82.6 hours for the following year, and 68.2 hours for the next year—if nothing else about the application changed.

No other variable explained any additional variance in annual corrective maintenance effort. It is of interest to note that the defect-related variable does not appear in the multi-variable model. This is because defects were strongly correlated with application size. The bigger the application, the more defects. Thus, once the effect of size was added to the annual corrective maintenance effort model, the number of defects was no longer significant. Defects alone explained 14% of the variance in effort, while size alone explained 27% of the variation. Application size was a more important indicator of effort than the number of defects.

3.1.2. The Predictive Value of the Model

Although the model is very useful to better understand the cost drivers of annual corrective maintenance, it is of limited use as a predictive model. We used this model to predict the 1994 annual corrective maintenance effort of 19 applications for which the actual 1994 effort was known. We compared its performance with simply using the actual value of the 1993 effort as an estimate of the 1994 effort. We found that better results were achieved by merely using the previous year's effort to estimate the next year's effort (see Table 5.5).

Nonetheless, one of the biggest problems facing the bank was estimating the first year of maintenance effort (which was often the biggest over the lifetime of the application). In this case, actual data from previous years cannot be used. Knowing which cost drivers are important simplifies the task of finding similar projects on which to base an estimate. In practice, we would recommend that the bank use the model to provide one estimate, and then compare this with the average effort needed for projects of a similar size for each key classification variable.

Of the 19 applications that had comparable data in 1994, 17 had also been maintained in 1993, and maintenance was started on 2 applications. In Table

TABLE 5.5
Comparison of Model Prediction vs. Using Previous Year's Effort

Predicted Using:	On 1994 Applications:	Num Obs	MMRE (%)	MedMRE (%)	Pred(.25) (%)
1993 actuals	Ongoing	17	76	42	35
	New	2	NA	NA	NA
1993 model	Ongoing	17	102	56	29
	New	2	48	48	50

5.5, Num Obs is the number of observations, MMRE[4] is the mean magnitude of relative error, and MedMRE is the median magnitude of relative error. The mean is the arithmetic average, and the median refers to the value for which 50% of observations are above, and 50% below. The mean is very sensitive to outliers, which is why it is a good idea to use both metrics. Acceptable values of MMRE and MedMRE are 25%. This means that on average, the estimate is within 25% of the actuals. Pred(.25) is the percentage of predicted efforts that are within 25% of the actuals. 75% or more is considered an acceptable value.

Neither of the methods used resulted in acceptable accuracy. For example, when the 1993 model was used to predict the 1994 effort of the 17 ongoing applications, there was a mean error of 102% and a median error of 56%. There was a big difference in the mean and median because one application had a very large error, 805% (an overestimate), which had a big influence on the mean value. Only 29% of the predictions were within 25% of the actuals.

3.2. The Choice of Development Tools

*"The Telon salesperson said that it would be more productive
both in the development project and especially in maintenance."*

If you are going to develop 250 integrated software applications that you plan to maintain for 20 years on average, it is very important to select the right strategic tools—the earlier the better. It is very expensive, and in most real-world cases, almost impossible to change tools later. Not enough is known

---

4. These measures are discussed in detail in Chapter 4.

about the real impact on effort until you have trained many people to use the tools and implemented approximately 50% of the applications. The most important reason why Telon was selected as a tool was that it was purported to be more productive in the development phase, and especially in the maintenance phase, compared to COBOL. Was the decision to select Telon a good one?

Of the 67 applications in the data set, 11 were developed using Telon. We found that less corrective maintenance hours per function point were required for Telon applications; 1.19 hours/function point compared with 2.47 hours/function point for applications that were not developed using Telon. However, this result is not statistically significant. Thus, we decided to study the 11 Telon applications in more detail.

The Telon models are presented in Table 5.6. We found a very strong relationship between the percentage of Telon code and the annual corrective maintenance effort. Using more Telon decreased corrective maintenance effort (see Figure 5.4). The relationship when corrective effort was adjusted for size was also very strong.

We were also interested to know if the use of Telon increased the quality of the applications. We found evidence of a non-linear relationship between the number of defects and the percentage of Telon code used (Figure 5.5). Figure 5.5 shows that the relationship appears U-shaped, and suggests that the number of defects decreased with the percentage of Telon used up to about 50%,

TABLE 5.6
Results for Applications Using Telon

Dependent Variable	Significant Variable	Effect on Dependent Variable	Total Variance Explained
Corrective effort (11 observations)	Percentage of Telon code	Negative	72%
Corrective effort per function point (11 observations)	Percentage of Telon code	Negative	64%

All variables are significant at the 5% level.

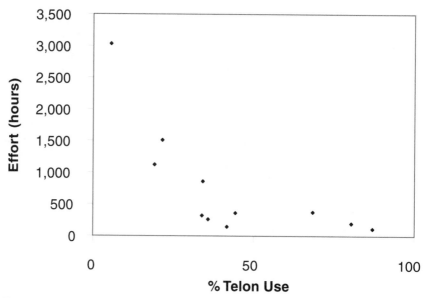

FIGURE 5.4
Corrective effort vs. % Telon use

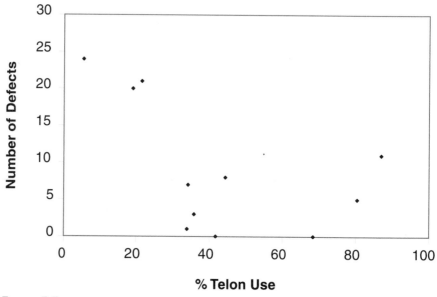

FIGURE 5.5
Number of defects vs. % Telon use

was the lowest between 50-70%, and increased again after 70%. The same relationship was observed even when the number of defects was adjusted for application size.

4. Conclusions—Lessons Learned

Software managers often find it difficult to plan for maintenance work, and there is little quantitative empirical research devoted to improving performance in this area [7]. Through the statistical analysis of one commercial bank's data, we have determined which factors had a real impact on the bank's annual corrective maintenance effort. While it is interesting to know which factors are important, it is even more valuable for software managers to be able to reduce future software maintenance cost by changing their practices. Which of these factors are within the manager's control, and what would Pekka have done differently?

The percentage of Telon use can be modified. For applications that used Telon, using it more appeared to decrease annual maintenance effort. Pekka would prefer to use Telon in all new development projects, but not for all kinds of functionality. He would increase the percentage to within the optimal range. Although we only studied 11 projects, this was enough evidence for him, as it confirmed his intuition based on experience with 19 other Telon projects that did not collect detailed data and were not included in the analysis. In addition, Kemerer and Slaughter [7] found in their study that modules generated by a backend CASE tool that generated COBOL code were significantly less likely to need repair. There is also evidence that using Telon (compared to traditional COBOL coding) improves development productivity. The International Software Benchmarking Standards Group database shows a median delivery rate of 8.6 hours/function point for Telon as opposed to 11.8 hours/function point for COBOL [8] for mainframe platforms. Thus, it appears that the salesperson was right and that using Telon can improve the productivity of the software lifecycle.

Corrective maintenance effort increased with a higher integration of batch processing. This factor can be controlled to some extent. If all possible interconnections are not implemented, the application itself will be simpler, but will need much more manual effort and human control from the user organization. The more automated the process, the smaller the total effort, although the corrective maintenance effort may increase slightly. Batch processing also causes more problems compared to online transaction processing. It is usually done at night when the online processing system is off. 50% of the applications were integrated in online processing. 80% of the applications had high batch integration. Because batch processing integration was important in the model, and integration of online transaction processing was not a significant factor, Pekka would recommend moving some interfaces from batch processing to online processing.

The risk factor of change management flexibility can be partially con-trolled. Pekka was surprised to learn that less corrective effort was required by applications that were dependent on other applications, had more owners, and for which no quick decisions could be made. He wondered if this had anything to do with the number of defects. Were the applications with fewer owners, less dependence on other applications, and which could be changed quickly also the ones with the most defects? Close inspection of the data revealed that this was not the case. He couldn't see why more dependent applications would be easier to maintain, so he concluded that this result was due to the change management process: He couldn't change the applications' dependency, he couldn't change the number of owners, but he could change the decision-making process. He would not allow quick decisions. He would recommend a more formal, controlled change management process. He believes this would lead to better reasoning for change requests, which would be analyzed and formulated better.

Part of the problem with interpreting this variable is that the definition is complicated and includes three different factors: dependence of changes, number of owners, and quickness of decisions. We recommend splitting this variable into three different variables in the future.

The business sector classification cannot be changed, but it is useful to know that different productivities can be expected for the various internal business sectors. This could help in the negotiations between the mainte-nance staff and the application owners.

We also found that maintenance effort adjusted for size (hours/function point) decreased with increasing size. This was an interesting result, as Pekka was concerned that developing big applications would have a negative impact on maintenance productivity. We have now found economies of scale both in the development productivity [9] and maintenance productivity of COBOL applications in banks.

Since application age was found to be important, Pekka would start recording actual efforts and number of defects every month during the first years of maintenance. Although we have no empirical evidence, he believes that the first months are critical. Some of the highest 1993 defect levels were found in older applications, which had caused problems from the start. He believes that if these applications had been better controlled in the beginning, their lifetime maintenance costs would have been much lower.

He also found it interesting that the status of documentation did not emerge as being important. This was probably because there were no appli-cations without documents and for which even understanding the code was difficult. Another probable explanation could be the very low volatility of staff in the early 1990s—something clear and understandable to the original developer could be very difficult for any new maintainer to understand.

Unfortunately, the lessons learned were not put into practice at this bank. Although the bank had developed a very good understanding of its software development and maintenance activities, and one could even say that they were ahead of their time as far as software measurement goes, strategic decisions made by the upper management of the bank changed everything. In early 1995, near the end of the banking crisis in Finland, and just a couple of months before the large migration project was successfully completed, the bank merged with another bank. A major motive for the merger was to benefit from economies of scale by eliminating overlapping operations. This resulted in the adoption of nearly all of the other bank's Information Systems. Thus, only a few of the applications studied still exist today. It is for this reason that we are able to make these results public.

5. Acknowledgments

We would like to thank Chris Kemerer for his comments on an earlier version of this paper.

6. References

[1] Carr, D. and R.J. Kizior, "The Case for Continued COBOL Education," *IEEE Software*, Volume 17, Number 2, March/April 2000, pp. 33-36.

[2] Arranga, E., "In COBOL's Defense," *IEEE Software*, Volume 17, Number 2, March/April 2000, pp. 70-75.

[3] Jones, C., "A New Look at Languages," *Computerworld*, November 7, 1988, pp. 97-103.

[4] Ramaswamy, R., "How to Staff Business-Critical Maintenance Projects," *IEEE Software*, May/June 2000, pp. 90-94.

[5] Kemerer, C.F. and S. Slaughter, "Methodologies for Performing Empirical Studies: Report from the International Workshop on Empirical Studies of Software Maintenance," *Empirical Software Engineering*, Volume 2, 1997, pp. 109-118.

[6] Kemerer, C.F. and S. Slaughter, "An Empirical Approach to Studying Software Evolution," *IEEE Transactions on Software Engineering*, Volume 25, Number 4, July/August 1999, pp. 493-509.

[7] Kemerer, C.F. and S. Slaughter, "Determinants of Software Maintenance Profiles: An Empirical Investigation," *Software Maintenance Research and Practice*, Volume 9, 1997, pp. 235-251.

[8] ISBSG, *The Benchmark Release 6, International Software Benchmarking Standards Group Limited*, Australia, 2000, p. 55.

[9] Maxwell, K. and P. Forselius, "Benchmarking Software Development Productivity," *IEEE Software*, Volume 17, Number 1, January/February 2000, pp. 80-88.

Appendix A
A Risk Analysis Method for Annual Maintenance of Software

This method, developed by Pekka Forselius and Maritta Tynninen, was in use in a Finnish commercial bank in the 1990s. It was developed to help the Information Systems Division (ISD) management focus improvement activities on the riskiest applications. It was applied to all software applications maintained by the ISD staff in the bank's IBM mainframe environment. The risk score of each application was calculated every September to find the riskiest applications.

This method consists of 10 risk factors, each of them with equal weight and five-point scale metrics. For each factor, a higher score means a riskier situation. The score of each factor was determined by the application manager. The overall risk score was calculated in the following way:

$$Overall\ Risk = ((1 * the\ number\ of\ 1\ scores) + (2 * the\ number\ of\ 2\ scores)$$
$$+ (4 * the\ number\ of\ 3\ scores) + (7 * the\ number\ of\ 4\ scores)$$
$$+ (10 * the\ number\ of\ 5\ scores)) / 10$$

The lowest possible score is 1 (lowest risk), and the highest possible score is 10 (highest risk). Each application with an overall score of 6 was examined carefully. Additionally, any single factor having a value of 5 was analyzed and improved when possible.

1. **Number of Users**
   = 1 if less than 20 users, all working in one place (e.g., in same department)
   = 2 if tens of users, working in several departments at headquarters
   = 3 if hundreds of users, working at several sites at many locations
   = 4 if thousands of users, working at most sites and locations everywhere
   = 5 if tens of thousands of users; self-service applications for customers

2. **Flexibility of Configuration Management**
   = 1 if changes could be implemented very fast, without any technical break
   = 2 if running of the application had to be stopped during version upgrade
   = 3 if new version had to be published and planned one week beforehand
   = 4 if new versions had to be synchronized with one or two other applications

= 5 if new versions were bound with a large set of other software applications

3. **Flexibility of Change Management**
   = 1 if changes were independent of other applications, had no more than one owner, and had a defined procedure for quick decision-making
   = 2 if proposed change decisions could usually be made in the first meeting of the board, applications had one owner, but no procedure for quick decisions
   = 3 if board meetings were organized once a month or less, applications had one or two owners, and no quick decisions were made
   = 4 if changes were dependent on other applications managed by other boards, applications had one or two owners, and no quick decisions were made
   = 5 if changes were dependent on other applications managed by other boards, applications had many owners, and no quick decisions were made

4. **Structural Flexibility**
   = 1 if structure of application was simple, use of parameters was efficient, environment was standard, and test package existed
   = 2 if complexity of application was typical, structure was based on common modules and components, use of parameters was efficient, environment was standard, and test package existed
   = 3 if original development process applied structural methods, environment was standard, and no test package existed
   = 4 if average module size was large, similar processing occurred in many parts of application, and application was completed by setting only a few parameters or creating a special development environment
   = 5 if even very common changes in the business required programming and the environment was uncommon

5. **Documentation Quality**
   = 1 if Systems Requirement Specification (SRS) and all data repository elements were updated and source code was well-commented
   = 2 if most important parts of SRS were updated and code was well-commented
   = 3 if some parts of SRS were not updated, but programming code was easy to read
   = 4 if some parts of SRS were missing, but programming code was easy to read
   = 5 if there were no documents and understanding the code was difficult

6. Dependence on People

= 1 if several people knew and understood the functionality of the application and an experienced application manager and permanent substitute existed

= 2 if experienced application manager and permanent substitute existed

= 3 if experienced application manager and nominal substitute existed and application environment was known by many

= 4 if there was only one person who knew and understood the functionality and his/her presence was essential for uninterrupted operation

= 5 if no one in organization knew the functionality

7. Shutdown Time Constraints

= 1 if operation was completely independent of timing, for example, no batch processing

= 2 if need for batch processing was daily, but it could be done anytime during the day or night

= 3 if timing was dependent on opening hours of offices in one country only

= 4 if timing of batch processing depended on opening hours and one certain break (like change of calendar day or point of time in mailing timetable)

= 5 if batch processing had to be done between two fixed points of time

8. Integration of Online Transaction Processing

= 1 if all transaction processing programs and databases were for this application only, or there was no online processing

= 2 if database was shared with other applications, but no transaction processing services shared with any other application

= 3 if application needed some shared processing services and may have caused a decrease in service levels to other applications

= 4 if application needed a lot of common services and provided them to some others

= 5 if many widely used applications needed online processing services from this application

9. Integration of Batch Processing

= 1 if there was no batch processing or an occasional delay in batch processing did not cause problems with any other application

= 2 if occasional delay in batch processing may have caused problems only to some non-critical applications

= 3 if start of batch processing was dependent on other applications or an interruption of online processing

= 4 if any critical application had to wait for successful completion of this batch processing

= 5 if end-users and their customers would have noticed problems in batch processing (i.e., high visibility)

10. **Capacity Flexibility**

= 1 if volatility in numbers of transactions and data records was predictable and easy to plan for

= 2 if occasional changes in volumes could be managed by external means (operational priorities, etc.)

= 3 if occasional increase in volumes could be managed by parameters and other means

= 4 if occasional increase in volumes may have caused remarkable decrease in service level

= 5 if occasional increase in volumes could not be managed without programming and changing database structure

From Data to Knowledge

Now that you have read the results, I'll explain how we got there. This section contains the data the software maintenance cost driver case study was based on and explains in detail how it was analyzed.

Data Validation

First of all, I interviewed Pekka to understand what the data was, how it was collected, and what the definitions of the variables were. Data validation was further complicated by the fact that the initial data labels and written definitions were in Finnish, a language I do not understand. Although Pekka speaks English well, I still had to be very careful throughout the analyses to make sure that we were really talking about the same thing. I found it useful to make an initial definition table that included my assumptions about what missing values and zeros meant for each variable after our first interview and then had him correct it. I took notes at each face-to-face meeting and further clarified points via email. I found it very beneficial to meet again face-to-face to discuss the results of the preliminary analyses (Steps 1-3 of Chapter 1) to make sure everything was okay before building the multi-variable model. Another difficulty we faced was that I had never developed software in a bank myself and was thus unfamiliar with the types of applications found in banks, and unsure of the correct English banking terminology. It is interesting to note that although **we** finally understood what we were talking about, some of our initial variable definitions were not clear to other English speakers with whom we shared our results.

The original data was in three different spreadsheets. Sorting through the different spreadsheets to find complete and useful data was very complicated. This was a long, painstaking process that I have briefly summarized here so as not to bore you with too many details. One spreadsheet contained 26 variables, including different types of effort data from 1990-1993 and the starting date of maintenance for 426 applications. A second spreadsheet contained 11 variables concerning 1993 size data for 205 applications. A third spreadsheet contained 28 variables, including 10 risk factors and application defects found in 1993 and 1994 for 191 applications. When these three spreadsheets were merged, we found that only 169 applications were present in all three files. There were many missing values. Only 99 of the 169 applications had data for the risk factors. The most complete data was available for 1993. Of the 99 applications, Pekka decided that we should only trust the data that had nonzero values for all three types of maintenance effort, corrective, change, and running effort, for 1993. Finally, after Pekka was able to find some missing maintenance start dates, we ended up with 67 applications with corrective maintenance effort, size, maintenance age, and application programming defects for 1993. Risk factor data was available for 56 of the 67 applications. We decided to study the factors that could be related to corrective effort and selected the 28 variables presented in Table 5.7 for our analysis. The raw data can be found in Appendix C.

TABLE 5.7
Variable Definitions

Variable	Full Name	Definition
mid	maintenance identification number	I gave each application a unique identification number. (Originally, each application was given a name instead of a number, but I replaced these names for data confidentiality reasons.)
correff	corrective maintenance effort	Changes necessary to keep application running during 1993, measured in hours.
totfp	application size	Function points; calculated by adding the number of COBOL, Telon, Easytrieve+, and JCL function points (which were originally backfired from lines of code). Size counted in summer 1993; represents average size during 1993.

Variable	Full Name	Definition
pcobol	percentage COBOL code	Number of COBOL function points/*totfp*
ptelon	percentage Telon code	Number of Telon function points/*totfp*
peasy	percentage Easytrieve+ code	Number of Easytrieve+ function points/*totfp*
pjcl	percentage JCL code	Number of JCL function points/*totfp*
ageend	total months maintained	Total number of months maintained at end of 1993 (calculated from start date of application's maintenance)
avetrans	ave. no. transactions	Average number of thousands of transactions per 24 hours
disksp	disk space	Measured in MB
cpu	cpu	Seconds/24 hours
appdef	number of application programming defects	Total number of application programming defects found during 1993
borg	business organization type	BigCorp = Selected large corporate customers Corp = Other corporate customers Group = Group accounting/management ITServ = IT services InHServ = In-house services Retail = Retail/people
morg	internal business unit	Account = Accounting BUC = Business unit counting Common = Common banking service CusInt = Customer interconnection DecSup = Decision support Deposit = Deposit ITInfra = IT infrastructure ITServ = IT services ITSupp = IT technical support IntlBank = International banking LetCred = Letter of credit Loan = Loan security Payment = Payment Person = Personnel

(Continued)

TABLE 5.7 *(Continued)*

Variable	Full Name	Definition
		Resto = In-house restaurant SecTrade = Securities trading system Treasury = Treasury
apptype	application type	BackOff = Backoffice database Connect = Customer interconnection service Core = Core banking business system InfServ = Information service/decision support
dbms	database management system	DB2, IDSN
tpms	transaction processing management system	BATCH, IIMS, IMS, PTCICS, RECICS
t	recovery capability	1 = Not important 2 = Bad 3 = Satisfactory 4 = Good 5 = Excellent
r1	number of users	Values of risk factors range from 1 to 5. 1 = least
r2	configuration management flexibility	risky situation; 5 = most risky situation; 3 does not mean average, it represents a situation some-
r3	change management flexibility	where between least and most risky.
r4	structural flexibility	Risk factor definitions provided in full at end of
r5	documentation quality	earlier paper titled "Cost Drivers of Annual of
r6	people dependence	Corrective Maintenance: One Commercial Bank's
r7	shutdown time constraints	Experience."
r8	online transaction processing integration	
r9	batch processing integration	
r10	capacity flexibility	

Once we had selected the variables, I was ready to start looking in more detail at the data. I used the summary function to check for missing or strange values (Example 5.1).

Example 5.1

```
                          .  summarize
```

Variable	Obs	Mean	Std. Dev.	Min	Max
mid	67	34	19.48504	1	67
correff	67	515.0746	720.5377	22	3031
totfp	67	470.6119	514.5435	18	2328
pcobol	67	.3792537	.2943773	0	1
ptelon	67	.0704255	.1888824	0	.8691589
peasy	67	.0943003	.1332916	0	.5244565
pjcl	67	.4561443	.2620808	0	1
t	59	3.322034	.7529409	1	4
ageend	67	39.35821	20.5903	8	85
avetrans	67	14.10448	46.84149	0	345
disksp	67	1817	6019.997	0	39012
cpu	67	312.5672	535.797	0	2197
r1	56	3.392857	1.302844	1	5
r2	56	2.660714	1.391883	1	5
r3	56	2.375	1.272971	1	5
r4	56	2.375	.9256447	1	4
r5	56	2.160714	.968162	1	4
r6	56	2	.6875517	1	4
r7	56	4.053571	.9614316	1	5
r8	56	2.928571	1.616474	1	5
r9	56	3.660714	1.32496	1	5
r10	56	1.839286	.9298443	1	3
appdef	67	9.432836	22.3825	0	163
borg	67	3.567164	1.940196	1	6
morg	67	9.492537	6.013553	1	17
apptype	67	2.298507	.853068	1	4
dbms	59	1.033898	.1825208	1	2
tpms	66	2.772727	.7604746	1	5

The minimum (*Min*) and maximum (*Max*) values for all the variables do not make sense. There is a problem with the minimum value of average number of transactions (*avetrans*), disk space (*disksp*), and *cpu*. How could the minimum value be 0 for these variables? I asked Pekka and learned that these values were not really zero, but had been rounded or truncated to zero at some point during the data collection process. So, in these cases, zero does not really signify 0, just a number less than 1.

I also noted that four of the ten risk factors were missing the higher, riskier values. The variables *r1-r10, t, dbms,* and *tpms* all contained missing values for some applications. In all of these cases, missing data means "unknown" as Pekka and I had already filled in the missing values when possible, during the merging of the initial spreadsheets.

The summary statistics of *correff, totfp,* and *ageend* are of special interest. The size of projects (*totfp*) in this database range from 18 function points to

2328 function points. The average project size is 471 function points. Annual corrective effort (*correff*) ranges from 22 hours to 3031 hours, with an average of 515 hours. The number of months maintained (*ageend*) ranges from 8 months to 85 months. The average number of months maintained is 39 months. Therefore, my conclusions will not apply to projects in this bank that were smaller than 18 function points, or that used less than 22 hours of effort, or that were maintained less than 8 months. They will also not apply to projects bigger than 2328 function points, or that used more than 3031 hours effort, or that were maintained more than 85 months.

The reason why *borg, morg, apptype, dbms*, and *tpms* appear as numerical values in these summary statistics is that Stata automatically sorts category-level names in alphabetical order and assigns them a number starting with 1. This number also appears in the regression statistical output. The maximum (*Max*) for these variables corresponds to the number of different levels. As I already checked for spelling mistakes while working with the raw data, I do not need to tabulate the categorical data at this point in my analysis.

Variable and Model Selection

This section includes the creation of new variables, data modifications, identification of categorical variable subsets, and the selection of the model to be studied.

Creation of New Variables

Because corrective maintenance effort, *correff*, is the effort expended on corrective maintenance during one calendar year, a problem is posed by applications that started maintenance during the year. These applications are not strictly comparable with applications maintained during the entire year. I decided to resolve this problem by adjusting the effort of partial-year applications to a full-year equivalent. Thus, an application that was maintained for 10 months during 1993 and which required 30 hours of effort had an annual equivalent effort of 36 hours (=(30 hours/10 months)*12 months). I named this new variable *acorreff*, annual corrective maintenance effort. It follows that I will need to transform *acorreff* back to *correff* should I ever wish to estimate the effort actually required by applications that began maintenance during the year.

After I learned that the zero values of the variables *avetrans, disksp*, and *cpu* did not really mean zero but just a number less than 1, I decided to transform them into categorical variables based on their levels. For example, I did not know if a 0 was really 0.0001 or 0.9, but I did know for certain that it was a number less than 1. Therefore, if I created a categorical variable with a level called "values < 1," I did not need to make any assumptions about the actual value. I named these transformed variables *avetlev, dsplev*, and *cpulev*. Their levels are defined in Table 5.8.

I knew from experience that variables containing many zero values cause problems in statistical analyses of software project data. They are usually not normally distributed, and when you try to transform them by taking their natural log, all the applications with a value of 0 are dropped because *ln(0)* is undefined. *ptelon, peasy*, and *appdef* contained many zero values.[5] To get around this problem with *ptelon* and *peasy*, I decided to create two new categorical variables that signaled if a language was used or not: *telonuse* and *easyuse*. For *appdef*, I decided to create a new variable, *adefect*, which equaled *appdef + 1*. (Should I need to interpret the relationship between corrective

TABLE 5.8
Summary of Variables Created

Variable	Full Name	Definition
acorreff	annual corrective maintenance effort	Changes necessary to keep application running during one full calendar year, measured in hours
avetlev	level of average transactions (000s/24 hours)	1 = Less than 1 2 = From 1 through 9 3 = 10 or more
dsplev	level of disk space use (MB)	1 = Less than 10 2 = From 10 through 99 3 = From 100 through 999 4 = 1000 or more
cpulev	level of cpu (seconds/24 hours)	1 = Less than 10 2 = From 10 through 99 3 = From 100 through 999 4 = 1000 or more
telonuse	Telon use	no = Telon not used yes = Telon used
easyuse	Easytrieve+ use	no = Easytrieve+ not used yes = Easytrieve+ used
adefect	adjusted application defects	*adefect = appdef + 1*

---

5. Problems with *ptelon, peasy,* and *appdef* became apparent to me after I looked at their histograms and two-dimensional graphs. Sometimes it is necessary to loop back to Step 1, variable and model selection, after looking at the graphs. I present the new variables here for clarity.

maintenance effort and number of applications defects at a later stage, I will need to remember to transform *adefect* back to *appdef*.) Definitions for the variables I created can be found in Table 5.8.

Data Modifications

Before analyzing the data further, I added the new variables I created to the original data.

Identifying Subsets of Categorical Variables

As I did not need to check for spelling mistakes in the data validation step, I will tabulate the categorical variables now to see how many applications are in each category (Example 5.2).

Example 5.2

```
                              . tabulate borg

        Business
        Organization
        Type              Freq.       Percent        Cum.
        BigCorp               9         13.43        13.43
        Corp                 19         28.36        41.79
        Group                11         16.42        58.21
        ITServ                4          5.97        64.18
        InHServ               1          1.49        65.67
        Retail               23         34.33       100.00

        Total                67        100.00
```

The majority of applications are Retail. There is only one in-house service (*InHServ*) application in this database. As I do not believe that one project is enough to base any conclusions on, I created a subset of the *borg* variable (*subborg*), which excluded the *InHServ* organization type.

Example 5.3

```
                              . tabulate morg

        Internal
        Business
        Unit             Freq.        Percent        Cum.
        Account            13          19.40        19.40
        BUC                 1           1.49        20.90
        Common              4           5.97        26.87
        CusInt              2           2.99        29.85
        DecSup              1           1.49        31.34
```

```
Deposit              6       8.96       40.30
ITInfra              1       1.49       41.79
ITServ               1       1.49       43.28
ITSupp               1       1.49       44.78
IntlBank             1       1.49       46.27
LetCred              1       1.49       47.76
Loan                 1       1.49       49.25
Payment             15      22.39       71.64
Person               1       1.49       73.13
Resto                1       1.49       74.63
SecTrade            10      14.93       89.55
Treasury             7      10.45      100.00

Total               67     100.00
```

From Example 5.3, we see that the majority of applications are in the payment (*Payment*), accounting (*Account*), and securities trading systems (*SecTrade*) business units. I created a subset of the internal business unit variable (*submorg*), which excluded the 11 categories with less than 3 observations.

Example 5.4

```
                  . tabulate apptype

    Application
    Type              Freq.     Percent      Cum.
    BackOff             15       22.39      22.39
    Connect             19       28.36      50.75
    Core                31       46.27      97.01
    InfServ              2        2.99     100.00

    Total               67      100.00
```

In Example 5.4, we see that nearly half the applications were core banking business system applications (*Core*). I created a new variable, *subapp*, which excluded the information service/decision support (*InfServ*) category, which contained less than three applications.

Example 5.5

```
                  . tabulate dbms

    Database
    Management
    System            Freq.     Percent      Cum.
    DB2                 57       96.61      96.61
    IDSN                 2        3.39     100.00

    Total               59      100.00
```

As nearly all the applications used the *DB2* database management system (Example 5.5), it was impossible to look at the effect of changes in this variable on maintenance effort. Thus, I decided to drop this variable from my analysis.

Example 5.6

```
                    . tabulate tpms

    Trans.
    Process.
    Mgmt.
    System          Freq.        Percent         Cum.
    BATCH              8          12.12          12.12
    IIMS               3           4.55          16.67
    IMS               52          78.79          95.45
    PTCICS             2           3.03          98.48
    RECICS             1           1.52         100.00
    Total             66         100.00
```

Most applications used the *IMS* transaction management system (Example 5.6). I created a subset of *tpms*, *subtpms*, which excluded the *PTCICS* and *RECICS* categories.

Example 5.7

```
                    . tabulate t

    Recovery
    Capability      Freq.        Percent         Cum.
        1              3           5.08           5.08
        2              1           1.69           6.78
        3             29          49.15          55.93
        4             26          44.07         100.00
    Total             59         100.00
```

Example 5.7 shows that most applications had a recovery capability of either satisfactory (3) or good (4). As there are no excellent recovery capabilities (5) and only one bad (2), I can only study the difference between satisfactory and good in the database. This did not seem very interesting to me, so I decided to drop this variable from my analysis.

Example 5.8

```
                    . tabulate avetlev

    Level of
    Ave.
    Transactions    Freq.        Percent         Cum.
        1             31          46.27          46.27
        2             22          32.84          79.10
        3             14          20.90         100.00
    Total             67         100.00
```

The majority of applications had less than 1000 transactions per 24 hours (Level 1 in Example 5.8).

Example 5.9

```
. tabulate dsplev
```

Level of Disk Space Use	Freq.	Percent	Cum.
1	14	20.90	20.90
2	13	19.40	40.30
3	26	38.81	79.10
4	14	20.90	100.00
Total	67	100.00	

Most applications used between 100 and 999 MB of disk space (Level 3 in Example 5.9).

Example 5.10

```
. tabulate cpulev
```

Level of CPU	Freq.	Percent	Cum.
1	14	20.90	20.90
2	22	32.84	53.73
3	23	34.33	88.06
4	8	11.94	100.00
Total	67	100.00	

From Example 5.10, nearly an equal number of applications had a CPU level of either between 10 to 99 seconds/24 hours (Level 2) or between 100 to 999 seconds/24 hours (Level 3).

Example 5.11

```
. tabulate telonuse
```

Telon Use	Freq.	Percent	Cum.
no	56	83.58	83.58
yes	11	16.42	100.00
Total	67	100.00	

Only 11 applications were developed using Telon (Example 5.11).

Example 5.12

```
                     . tabulate easyuse
        Easy Use      Freq.      Percent      Cum.
          no            27        40.30       40.30
          yes           40        59.70      100.00
        Total           67       100.00
```

Example 5.12 shows that 40 applications were developed using Easytrieve+.

Model Selection

My goal in this study is to determine which variables explain the differences in annual corrective maintenance effort among software applications in the bank. After carefully studying the data, I decided to use the following variables:

$$acorreff = f(totfp, pcobol, pjcl, ageend, adefect, subborg,$$
$$submorg, subapp, subtpms, r1\text{-}r10, avetlev,$$
$$dsklev, cpulev, telonuse, easyuse)$$

What are the relationships between annual corrective maintenance effort (*acorreff*) and the size of an application (*totfp*), the percentage of COBOL used (*pcobol*), the percentage of JCL used (*pjcl*), the application's maintenance age (*ageend*), the number of application defects (*adefect*), the business organization type (*subborg*), the internal business unit (*submorg*), the type of application (*subapp*), the transaction processing management system (*subtpms*), the 10 different risk factors (*r1-r10*), the transaction level (*avetlev*), the level of disk space use (*dsklev*), the level of CPU (*cpulev*), whether or not Telon was used (*telonuse*), and whether or not Easytrieve+ was used (*easyuse*)? Note that "*sub*" before a variable refers to a subset of the variable, which contains only categories with three or more observations.

Preliminary Analyses

Graphs

I always look at two type of graphs: histograms and two-dimensional graphs.

Histograms

Effort (*acorreff*) and size (*totfp*) are not normally distributed (Figures 5.6 and 5.7). To more closely approximate a normal distribution, I transformed these variables by taking their natural log. These transformed variables are shown in Figures 5.8 and 5.9.

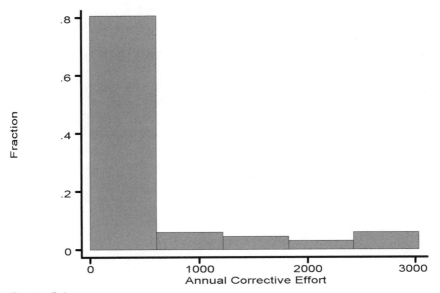

FIGURE 5.6
Distribution of *acorreff*

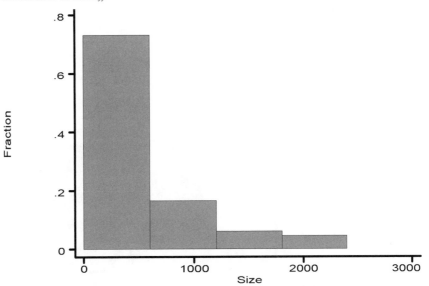

FIGURE 5.7
Distribution of *totfp*

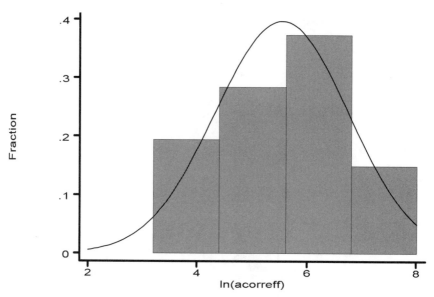

FIGURE 5.8
Distribution of *ln(acorreff)*

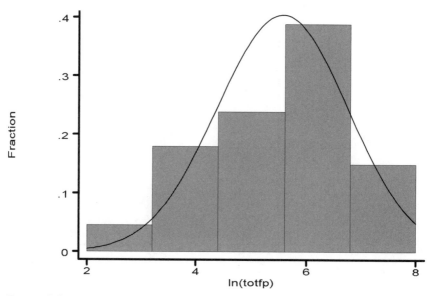

FIGURE 5.9
Distribution of *ln(totfp)*

The distributions of the percentage of COBOL used (*pcobol*) and the percentage of JCL used (*pjcl*) are closer to a normal distribution without any transformation (see Figures 5.10 through 5.13). Therefore, I did not need to take the natural log of these variables in my analysis.

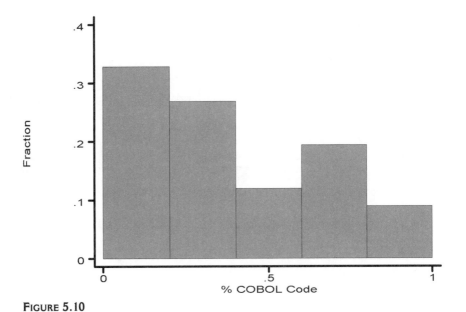

FIGURE 5.10
Distribution of *pcobol*

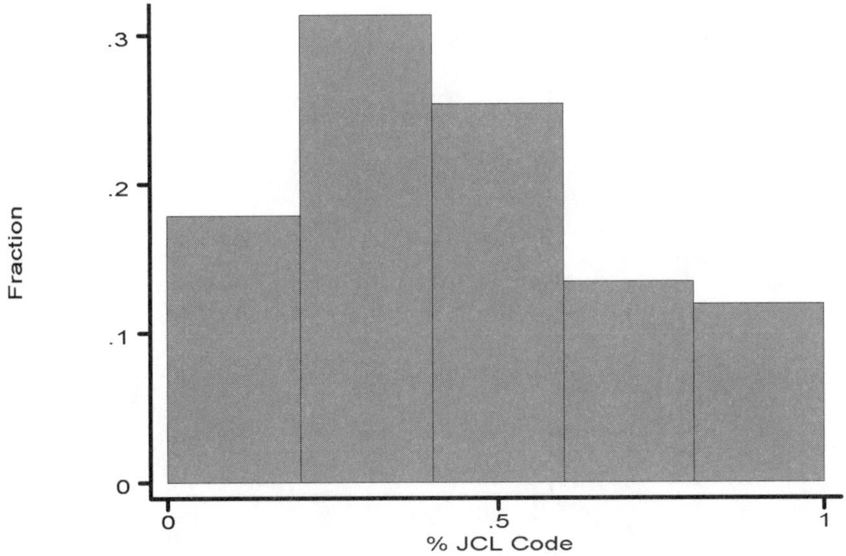

FIGURE 5.11
Distribution of *pjcl*

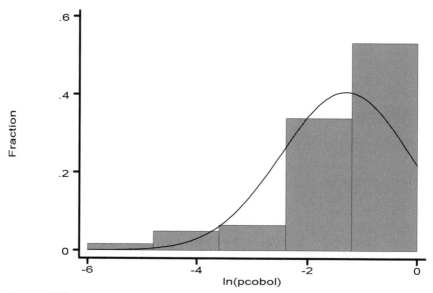

FIGURE 5.12
Distribution of *ln*(*pcobol*)

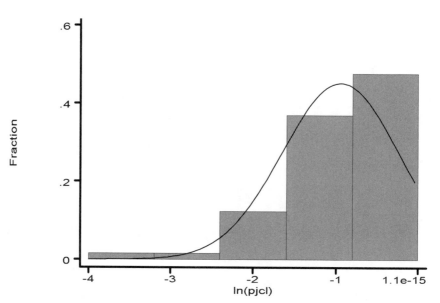

FIGURE 5.13
Distribution of *ln*(*pjcl*)

After looking at the distributions of the percentage of Easytrieve+ used (*peasy*) and the percentage of Telon used (*ptelon*) in Figures 5.14 and 5.15, I realized they were skewed to the left because they contained numerous zeros. Therefore, I decided to transform these two variables into categorical variables (see "Creation of New Variables" section).

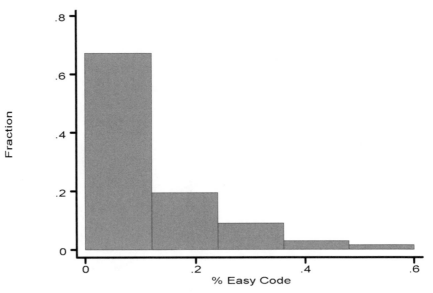

FIGURE 5.14
Distribution of *peasy*

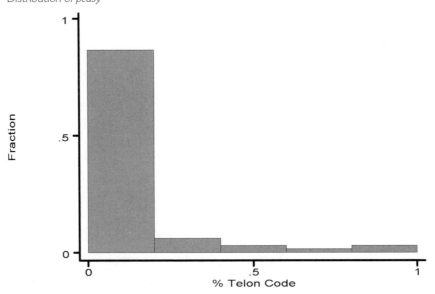

FIGURE 5.15
Distribution of *ptelon*

The total number of months maintained (*ageend*) is approximately normally distributed (see Figure 5.16).

The number of application programming defects (*appdef*) is skewed to the left (Figure 5.17). Transforming *appdef* to *adefect* (recall that *adefect*

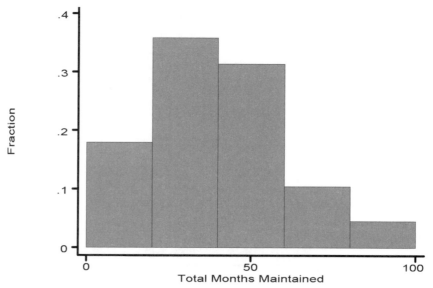

FIGURE 5.16
Distribution of *ageend*

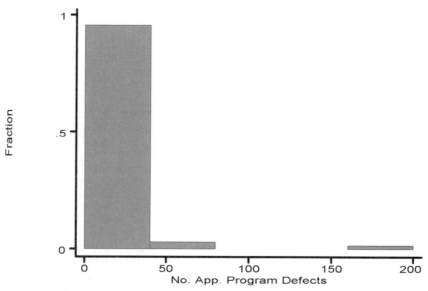

FIGURE 5.17
Distribution of *appdef*

= *appdef* + *1*) and then taking the natural log of *adefect* more closely approximates a normal distribution (Figure 5.18).

Most risk factors are not normally distributed in the sample (see Figures 5.19 through 5.28). In addition, the definitions of the factors were not chosen

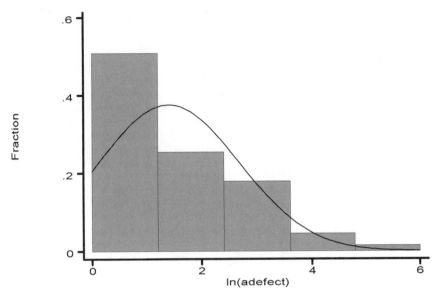

FIGURE 5.18
Distribution of *ln(adefect)*

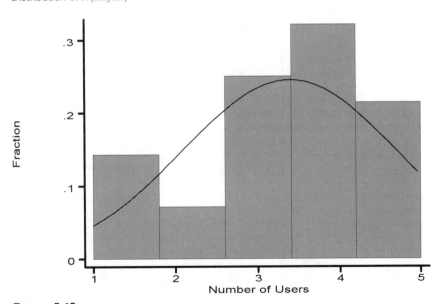

FIGURE 5.19
Distribution of *rl*

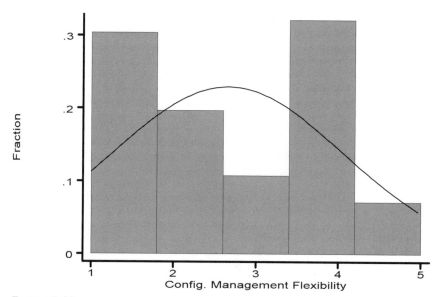

FIGURE 5.20
Distribution of *r2*

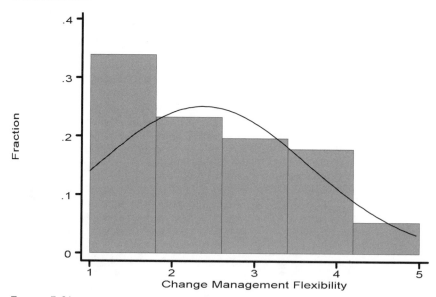

FIGURE 5.21
Distribution of *r3*

especially so that most projects would be average. The risk factors were not measured using a Likert scale and thus cannot be considered quasi-interval variables. They are ordinal variables, and I will treat them as categorical variables in the ANOVA step. (See Chapter 6 for a complete discussion of variable types.)

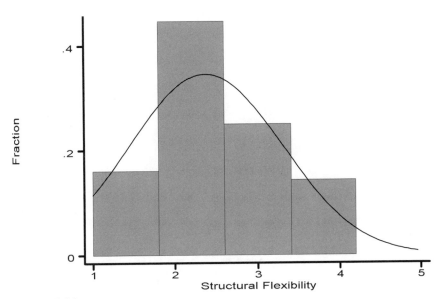

FIGURE 5.22
Distribution of *r4*

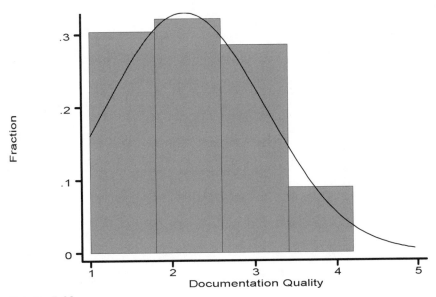

FIGURE 5.23
Distribution of *r5*

Two-Dimensional Graphs   I plotted the relationships between the transformed effort variable, *lacorref*,[6] and each numerical-type variable. The variables were transformed as described in the previous section.

---

6. Because there is an 8 character limit to variable names, I decided to name $ln(acorreff) = lacorref$.

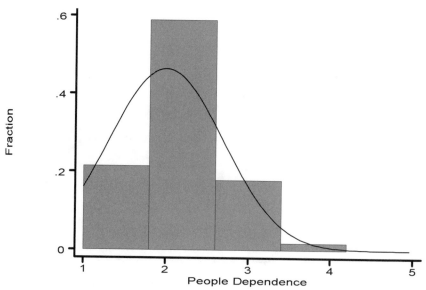

FIGURE 5.24
Distribution of *r6*

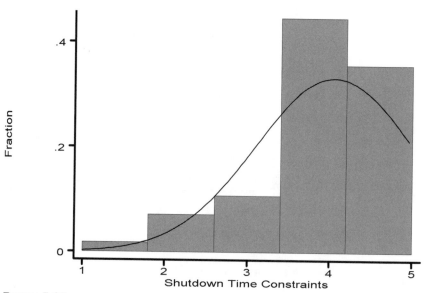

FIGURE 5.25
Distribution of *r7*

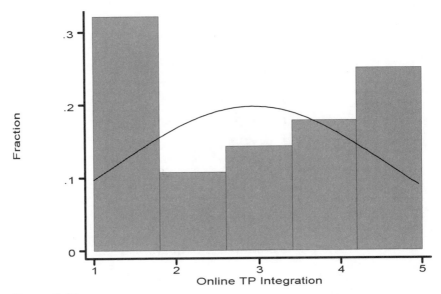

FIGURE 5.26
Distribution of *r8*

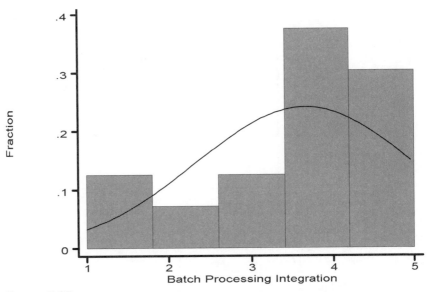

FIGURE 5.27
Distribution of *r9*

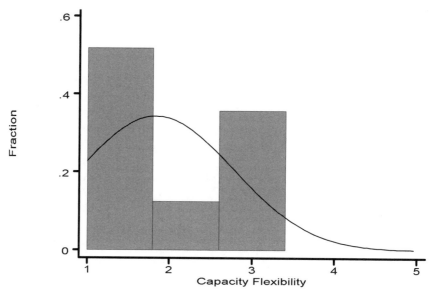

FIGURE 5.28
Distribution of *r10*

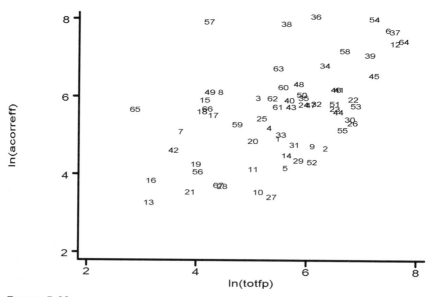

FIGURE 5.29
ln(acorreff) vs. *ln(totfp)*

Figure 5.29 shows a linear relationship between *ln(acorreff)* and *ln(totfp)*; thus, annual corrective maintenance effort appears to increase with application size. In Figure 5.30, it appears that applications developed using more

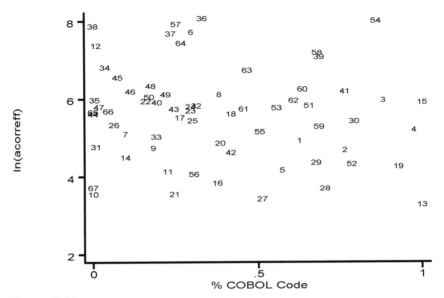

FIGURE 5.30

ln(acorreff) vs. *pcobol*

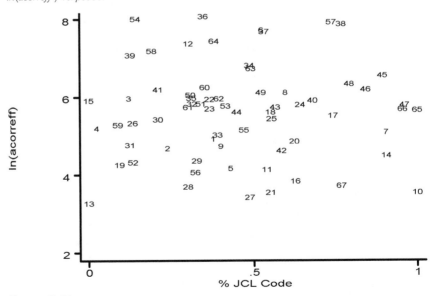

FIGURE 5.31

ln(acorreff) vs. *pjcl*

COBOL require a slightly lower maintenance effort. Figure 5.31 shows no obvious relationship between maintenance effort and percentage of JCL code.

I don't see any clear relationship between maintenance effort and total number of months maintained (Figure 5.32).

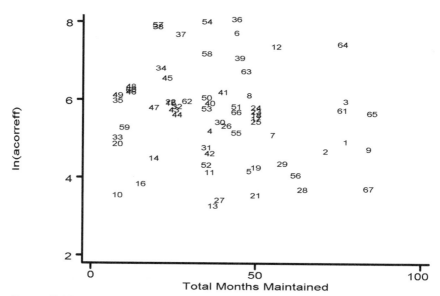

FIGURE 5.32

ln(acorreff) vs. *ageend*

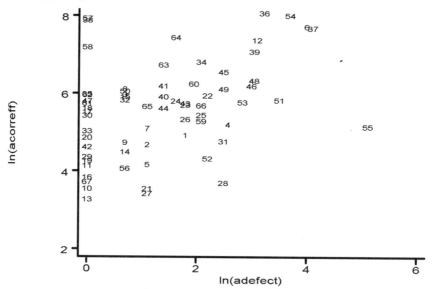

FIGURE 5.33

ln(acorreff) vs. *ln(adefect)*

In Figure 5.33, especially if I ignore all the applications with zero defects,[7] it looks like applications with more defects require more corrective maintenance. This makes sense.

---

7. $ln(adefect) = 0$ when $adefect = 1$; thus, $appdef = 0$. (Recall that $adefect = appdef + 1$.)

In Figures 5.34 through 5.37, I don't see any clear relationships between maintenance effort and number of users (*r1*), configuration management flexibility (*r2*), change management flexibility (*r3*), or structural flexibility (*r4*).

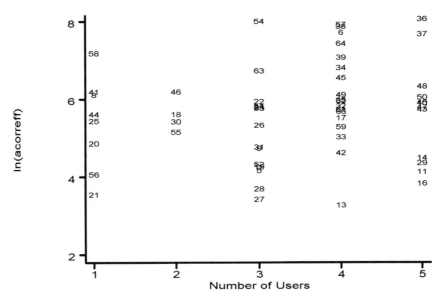

FIGURE 5.34

ln(acorreff) vs. *r1*

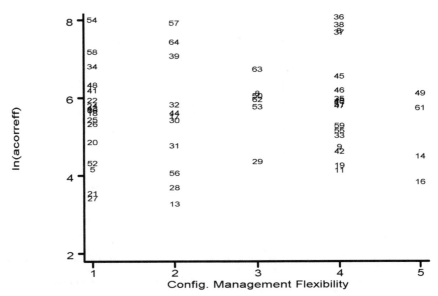

FIGURE 5.35

ln(acorreff) vs. *r2*

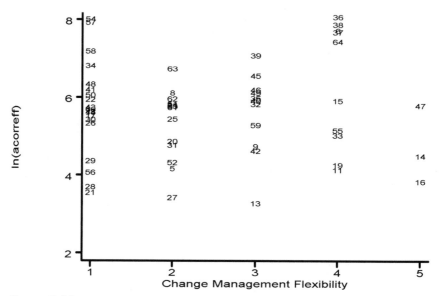

FIGURE 5.36

ln(acorreff) vs. *r3*

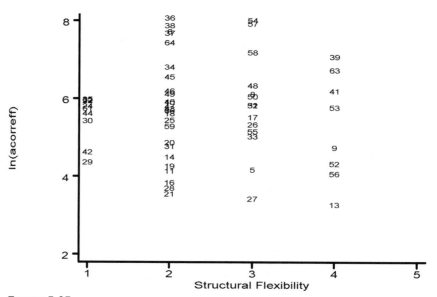

FIGURE 5.37

ln(acorreff) vs. *r4*

In Figures 5.38 through 5.41, there are no obvious relationships between maintenance effort and documentation quality (*r5*), people dependence (*r6*), shutdown time constraints (*r7*), or online transaction processing integration (*r8*).

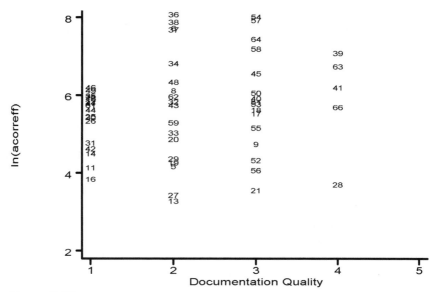

FIGURE 5.38
ln(acorreff) vs. *r5*

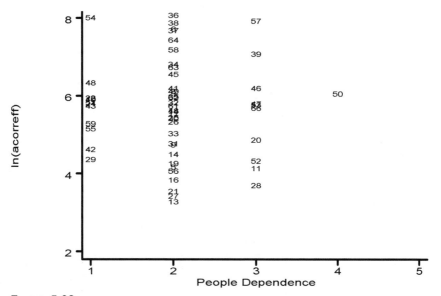

FIGURE 5.39
ln(acorreff) vs. *r6*

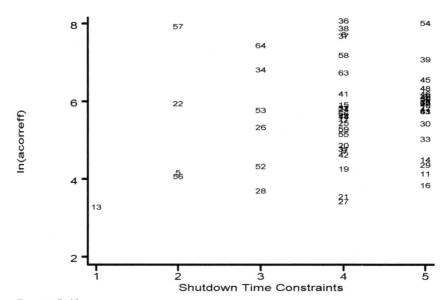

FIGURE 5.40

ln(acorreff) vs. *r7*

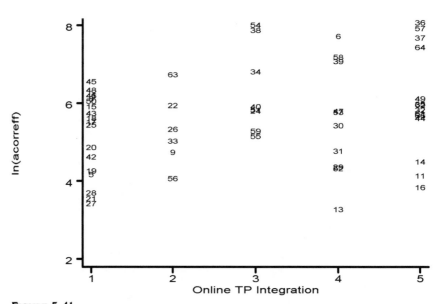

FIGURE 5.41

ln(acorreff) vs. *r8*

In Figure 5.42, it appears that more maintenance effort is needed for higher levels of batch processing integration (*r9*). Figure 5.43 shows no clear relationship between maintenance effort and capacity flexibility (*r10*).

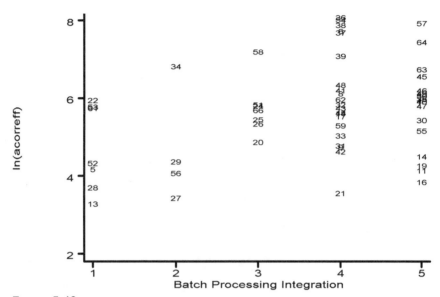

FIGURE 5.42
ln(acorreff) vs. *r9*

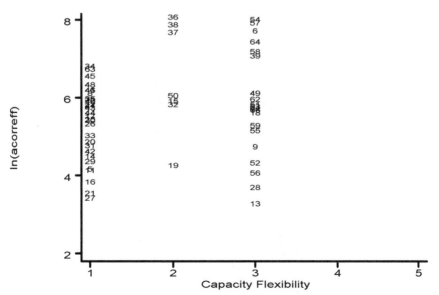

FIGURE 5.43
ln(acorreff) vs. *r10*

In Figure 5.44, maintenance effort appears to increase slightly with increasing transaction levels (*avetlev*). From Figures 5.45 and 5.46, there are no obvious relationships between maintenance effort and level of disk space use (*dsplev*) or level of CPU (*cpulev*).

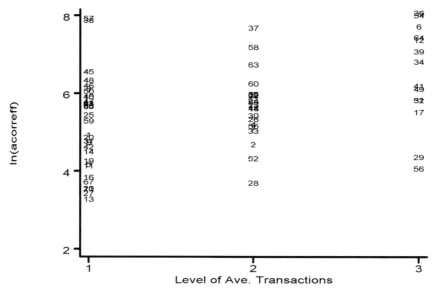

FIGURE 5.44

ln(acorreff) vs. *avetlev*

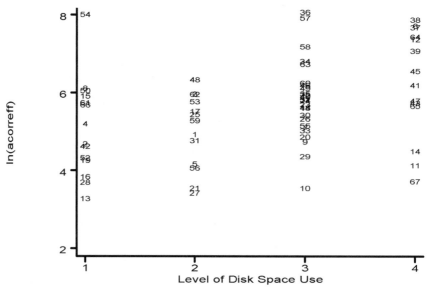

FIGURE 5.45

ln(acorreff) vs. *dsplev*

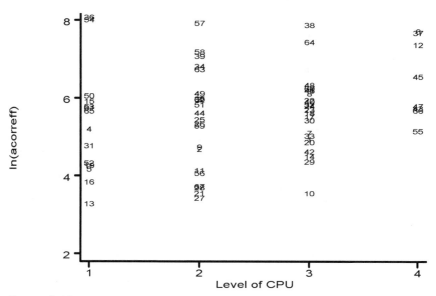

FIGURE 5.46
ln(acorreff) vs. *cpulev*

Tables

What is the average annual corrective maintenance effort for each categorical variable? In the previous step, we saw that the strongest linear relationship appeared to be between maintenance effort and application size. So, keep in mind that the explanation behind many of the effort differences in the following tables may be due to application size. Note that I limited my comparisons to categories with three or more observations.

Example 5.13

```
. table borg, c(n acorreff mean acorreff)

Business
Organization
Type              N(acorreff)      mean(acorreff)
BigCorp                9                 381
Corp                  19                 403
Group                 11                 188
ITServ                 4                 193
InHServ                1                  29
Retail                23                 911
```

On average, applications for the retail customers (*Retail*) required the highest corrective maintenance effort (Example 5.13). Applications for group accounting/management (*Group*) and IT services (*ITServ*) required the lowest effort. As there is only one in-house service application (*InHServ*), there is not enough information to make any generalizations about this type. However, I printed out its effort as it might be of interest to the bank.

Example 5.14

```
. table morg, c(n acorreff mean acorreff)
```

Internal Business Unit	N(acorreff)	mean(acorreff)
Account	13	186
BUC	1	282
Common	4	283
CusInt	2	144
DecSup	1	1508
Deposit	6	1891
ITInfra	1	271
ITServ	1	39
ITSupp	1	112
IntlBank	1	795
LetCred	1	463
Loan	1	1122
Payment	15	328
Person	1	196
Resto	1	29
SecTrade	10	819
Treasury	7	255

In Example 5.14, applications for the deposit business unit (*Deposit*) required the highest amount of corrective maintenance effort. Accounting business unit applications (*Account*) required the lowest amount.

Example 5.15

```
. table apptype, c(n acorreff mean acorreff)
```

Application Type	N(acorreff)	mean(acorreff)
BackOff	15	191
Connect	19	411
Core	31	730
InfServ	2	808

Core banking applications (*Core*) required the highest amount of corrective maintenance effort (Example 5.15). Backoffice (*BackOff*) database applications required the lowest amount.

Example 5.16

```
. table tpms, c(n acorreff mean acorreff)
```

Trans. Process. Mgmt. System	N(acorreff)	mean(acorreff)
BATCH	8	333
IIMS	3	548
IMS	52	565
PTCICS	2	144
RECICS	1	463

Applications that used the *IMS* or *IIMS* transaction processing management system required the highest amount of corrective maintenance effort (Example 5.16). Batch transaction processing management system applications (*BATCH*) required the least maintenance effort.

Example 5.17

```
. table avetlev, c(n acorreff mean acorreff)
```

Level of Ave. Transactions	N(acorreff)	mean(acorreff)
1	31	361
2	22	397
3	14	1071

Applications with higher transaction levels required more maintenance effort (Example 5.17).

Example 5.18

```
. table dsplev, c(n acorreff mean acorreff)
```

Level of Disk Space Use	N(acorreff)	mean(acorreff)
1	14	372
2	13	203
3	26	537
4	14	936

Example 5.18 shows that on average, applications that used more than 1000 MB of disk space (Level 4) required the most maintenance effort. Applications that used between 10 to 99 MB of disk space (Level 2) required the least maintenance effort.

Example 5.19

```
. table cpulev, c(n acorreff mean acorreff)
  Level of CPU      N(acorreff)       mean(acorreff)
            1            14                574
            2            22                446
            3            23                420
            4             8                925
```

Applications with CPU levels of more than 1000 seconds/24 hours (Level 4) required the most maintenance effort on average (Example 5.19). Applications with CPU levels of 100 to 999 seconds/24 hours (Level 3) required the lowest amount of effort.

Example 5.20

```
. table telonuse, c(n acorreff mean acorreff)
  Telon Use       N(acorreff)       mean(acorreff)
  no                  56                 475
  yes                 11                 753
```

On average, applications developed using Telon required more maintenance effort than applications that did not use Telon (Example 5.20).

Example 5.21

```
. table easyuse, c(n acorreff mean acorreff)
  Easy Use        N(acorreff)       mean(acorreff)
  no                  27                 286
  yes                 40                 680
```

Applications developed using Easytrieve+ required more than twice the amount of maintenance effort on average as applications that did not use Easytrieve+ (Example 5.21).

Correlation Analysis

In Chapter 1, I explained why I look at the correlation of the independent variables and showed you how to interpret correlation analysis output. Because this study had 19 numerical variables that resulted in 171 Spearman's correlation output tables (using my statistical analysis tool), I will not show all of the output from the correlation analysis as it would take far

TABLE 5.9
Summary of Correlation Coefficients

Variables	Num Obs	Correlation
r2 and *r9*	56	0.53
r7 and *r9*	56	0.52
adefect and *totfp*	67	0.52
dsplev and *cpulev*	67	0.53
acorreff and *totfp*	67	0.52
r4 and *r5*	56	0.60
r2 and *r3*	56	0.74

too many pages. Instead, I searched the correlation output for any significant correlation coefficients greater than |0.5|. My summary is presented in Table 5.9. (Note that the Spearman's rank correlation coefficient does not require that variables be normally distributed. Thus, I included *avetlev, dsplev, cpulev,* and *r1-r10* in the correlation analysis.)

The risk factor relationships were interpreted by referring to their definitions in Appendix A of the paper "Cost Drivers of Annual Corrective Maintenance: One Commercial Bank's Experience" contained in this chapter. Applications with lower flexibility of configuration management (*r2*) often had a higher integration of batch processing (*r9*) and a lower flexibility of change management (*r3*). Higher shutdown time constraints (*r7*) were often associated with a higher integration of batch processing (*r9*). Bigger applications (*totfp*) often had more application programming defects (*adefect*) and required more annual corrective maintenance effort (*acorreff*). Higher disk space needs (*dsplev*) were often associated with higher CPU levels (*cpulev*). Applications with less structural flexibility (*r4*) very often had lower documentation quality (*r5*). As 0.74 is very close to my cut-off level of 0.75, I would prefer a model that does not include both *r2* and *r3* (risk of multicollinearity).

Stepwise Regression Analysis

The stepwise regression analysis was run using the following non-categorical variables: *ltotfp, pcobol, pjcl, ageend,* and *ladefect* (Example 5.22). The forward and backward stepwise regression procedures found the same model. Only one variable, application size (*ltotfp*), explained any variation (27%) in annual corrective maintenance effort (*lacorref*). Annual corrective maintenance effort increased with increasing application size, which makes sense to me.

Example 5.22

```
Source          SS       df       MS              Number of obs =      67
Model      27.1097401    1    27.1097401          F(1,65)       =   25.37
Residual   69.4586695   65    1.06859492          Prob > F      =  0.0000
                                                  R-squared     =  0.2807
Total      96.5684097   66    1.46315772          Adj R-squared =  0.2697
                                                  Root MSE      =  1.0337

lacorref      Coef.    Std. Err.      t       P>|t|     [95% Conf. Interval]
ltotfp      .5410196    .107413     5.037    0.000     .326501     .7555381
_cons       2.532008    .6108209    4.145    0.000    1.312115    3.751902
```

Building the Multi-Variable Model_____

The best regression model explained only 27% of the variance in maintenance effort. It is highly likely that the categorical variables, *subborg, submorg, subapp, subtpms, avetlev, dsklev, cpulev, telonuse, easyuse*, and the ten risk factors (*r1-r10*), will help explain more of the variation in maintenance effort. I used the stepwise ANOVA procedure explained in Chapter 1 to see if an improvement in the R-squared value could be made. The results are shown in Sidebar 5.1.

SIDEBAR 5.1
STATISTICAL OUTPUT SUMMARY SHEET

Date: 31/08/2001
Directory: C:\my documents\data analysis book\maintenance\
Data File: main1993.dta
Procedure Files: *var.do (* = one, two, three, etc.)
Output Files: *var.log
Dependent variable: *lacorref*

Variables	Num Obs	Effect	Adj R²	Significance of Added Variable	Comments
1-variable models					
* *ltotfp*	67	+	.27		
ladefect	67	+	.14		
telonuse	67		.03	.089	
easyuse	67		.14		
r9	56		.10		

Variables	Num Obs	Effect	Adj R^2	Significance of Added Variable	Comments
r10	56		.07		
avetlev	67		.14		
dsplev	67		.11		
submorg	55		.16		
subapp	65		.08		
2-variable models with *ltotfp*					
easyuse	67		.30	.066	
* *r1*	**56**		**.39**		**continue on this path (Path A)**
* *r9*	56		.38		follow Path B
r10	56		.37		
3-variable models with *ltotfp, r1*					
easyuse	56		.42	.073	
r9	56		.44	.094	
* *r10*	**56**		**.46**		
4-variable models with *ltotfp, r1, r10* * *pjcl*	56		.50		**r1 = .076, best Model A: sign. = 0.0000**
5-variable models with *ltotfp, r1, r10, pjcl*					
none significant					no further improvement possible
Path B:					
3-variable models with *ltotfp, r9*					
r1	56		.44	.069	r9 = .094
* *r10*	56		.46		follow Path C
* *submorg*	**48**		**.49**	**.070**	
* *subtpms*	53		.44		Result: This path leads to Model C.

SIDEBAR 5.1 (*Continued*)

Variables	Num Obs	Effect	Adj R²	Significance of Added Variable	Comments
4-variable models with *ltotfp, r9, submorg*					
ageend	48		.52	.084	
* r3	**48**		**.56**	**.061**	
5-variable models with *ltotfp, r9, submorg, r3*					
* *ageend*	48		.61		
rl	48		.61	.097	
6-variable models with *ltotfp, r9, submorg, r3, ageend*					
* *r10*	48		.65	.089	**best Model B: sign. = 0.0000**
7-variable models with *ltotfp, r9, submorg, r3, ageend, r10*					
none significant					no further improvement possible
Path C:					
4-variable models with *ltotfp, r9, r10*					
pjcl	56		.51		*r9* = .066
* *subtpms*	**53**		**.51**		
5-variable models with *ltotfp, r9, r10, subtpms*					
* *pjcl*	53		.56		**r9 = .060, best Model C: sign. = 0.0000**
6-variable models with *lsize, r9, r10, tpms, pjcl*					
none significant					no further improvement possible

From the summary of one-variable models, I learn that there are significant relationships between annual corrective maintenance effort (*lacorref*) and *ltotfp* (size), *ladefect* (defects), and eight categorical variables: *telonuse, easyuse, r9, r10, avetlev, dsplev, submorg*, and *subapp*. Maintenance effort increases with increasing numbers of defects and with increasing application size. This makes sense to me.

As the relationships between the multi-level categorical variables and corrective maintenance effort are much more complicated to interpret, I will interpret these relationships only when I have found the best overall model (see the "Choosing Baseline Categorical Variables" and "Interpreting the Equation" sections of this chapter for further explanation). The best one-variable model is based on application size (*ltotfp*) and explains 27% of the variation in effort.

Choosing the best two-variable model is not so easy. The best two-variable model includes *r1* along with *ltotfp* and explains 39% of the variation in effort. Another model, which includes *r9* along with *ltotfp*, explains 38% of the variation in effort. I decided to continue building the model with *r1* (Path A), but will return to build a three-variable model with *r9* (Path B) to see where it leads. Finally, the best Path A model includes four variables: *ltotfp, r1, r10*, and *pjcl*, and explains 50% of the variance in effort using data from 56 applications.

Now I build the best Path B model. Once again, the choice of the best three-variable Path B model is not easy. The internal business unit subset, *submorg*, explains the most variation in effort (49%), but only for 48 applications. Capacity flexibility (*r10*) explains less variation (46%), but for more applications and with a higher significance level. I decide to continue building the Path B model with *submorg*, and will return to build a four-variable model with *r10* (Path C) to see where it leads. Finally, the best Path B model includes six variables: *ltotfp, r9, submorg, r3, ageend*, and *r10*. The combination of these variables explains 65% of the variation in effort for 48 observations.

Next, I return to build the best Path C model. The best Path C model includes five variables: *ltotfp, r9, r10, subtpms*, and *pjcl*. The combination of these variables explains 56% of the effort for 53 observations. Finally, I have three models to choose from. Which model is the best: a higher R-squared model based on a smaller number of applications or a lower R-squared model that applies to more applications? I prefer the higher R-squared model as long as the number of observations is still reasonable. In addition, as you know from the presentation of results at the beginning of this chapter, the bank no longer existed when we analyzed the data. Thus, the real goal of this analysis was not to help the bank, but to find relationships in the data that would be of interest to the software community at large. At the time of this analysis, there was little quantitative empirical research devoted to improving the performance of software maintenance planning. As Pekka and I thought that software managers would be very interested in the effect of maintenance age on annual corrective maintenance effort, we decided to focus on Model B in the paper.

Models A and C would have been useful as alternative models in the bank. For example, if the bank wanted to estimate the annual corrective maintenance effort of an application that had no comparable *submorg* in Model B, it could have estimated its effort using Model C. If Model C was not suitable because the *tpms* was not comparable, it could have used Model A. In addition, the bank could have learned even more about its maintenance effort by looking closely at the relationships among the variables in these models, too.

ANOVA Output for Six-Variable Model B

Example 5.23

```
. anova lacorref ltotfp r9 submorg r3 ageend r10,
          category(r9 submorg r3 r10)

          Number of obs =      48      R-squared     = 0.7747
          Root MSE      = .735489      Adj R-squared = 0.6470

Source      Partial SS    df       MS         F      Prob > F
Model       55.8055923    17    3.2826819    6.07     0.0000
ltotfp      16.4190487     1    16.4190487  30.35     0.0000
r9          12.710063      4    3.17751576   5.87     0.0013
submorg     11.5337127     5    2.30674255   4.26     0.0048
r3          8.27639071     4    2.06909768   3.82     0.0125
ageend      5.1104289      1    5.1104289    9.45     0.0045
r10         2.84103198     2    1.42051599   2.63     0.0889
Residual    16.2283348    30    .540944492
Total       72.033927     47    1.53263675
```

As shown in Example 5.23, the best Path B model is based on size (*ltotfp*), batch processing integration (*r9*), internal business unit (*submorg*), change management flexibility (*r3*), total months maintained (*ageend*), and capacity flexibility (*r10*).

We can also see in the ANOVA output (Example 5.23) that the significance of *r10* is borderline (i.e., significant at the 8.89% level instead of at the 5% level). This model explains 64.7% of the variance in annual corrective maintenance effort and is based on 48 observations.

Regression Output for Six-Variable Model B

Example 5.24

```
                                    . regress
```

Source	SS	df	MS				
Model	55.8055923	17	3.2826819				
Residual	16.2283348	30	.540944492				
Total	72.033927	47	1.53263675				

```
Number of obs =      48
F(17,30)      =    6.07
Prob > F      =  0.0000
R-squared     =  0.7747
Adj R-squared =  0.6470
Root MSE      = .73549
```

lacorref		Coef.	Std. Err.	t	P >|t|	[95% Conf.	Interval]
_cons		2.442969	1.074631	2.273	0.030	.2482794	4.637658
ltotfp		.5860707	.1063781	5.509	0.000	.3688175	.8033238
r9							
	1	-2.240367	.5449797	-4.111	0.000	-3.353364	-1.12737
	2	-.7792491	.6314828	-1.234	0.227	-2.068909	.5104108
	3	-.6871665	.6041535	-1.137	0.264	-1.921013	.5466796
	4	-.4227012	.3334358	-1.268	0.215	-1.103668	.2582656
	5	(dropped)					
submorg							
	1	.7259922	1.044153	0.695	0.492	-1.406452	2.858437
	3	1.907546	.998899	1.910	0.066	-.1324775	3.94757
	6	2.409136	1.07909	2.233	0.033	.2053399	4.612931
	13	.6332993	1.063693	0.595	0.556	-1.539052	2.80565
	16	.2875977	.9113605	0.316	0.755	-1.573649	2.148844
	17	(dropped)					
r3							
	1	1.640698	.5984494	2.742	0.010	.4185009	2.862894
	2	1.401475	.7751105	1.808	0.081	-.1815121	2.984461
	3	.5555655	.5226528	1.063	0.296	-.5118339	1.622965
	4	.0367716	.6189603	0.059	0.953	-1.227314	1.300857
	5	(dropped)					
ageend		-.0229887	.0074793	-3.074	0.004	-.0382636	-.0077139
r10							
	1	-.9229493	.4120375	-2.240	0.033	-1.764442	-.0814565
	2	-.1959403	.4267353	-0.459	0.649	-1.06745	.6755693
	3	(dropped)					

Choosing Baseline Categorical Variables

As you can see in Example 5.24, Stata automatically drops the highest numbered category of each categorical variable. Therefore, when you interpret this output, you are forced to compare the effect on corrective maintenance effort of each category with the dropped category, even though the dropped category may not be a reasonable baseline. For example, in the regression table, we see that compared with the automatically dropped variable *submorg* = 17 (*Treasury*),[8] only *submorg* = 3 (*Common* banking service) and *submorg* = 6 (*Deposit*) are significantly different from *Treasury* at the 10% level ($P > |t|$ less than 0.100). Does it make sense for the bank to interpret *submorg* in terms of the Treasury business unit applications? The answer is no. Why not? Because most applications in the bank's database are not owned by the Treasury business unit. Before checking and interpreting the model, we need to reorder the categorical data to force Stata to omit the category with the most observations, or the category with which we want to compare. You could reorder all categorical data before analyzing it; however, if there are missing observations and many categorical variables, it will save time to just reorder the ones that are important at this stage. Making these changes does not alter the ANOVA output, only the regression output.

Let's look now at the number of observations for each significant categorical variable for the 48 applications in Model B and decide what to omit. We'll start with *rg* (Table 5.10).

As you can see in Example 5.24, Stata automatically omits 5. I will leave *r9* as it is because I think it would be best to compare everything with a value at one end of the scale, and there are more observations for 5 than for 1. If 3 had meant average, I would make average the comparable value.

I also see that there are only two applications with *r9* = 2 for this 48-observation model. I will not drop these applications. Why not? At the beginning of the analysis, I already dropped applications with a *morg* category of less than three observations to create a more meaningful model. However, with a limited number of observations to work with, at some point, I have to stop dropping applications or I will run out. If I drop the *r9* = 2 applications,

TABLE 5.10
Number of Observations by Batch Processing Integration Level (*r9*)

Batch Processing Integration	Frequency
1	7
2	2
3	6
4	18
5	**15**

---

8. You can easily determine each business unit's internal Stata number from the tabulation of *morg* in the "Identifying Subsets of Categorical Variables" section. They are listed in increasing order: *Account* = 1, *BUC* = 2, and so on.

this may have an effect on another categorical variable, which may end up having less than three observations for one of its categories. This is an area where you need to use your judgment. Another option would be to combine $r9 = 2$ with either $r9 = 1$ or $r9 = 3$, depending on the definitions of these categories. Combine the two categories that make the most sense to combine. My decision is to leave things as they are.

Payment has the most applications (Table 5.11). I will tell Stata to add 50 to its internal number of 13 for *Payment*. The new number for payment will be 63. As this is the highest number, *Payment* will be omitted. I chose to add 50 because I wanted a new number that was much higher than the original number to remind me that I made the change when I looked at the output. I also see something important that I did not notice before. Out of the initial seven *Treasury* applications, only one *Treasury* application ($mid = 62$) had risk factor data. I thus decide to drop the *Treasury* subset from the final model.

TABLE 5.11
Number of Observations by Internal Business Unit Subset (*submorg*)

Internal Business Unit	Frequency	Old Stata Number	New Stata Number
Account	12	1	1
Common	4	3	3
Deposit	6	6	6
Payment	15	13	63
SecTrade	10	16	16
Treasury	1	17	17

TABLE 5.12
Number of Observations by Change Management Flexibility Level (*r3*)

Change Management Flexibility	Frequency
(now 51) 1	15
2	10
3	10
4	10
5	3

TABLE 5.13
Number of Observations by Capacity Flexibility Level (r10)

Capacity Flexibility	Frequency
(now 51) 1	22
2	7
3	19

In Table 5.12, Level 1 has the most observations. I will tell Stata to add 50 to its internal number of 1. Thus, the new number for Level 1 will be 51.

Level 1 has the most observations (Table 5.13). I will tell Stata to add 50 to its internal number of 1. The new number for Level 1 will be 51. Making these three adjustments to the internal numbering of *submorg, r3,* and *r10* leads to the model shown in Example 5.25.

Adjusted Regression Output for Six-Variable Model B Without Treasury Business Unit Category

Example 5.25

```
                                       . regress
```

Source	SS	df	MS			Number of obs =	47
Model	55.7361852	16	3.48351158			F(16,30) =	6.44
Residual	16.2283348	30	.540944492			Prob > F =	0.0000
						R-squared =	0.7745
Total	71.96452	46	1.56444609			Adj R-squared =	0.6542
						Root MSE =	.73549

lacorref	Coef.	Std. Err.	t	P>|t|	[95% Conf.	Interval]
_cons	3.794017	.7724745	4.912	0.000	2.216413	5.37162
ltotfp	.5860707	.1063781	5.509	0.000	.3688175	.8033238
r9						
1	-2.240367	.5449797	-4.111	0.000	-3.353364	-1.12737
2	-.7792491	.6314828	-1.234	0.227	-2.068909	.5104108
3	-.6871665	.6041535	-1.137	0.264	-1.921013	.5466796
4	-.4227012	.3334358	-1.268	0.215	-1.103668	.2582656
5	(dropped)					
submorg						
1	.0926929	.445713	0.208	0.837	-.8175746	1.00296
3	1.274247	.6409948	1.988	0.056	-.034839	2.583333
6	1.775836	.6023633	2.948	0.006	.5456463	3.006026
16	-.3457016	.5182728	-0.667	0.510	-1.404156	.7127526
63	(dropped)					
r3						
2	-.239223	.4738759	-0.505	0.617	-1.207007	.7285606

```
         3  -1.085132   .390299    -2.780   0.009   -1.882229   -.2880352
         4  -1.603926  .4682943    -3.425   0.002   -2.560311   -.6475415
         5  -1.640698  .5984494    -2.742   0.010   -2.862894   -.4185009
        51  (dropped)
ageend     -.0229887  .0074793    -3.074   0.004   -.0382636   -.0077139
r10
         2   .7270089  .4584794     1.586   0.123    -.209331    1.663349
         3   .9229493  .4120375     2.240   0.033    .0814565    1.764442
        51  (dropped)
```

Checking the Model

Before accepting the final model, we must first check that the assumptions underlying the statistical tests have not been violated.

Numerical Variable Checks

We already checked the Spearman's rank correlation coefficients of all pairwise combinations of *totfp*, *r3*, *r9*, *r10*, and *ageend* in the preliminary analysis. However, these were correlations for the entire data set. We need to check these again because our model is now based on a subset of the data. I redid the correlation analysis using the 47 observations in the model and found that none of the variables were highly correlated with each other.

Categorical Variable Checks

First, let's look at the relationships between *submorg* and the non-categorical variables, *ltotfp* and *ageend*. As can be seen in the following statistical output, Example 5.26, the relationships between *submorg* and *ltotfp* and between *submorg* and *ageend* are not significant. Thus, *submorg* is not confounded with *ltotfp* or *ageeend*.

Example 5.26

```
                    . anova ltotfp submorg

            Number of obs =      47     R-squared     = 0.1495
            Root MSE      = 1.1702     Adj R-squared = 0.0685

    Source      Partial SS   df       MS          F      Prob > F
    Model       10.1126843    4    2.52817107    1.85     0.1380
    submorg     10.1126843    4    2.52817107    1.85     0.1380
    Residual    57.5135095   42    1.36936927
    Total       67.6261938   46    1.47013465
```

```
                      . anova ageend submorg

          Number of obs =      47      R-squared    =  0.1638
          Root MSE      = 18.0147      Adj R-squared =  0.0842

Source      Partial SS    df        MS         F      Prob > F
Model       2670.47163     4    667.617908    2.06     0.1037
submorg     2670.47163     4    667.617908    2.06     0.1037
Residual    13630.1667    42    324.527778

Total       16300.6383    46    354.361702
```

It is more difficult to determine if *submorg* is confounded with the categorical variables, *r3, r9,* and *r10.* First, I calculate the chi-square statistic to test for independence. (You can learn more about the chi-square statistic in Chapter 6.) From this I learn if there is a significant relationship between two categorical variables, but not the extent of the relationship. If there is a significant relationship, I need to look closely at the two variables and judge for myself if they are so related that there could be a problem with confounding.

Example 5.27

```
                 . tabulate submorg r3, chi2
Internal     Change Management Flexibility
Business
Unit         1        2        3        4        5      Total
Account      6        3        1        2        0       12
Common       0        3        0        1        0        4
Deposit      0        0        1        5        0        6
Payment      4        0        7        1        3       15
SecTrade     5        3        1        1        0       10
Total       15        9       10       10        3       47

           Pearson chi2(16) =   43.4489    Pr = 0.000

                 . tabulate submorg r9, chi2
Internal     Batch Processing Integration
Business
Unit         1        2        3        4        5      Total
Account      2        0        4        5        1       12
Common       2        0        0        1        1        4
Deposit      1        0        0        4        1        6
Payment      0        1        0        5        9       15
SecTrade     2        1        2        2        3       10
Total        7        2        6       17       15       47

           Pearson chi2(16) =   24.0955    Pr = 0.087
```

```
                  . tabulate submorg r10, chi2

Internal          Capacity Flexibility
Business
Unit              1        2        3       Total
Account           7        2        3        12
Common            2        1        1         4
Deposit           0        3        3         6
Payment          13        0        2        15
SecTrade          0        1        9        10
Total            22        7       18        47

         Pearson chi2(8)  =   30.9631    Pr = 0.000
```

Based on the output of Example 5.27, I have to reject the null hypotheses that *submorg* and *r3* and *submorg* and *r10* are independent at the 5% significance level ($Pr < 0.050$). Thus, I need to look closely at the dependency between these two sets of variables. To see any relationship, I make a 100% bar chart showing the percentage of each risk factor category for each internal business unit. I take care to rank the business units in order of increasing average corrective maintenance effort requirements to make interpretation easier.

I do not see any strong relationship between *submorg* and change management flexibility (*r3*) in Figure 5.47. However, there appears to be a strong relationship between *submorg* and capacity flexibility (*r10*). In Figure 5.48, we can

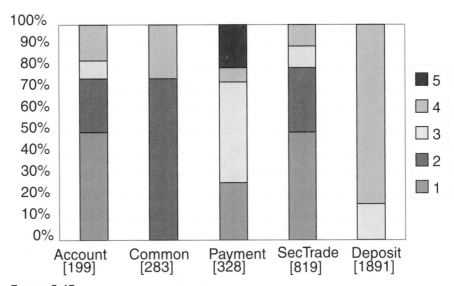

FIGURE 5.47
Change management flexibility (*r3*) distribution in internal business units

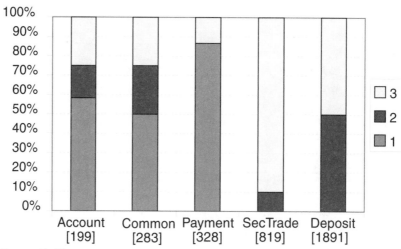

FIGURE 5.48

Capacity flexibility ($r10$) distribution in internal business units

see that the three business units with lower than average maintenance efforts all have mostly $r10 = 1$ (volatility predictable and easy to plan). The higher effort security trading (*SecTrade*) and *Deposit* business units do not have any $r10 = 1$. They have a majority of $r10 = 3$ (occasional volume increases can be managed by parameters and other means). Thus, there appears to be evidence of confounding between *submorg* and $r10$. In addition to this evidence, we can see in the ANOVA summary sheet (Sidebar 5.1) under Path B that $r10$ is always significant until *submorg* enters the model, then it is no longer significant in the next step. This is a sign that the two variables are related. When it enters the model in the last step, it is with a borderline significance level of 0.089. Because it may be confounded with *submorg*, I decided to remove $r10$ from Model B. My best model is now the five-variable model B in which all variables are significant at the 5% level (Example 5.28).

Final Model B: Adjusted Regression Output for Five-Variable Model B Without Treasury Business Unit Category

Example 5.28

```
                                        . regress
```

Source	SS	df	MS
Model	52.8951533	14	3.77822523
Residual	19.0693667	32	.595917711
Total	71.96452	46	1.56444609

Number of obs =	47
$F(14, 32)$ =	6.34
Prob > F =	0.0000
R-squared =	0.7350
Adj R-squared =	0.6191
Root MSE =	.77196

lacorref	Coef.	Std. Err.	t	P >│t│	[95% Conf.	Interval]
_cons	3.768108	.8106651	4.648	0.000	2.116837	5.419379
ltotfp	.5552824	.1104393	5.028	0.000	.330325	.7802398
r9						
1	-1.989677	.5434387	-3.661	0.001	-3.096625	-.8827284
2	-.8426482	.6620686	-1.273	0.212	-2.191238	.5059413
3	-.4391976	.6137379	-0.716	0.479	-1.689341	.8109456
4	-.4042459	.3488803	-1.159	0.255	-1.114892	.3064
5	(dropped)					
submorg						
1	.253708	.4401861	0.576	0.568	-.6429217	1.150338
3	1.620253	.6267326	2.585	0.014	.3436406	2.896865
6	2.288984	.5677226	4.032	0.000	1.132571	3.445397
16	.4844644	.3878234	1.249	0.221	-.3055061	1.274435
63	(dropped)					
r3						
2	-.6087856	.4676664	-1.302	0.202	-1.561391	.3438195
3	-.8350846	.3931705	-2.124	0.041	-1.635947	-.0342225
4	-1.433967	.480279	-2.986	0.005	-2.412263	-.4556708
5	-1.587721	.627651	-2.530	0.017	-2.866204	-.3092373
51	(dropped)					
ageend	-.0158791	.0068253	-2.327	0.026	-.0297817	-.0019765

Testing the Residuals

Figure 5.49 shows no pattern in the residuals of the final model. We can see in Figure 5.50 that the residuals are normally distributed.

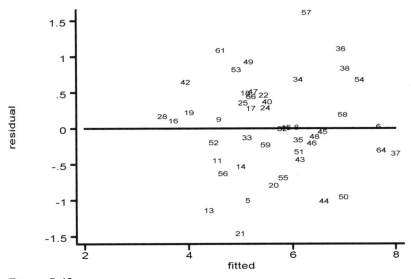

FIGURE 5.49
Residuals vs. fitted values

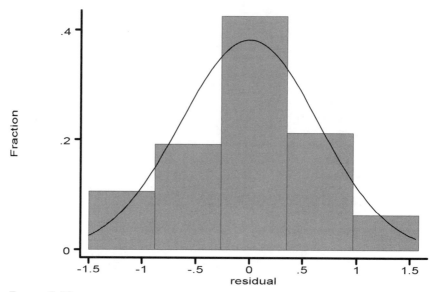

FIGURE 5.50
Distribution of residuals

Detecting Influential Observations

As the model is based on 47 applications, I printed the applications with a Cook's distance greater than 4/47 = .085 in Example 5.29.

Example 5.29

```
. list mid totfp acorreff cooksd if cooksd>4/47
```

	mid	totfp	acorreff	cooksd
1.	1	237	130	.
2.	2	569	102	.
3.	3	165	369	.
4.	4	203	171	.
7.	7	41	155	.
10.	10	167	32.99835	.
12.	13	23	25	.563312
27.	34	559	861	.1882778
47.	56	56	55	.1882778
48.	57	68	2600	.209702
51.	60	262	490	.
52.	61	237	292	.1031092

The application with the highest Cook's distance (0.56) is Application 13 (*mid* = 13). This retail application had a much lower effort and size than the other retail applications. I discussed this application with Pekka. He said that it was a temporary, quite technical application made for helping transaction processing in a double-mainframe environment. He did not want it, or any more applications, removed from the database. I agreed. When you have a small amount of data, every time you remove one application, another one becomes influential. At some point, you have to stop, and in my opinion, we had reached that point. Although some of the Cook's distances in the final model were greater than the cut-off value, the Cook's distance values would have been much, much worse had I not removed the *morg* categories with less than three observations at the beginning of the analysis. If I had left them all in, we would have had several Cook's distances over 10,000 in the list. This is because one application alone in its category is very influential.

Extracting the Equation

The equation as read from Final Model B's output is:

$$\ln(acorreff) = 3.768108 + 0.5552824 \ln(totfp) + r9\_coef + morg\_coef + r3\_coef - 0.0158791 \times ageend$$

where the values of *r9_coef*, *morg_coef*, and *r3_coef* for each category can be read directly off the statistical output in Example 5.28 (under *Coef.*).

This can be transformed into the following equation for corrective effort:

$$acorreff = 43.2981 \times totfp^{1.7424} \times r9\_mult \times morg\_mult \times r3\_mult \times e^{-0.0159 \times ageend}$$

where the values of *r9_mult*, *morg_mult*, and *r3_mult* can be found in Table 5.14. The baseline value is 1.

TABLE 5.14
Categorical Variable Multipliers

r3 level	r3_mult	r9 level	r9_mult	morg	morg_mult
1 (51)	1	1 (1)	0.1367*	*Account* (1)	1.2888
2 (2)	0.5440	2 (2)	0.4306	*Common* (3)	5.0544*
3 (3)	0.4338*	3 (3)	0.6446	*Deposit* (6)	9.8649*
4 (4)	0.2384*	4 (4)	0.6675	*Payment* (63)	1
5 (5)	0.2044*	5 (5)	1	*SecTrade* (16)	1.6233

* Significantly different from baseline value.

Numbers in parentheses refer to the Stata internal numbering in statistical output.

Interpreting the Equation

The coefficient of size is approximately 1.74. This means that for every 1% increase in size, the corrective maintenance effort will increase by 1.74% if all other variables remain constant. The maintenance age multiplier from Final Model B can also be written as $(0.9842)^{ageend}$. Thus, on average, the corrective maintenance of applications in this bank decreased at the rate of approximately 17.4% per year $(1 - 0.9842^{12})$, all other variables remaining constant. (Remember that *ageend* was measured in months).

The real effect of categorical variables is more difficult to discern because their interpretation depends on what you have chosen as the baseline value. If we look at the batch processing integration multipliers (*r9_mult*) in Table 5.14, we see that the effort needed increased with increasing levels of *r9*. However, only $r9 = 1$ was significantly different from $r9 = 5$. The effort needed decreased with increasing levels of change management flexibility (*r3*). The levels of $r3 = 3$, 4, and 5 were significantly different from $r3 = 1$. Applications with $r3 = 5$ require 80% less effort than those where $r3 = 1$, all other variables remaining constant. Once effort was adjusted for the other factors in the model, only applications in the common banking service and deposit business units (*morg* = 3 and 6) were significantly different from payment business unit applications (*morg* = 63).

Accuracy of Model Prediction

How accurately can the model predict next year's annual corrective maintenance effort? Is it better to use the model or to simply use last year's annual corrective maintenance effort to predict next year's effort?

There were 19 applications developed for the accounting (*Account*), payment (*Payment*), and securities trading system (*SecTrade*) business units with complete 1994 data; 17 of these applications had also been maintained during 1993, and two applications started maintenance in 1994. The data needed to calculate the accuracy of model prediction is shown in Table 5.15. The variables, *correff, totfp, ageend, r3*, and *r9*, are the 1994 values. For example, *ageend* means the maintenance age at the end of 1994.

Applications 70 and 71 started maintenance in 1994. Application 68 was maintained in 1993, but was not included in the 1993 analysis because it had a missing total function point count in 1993. Variable *aceff93* was the same as variable *acorreff* in 1993 (Table 5.8). It represented the annual corrective maintenance effort that was needed during the full calendar year of 1993, measured in hours.

TABLE 5.15
1994 Data and 1993 Annual Corrective Maintenance Effort

mid	correff	totfp	ageend	r3	r9	morg	aceff93
9	186	457	96	3	4	Payment	108.00
10	78	552	20	2	2	Account	33.00
11	9	163	48	4	5	Payment	59.00
14	103	457	31	5	5	Payment	85.00
16	62	93	27	5	5	Payment	44.00
34	676	752	33	1	2	Payment	861.00
35	254	479	20	3	5	Payment	371.98
40	283	296	48	3	5	Payment	350.00
42	111	36	48	3	4	Payment	96.00
43	338	304	37	1	4	Payment	292.00
44	256	859	38	3	4	Payment	260.00
45	376	1365	35	3	5	Payment	664.00
46	269	688	24	3	5	Payment	462.00
48	456	364	24	1	4	Payment	535.00
49	171	73	20	3	5	Payment	425.98
54	6322	1524	47	1	4	SecTrade	2840.00
68	406	652	38	3	4	Payment	53.00
70	248	169	11	2	4	Payment	
71	342	103	7	4	5	Payment	

Using the 1993 effort (*aceff93*) as an estimate of the 1994 effort (*correff*) for the 17 ongoing maintenance applications gives an MMRE of 75.6%, a MedMRE of 41.9%, and a Pred(.25) of 35.3%. (See Chapter 4 for definitions of these measurements.)

The estimates of Final Model B are shown below in Example 5.30. *mid* is the unique identification number, *est* is the estimate for the full year of maintenance in 1994, and *adjest* is the adjusted estimate for applications maintained less than 12 months in 1994. Thus, *est* and *adjest* are equal except for the two new maintenance applications; *mid* = 70 and *mid* = 71. *correff* is the actual 1994 maintenance effort, *mre* is the magnitude of relative error, and *ageend* is the number of months the application had been maintained at the end of 1994.

Example 5.30

. list mid est adjest correff mre ageend

	mid	est	adjest	correff	mre	ageend
1.	9	81.885	81.885	186	55.97581	96
2.	10	316.9053	316.9053	78	306.2889	20
3.	11	81.48471	81.48471	9	805.3857	48
4.	14	162.2381	162.2381	103	57.51273	31
5.	16	71.41623	71.41623	62	15.18747	27
6.	34	436.5659	436.5659	676	35.41924	33
7.	35	420.9351	420.9351	254	65.72247	20
8.	40	206.5587	206.5587	283	27.01106	48
9.	42	42.7961	42.7961	111	61.44495	48
10.	43	384.0995	384.0995	338	13.63889	37
11.	44	291.9938	291.9938	256	14.06008	38
12.	45	593.353	593.353	376	57.80664	35
13.	46	483.0034	483.0034	269	79.55516	24
14.	48	521.8345	521.8345	456	14.43738	24
15.	49	148.0957	148.0957	171	13.3943	20
16.	54	1302.092	1302.092	6322	79.4038	47
17.	68	250.5423	250.5423	406	38.29007	38
18.	70	227.9097	208.9172	248	15.7592	11
19.	71	121.0944	70.63843	342	79.34549	7

From this output, we can calculate that using the Final Model B to estimate the 1994 effort for the 17 ongoing maintenance applications results in an MMRE of 102.4, a MedMRE of 56.0, and a Pred(.25) of 29.4%. For the two new maintenance applications, we have an MMRE of 47.6, a MedMRE of 47.6, and a Pred(.25) of 50%. I conclude that Final Model B appears to be of limited use as a predictive model for ongoing maintenance projects. Using last year's effort to predict next year's effort is more accurate and easier to do. However, one of the biggest problems facing the bank was estimating the first year of maintenance effort. In this case, the model is more useful because last year's effort does not exist.

The Telon Analysis

Pekka and I discussed the maintenance data and our analyses with a business school professor who had published numerous papers in the area of software maintenance. He suggested that we study the Telon applications more carefully. He had already found that Telon use decreased defects and apparently did not cost more. He was interested to know if we would see the same effect in our data samples. In addition, the amount of Telon use is one the few variables in our database that managers could control.

Of the 67 applications in the data set, 11 were developed mainly using Telon. Because an application's size explained the most variation in corrective maintenance effort, I decided to adjust maintenance effort for size. I created a new variable, *mdrate*, the maintenance delivery rate, which I defined as annual corrective maintenance effort, *acorreff*, divided by application size, *totfp*. The units of *mdrate* are expressed in hours/function point.

In Example 5.31, we see that less corrective maintenance effort per function point was required for Telon applications; 1.19 hours/function point compared with 2.47 hours/function point for applications that were not developed using Telon.

Example 5.31

```
. table telonuse, c(n mdrate mean mdrate)

  Telon Use      N(mdrate)      mean(mdrate)
  no                56              2.47
  yes               11              1.19
```

I ran an ANOVA model to see if this result was statistically significant. Example 5.32 shows that the use of Telon explains no variance in the maintenance delivery rate. Note that *mdrate* requires a log transformation to more closely approximate a normal distribution (see Figures 5.51 and 5.52).

Example 5.32

```
. anova lmdrate telonuse

        Number of obs =      67    R-squared     = 0.0145
        Root MSE        = 1.16144  Adj R-squared = -0.0007
```

Source	Partial SS	df	MS	F	Prob > F
Model	1.28891773	1	1.28891773	0.96	0.3319
telonuse	1.28891773	1	1.28891773	0.96	0.3319
Residual	87.681119	65	1.34894029		
Total	88.9700367	66	1.34803086		

I decided to study the 11 Telon applications in more detail. First, I looked at the relationship between annual corrective maintenance effort and percentage of Telon used (*ptelon*). The strong linear relationship shown in Figure 5.53 between the natural logs of corrective effort and *ptelon* was

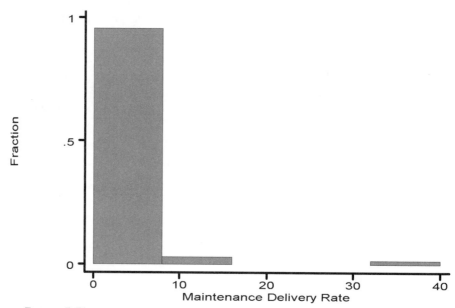

FIGURE 5.51
Distribution of *mdrate*

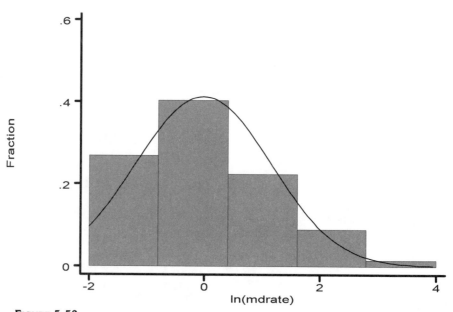

FIGURE 5.52
Distribution of *ln(mdrate)*

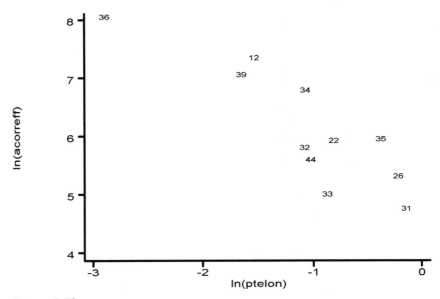

FIGURE 5.53
ln(acorreff) vs. *ln(ptelon)* for 11 Telon applications

confirmed by the regression output (Example 5.33). Telon use explained 72% of the variance of corrective effort. Applications that used more Telon had lower efforts.

Example 5.33

```
                              . regress lacorref lptelon

Source         SS        df      MS              Number of obs =      11
                                                 F(1, 9)       =   27.26
Model      8.10789042    1   8.10789042          Prob > F      = 0.0005
Residual   2.67710116    9   .297455684          R-squared     = 0.7518
                                                 Adj R-squared = 0.7242
Total      10.7849916   10   1.07849916          Root MSE      = .54539


lacorref     Coef.    Std. Err.      t      P>|t|    [95% Conf. Interval]

lptelon   -1.155974    .221414    -5.221    0.001   -1.656847   -.6551003
_cons      4.881305    .2871501   16.999    0.000    4.231726    5.530884
```

After adjusting for size, the relationship is still strong (see Figure 5.54 and Example 5.34). Thus, using Telon appears to reduce corrective maintenance costs.

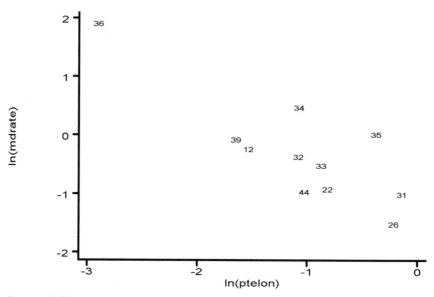

FIGURE 5.54

ln(mdrate) vs. *ln(ptelon)* for 11 Telon applications

Example 5.34

```
                          . regress lmdrate lptelon
Source        SS         df      MS              Number of obs =       11
Model     5.73266557      1   5.73266557         F(1, 9)        =    18.76
Residual  2.75060592      9    .30562288         Prob > F       =   0.0019
                                                 R-squared      =   0.6758
Total     8.48327149     10    .848327149        Adj R-squared  =   0.6397
                                                 Root MSE       =  .55283

lmdrate      Coef.    Std. Err.      t      P >|t|    [95% Conf. Interval]
lptelon   -.9720136    .2244331    -4.331    0.002   -1.479717   -.4643106
_cons     -1.368026    .2910656    -4.700    0.001   -2.026462   -.7095904
```

We were also interested to know if the use of Telon increased the quality of the applications (Example 5.35). There is a very weak significant relationship between the natural logs of number of defects and Telon use.[9] 19% of the variance in defects is explained by Telon use. Telon use is significant only at the 10% level, and the constant (*_cons*) is not significant. According to the model, more Telon use leads to less defects. However, one of the assumptions of

---

9. Defects and Telon use required a log transformation to more closely approximate a normal distribution.

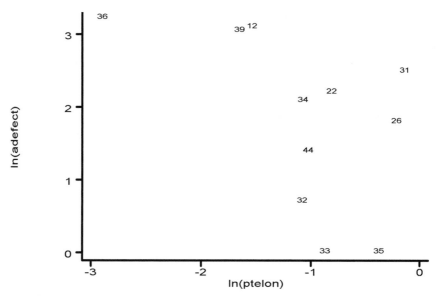

FIGURE 5.55

ln(adefect) vs. *ln(ptelon)* for 11 Telon applications

regression is that we are studying a linear relationship, and that is not the case here (see Figure 5.55).

Example 5.35

```
. regress ladefect lptelon
```

Source	SS	df	MS
Model	3.78062048	1	3.78062048
Residual	10.0263446	9	1.11403829
Total	13.8069651	10	1.38069651

```
Number of obs =      11
F(1, 9)       =    3.39
Prob > F      = 0.0986
R-squared     = 0.2738
Adj R-squared = 0.1931
Root MSE      = 1.0555
```

ladefect	Coef.	Std. Err.	t	P >|t|	[95% Conf. Interval]	
lptelon	−.7893608	.4284933	−1.842	0.099	−1.75868	.1799585
_cons	.9777928	.5557097	1.760	0.112	−.2793098	2.234895

If we look at the graph of defects vs. Telon use without log transformations (Figure 5.56), we find that the relationship is not linear at all, but appears U-shaped. Very high levels of Telon use result in more defects, too. This is a good example of why it is important to print graphs of the relationships you are studying. In Figure 5.57, we can see that even when defects have been adjusted for application size, the relationship is still U-shaped.

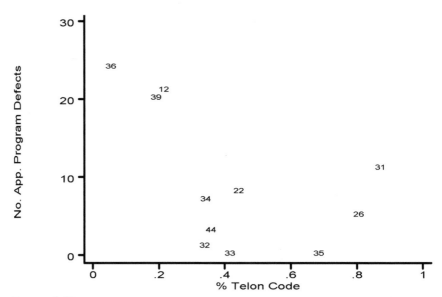

FIGURE 5.56
appdef vs. *ptelon* for 11 Telon applications

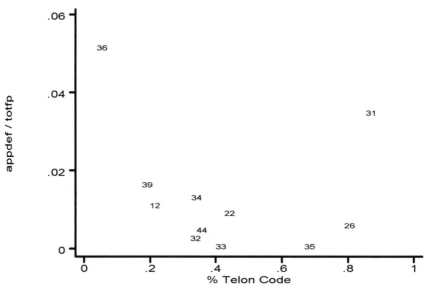

FIGURE 5.57
appdef/totfp vs. *ptelon* for 11 Telon applications

Further Analyses

In the conclusions of the paper, we briefly mention two additional analysis results. The first result answered Pekka's question: Are lower values of the change management variable linked with more application programming

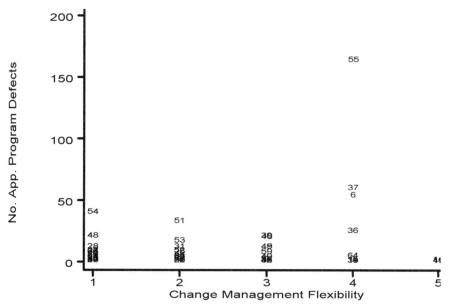

FIGURE 5.58
appdef vs. *r3*

defects? If so, this could partially explain why less corrective maintenance effort was required by applications with higher values of the change management variable. However, as you can see in Figure 5.58, this was not the case. In fact, $r3 = 4$ (i.e., changes were dependent on other applications managed by other boards, applications had one or two owners, and no quick decisions were made) for applications with the most defects.

The second result that we found was that maintenance effort adjusted for size (hours/function point) decreased with increasing size. The proof of this statement is in Example 5.36. As you can see, the model is significant and the coefficient of *ltotfp* is negative.

Example 5.36

```
                        regress lmdrate ltotfp
```

Source	SS	df	MS
Model	19.511371	1	19.511371
Residual	69.4586657	65	1.06859486
Total	88.9700367	66	1.34803086

Number of obs = 67
F(1, 65)   =   18.26
Prob > F   = 0.0001
R-squared   = 0.2193
Adj R-squared = 0.2073
Root MSE   = 1.0337

lmdrate	Coef.	Std. Err.	t	P>|t|	[95% Conf. Interval]
ltotfp	-.4589804	.107413	-4.273	0.000	-.673499 -.2444619
_cons	2.532008	.6108209	4.145	0.000	1.312115 3.751902

Final Comments

In this section, I showed you how to get from data to knowledge. This step is necessary, but not sufficient, to create value from data. You must also be able to transfer your knowledge to others. For that, you need to get out of your office during the analysis and discuss your results with the interested parties. Find out what others in your company think is important. Bring in comparisons from the world outside your company. Read relevant literature. Search the Web. Attend a software measurement conference. Much thought and many interviews were necessary to find the right angle to communicate the results presented in this chapter to the software community.

Starting with the simple, straightforward example in Chapter 1, each successive chapter has illustrated a progressively more difficult data analysis situation using four case studies. The case study in this chapter was the most realistic. By now, you should be aware that analyzing software project data is not an easy task. Statistics, like software development, is as much an art as it is a science. Validating data, creating new variables, selecting variables to put in the model, removing outliers, picking the best model(s), detecting confounded variables, choosing baseline categorical variables, and handling influential observations all require that you make many decisions during the data analysis process-decisions for which there are often no clear rules. Decisions that will have an impact on your results and which you should be able to justify.

What You Need to Know About Statistics

6

How do you measure the value of data? Not by the amount you have, but by what you can learn from it. Statistics provides a way to extract valuable information from your data. It is a science concerned with the collection, classification, and interpretation of data according to well-defined procedures. For a manager, however, statistics is simply one of many diverse techniques that may improve decision-making.

In Chapter 1, I presented my methodology for analyzing data as a simple recipe. In Chapters 2 through 5, we applied this recipe to determine the relationships among various factors and productivity, duration, development effort, and corrective maintenance cost. It was not necessary to have an in-depth understanding of statistics to apply the recipe. In this chapter, you will develop a deeper understanding of the statistical methods used. Notice that I use the word "deeper," not "complete." I don't believe a software manager needs a complete understanding of statistics. We'll leave that to the statisticians. I do see a need, however, to help software managers extract **what they need to know** from everything there is to know about statistics.

The methods I use to analyze software project data come from the branch of statistics known as multivariate statistical analysis. These methods investigate relationships between two or more variables. However, before we delve into detailed explanations of chi-square tests, correlation analysis, regression analysis, and analysis of variance, you need to understand some basic concepts.

Describing Individual Variables

In this section, you will learn how to categorize and meaningfully summarize data concerning individual variables.

Types of Variables

All data is not created equal. Information can be collected using different scales. This has an impact on what method you can use to analyze the data. There are four main types of scales: nominal, ordinal, interval, and ratio.

Nominal scales—Variables such as business sector, application type, and application language are nominal-scale variables. These variables differ in kind only. They have no numerical sense. There is no meaningful order. For example, let's say that business sector has four categories: bank, insurance, retail, and manufacturing. Even if we label these with numbers instead of names in our database (say 101, 102, 103, and 104), the values of the numbers are meaningless. Manufacturing will never be "higher" than bank, just different.

Ordinal scales—The values of an ordinal-scale variable can be ranked in order. The 10 risk factors discussed in Chapter 5 are ordinal-scale variables (see Table 5.7). It is correct to say that Level 5 is riskier than Level 4, and Level 4 is riskier than Level 3, and so on; however, equal differences between ordinal values do not necessarily have equal quantitative meaning. For example, even though there is an equal one-level difference between 3 and 4, and 4 and 5, Level 4 may be 50% more risky than Level 3, and Level 5 may be 100% more risky than Level 4.

Interval scales—The values of an interval-scale variable can be ranked in order. In addition, equal distances between scale values have equal meaning. However, the ratios of interval-scale values have no meaning. This is because an interval scale has an arbitrary zero point. The start date variable in Chapter 2 is an example of an interval-scale variable (see Table 2.1). The year 1993 compared to the year 1992 only has meaning with respect to the arbitrary origin of 0 based on the supposed year of the birth of Christ. We know that 1993 is one year more than 1992, and that 1991 is one year less than 1992. Dividing 1993 by 1992 makes no sense. For example, we could decide to make 1900 year zero and count from there. In this case, 1993 would simply become 93 and 1992 would become 92 in our new scale. Although in both cases there is a one-year difference, the ratio 1993/1992 does not equal the ratio 93/92.

Another example of an interval scale is a Likert-type scale. Factors are rated on a scale of equal-appearing intervals, such as very low, low, average, high, and very high, and are assigned numerical values of 1, 2, 3, 4, and 5, respectively. However, in real life, it is virtually impossible to construct verbal scales of exactly equal intervals. It is more realistic to recognize that these scales are approximately of equal intervals. Thus, a Likert scale is really somewhere between an ordinal scale and a true interval scale.

The 15 productivity factors from Chapter 2, *t01–t15*, can be considered quasi-interval variables (see Table 2.1). I treated *t01–t15* as interval variables when I analyzed the data because of the care that was taken when defining them to ensure that most projects fell into the average category, and that few projects fell into the very low or very high categories.

Ratio scales—Variables such as effort, application size, and duration are measured using a ratio scale. Ratio-scale variables can be ranked in order, equal distances between scale values have equal meaning, and the ratios of ratio-scale values make sense. For example, it is correct to say that an application that required 10 months to develop took twice as long as an application that took 5 months. Another ratio scale is a percentage scale. For example, the percentage of COBOL used in an application is also a ratio-type variable.

A summary of variable type definitions is presented in Table 6.1.

TABLE 6.1
Summary of Variable Type Definitions

Variable Type	Is There a Meaningful Order?	Do Equal Distances Between Scale Values Have Equal Meaning?	Does the Calculation of Ratio Make Sense?
Nominal	No	No	No
Ordinal	Yes	No	No
Quasi-interval	Yes	Approximately	No
Interval	Yes	Yes	No
Ratio	Yes	Yes	Yes

TABLE 6.2
Classification of Variable Types Using Data from Chapter 2

Non-Numerical Categorical Nominal	Numerical Categorical Ordinal	Numerical Categorical Quasi-Interval	Numerical Non-Categorical Interval	Numerical Non-Categorical Ratio
id		*t01-t15*	*syear*	*size*
app			*time*	*effort*
har				*duration*
dba				*prod*
ifc				*nlan*
source				
lan1-4				

Throughout this book, I often referred to variables as being either numerical or categorical. What do I mean by a numerical variable? I mean a variable that has numerical sense. It can be ordered in a meaningful way. Variables measured using the ordinal, interval, or ratio scales are numerical-type variables. What do I mean by a categorical variable? A categorical variable cannot be interpreted in a quantitative sense. We know there are different levels, but we cannot answer the question "How much of a difference exists between two levels?" Variables measured using the nominal or ordinal scales are categorical variables. Categorical variables are also referred to as qualitative or non-metric variables. Non-categorical variables are often described as quantitative or metric variables.

Table 6.2 classifies the software development project data presented in Table 2.1 of Chapter 2. As you can see in Table 6.2, ordinal and quasi-interval variables can be considered both categorical and numerical variables.

Descriptive Statistics

The purpose of descriptive statistics is to meaningfully summarize large quantities of data with a few relatively simple terms. It is important to fully understand these terms because they are used in many statistical methods. In addition, descriptive statistics can be used to present easily understandable summary results to decision-makers. They provide answers to questions such as: What was the percentage of projects developed using XYZ? This corresponds to how many projects? What is a typical project? What was the smallest or largest project we ever developed? Are our projects fairly similar in size or do they vary a lot? You can learn an enormous amount about your data just from descriptive statistics.

Describing the Average

Three measures, the mode, the median, and the mean, can be used to describe a typical project. These measures are often referred to as measures of central tendency.

Mean—Here, we are referring to the arithmetic mean, which is the most common measure. It is what we usually consider to be the "average" in our daily lives. It is computed by adding together the observed values and dividing by the number of observations. For example, consider the ages of five software developers: 20, 25, 25, 30, and 45. The mean is calculated by adding all the ages together and dividing by 5.

$$\frac{20 + 25 + 25 + 30 + 45}{50} = 29$$

The mean is 29 years.[1] The mean is expressed mathematically by the following formula:

$$\bar{x} = \frac{\Sigma x_i}{n}$$

The mean is represented by $\bar{x}$. The age of each software developer is considered to be an observation value (x_i). 20 is x_1, 25 is x_2, and so on. The summation sign, Σ, means that we should add (sum) the observation values. Finally, we divide by the number of observations (n). There were five software developers in this example, so we have five observations.

Median—This is the middle value when the data are ordered from smallest to largest value; it is also referred to as the 50th percentile. In the previous example, the median value is 25. If we have an even number of observations, we determine the median by averaging the two middle observation values. For example, the median of 20, 25, 30, and 45 is $(25 + 30)/2 = 27.5$ years.

Mode—This is the most frequent value. In our example of five software developers, the most frequent age is 25, so 25 years is the mode. Sometimes there is no mode, and sometimes there is more than one mode. For example, if the ages were 20, 24, 25, 29, and 45, there would be no mode. If the ages were 20, 20, 25, 35 and 35, there would be two modes: 25 years and 35 years.

---

1. It is important when dealing with numbers to identify the measurement units. Age is measured in years.

Describing the Variation   The variation of individual variables in our sample can be described by three commonly used variability measures: the range, the sample variance, and the sample standard deviation. "Sample" refers to the set of projects for which we have data.

Range—Technically, the range is the difference between the largest and smallest values. However, as the range is most useful for providing information about the values beyond which no observations fall, I describe a data set's range as "the smallest value to the largest value." If the ages of three software developers are 20, 25, and 30, the range is from 20 to 30 years.

Sample variance (s^2)—This measures the average distance between each value and the mean. It is the sum of the squared differences between each observation (x_i) and the mean value ($\bar{x}$) divided by the number of observations (n) minus one.[2] This is expressed mathematically by the following formula:

$$s^2 = \frac{\Sigma(x_i - \bar{x})^2}{n - 1}$$

For example, let's consider the ages of three software developers: 23, 25, and 27. The mean of their ages is 25 years. The sample variance is calculated as follows:

$$s^2 = \frac{[(23 - 25)^2 + (25 - 25)^2 + (27 - 25)^2]}{2} = 4$$

Thus, the sample variance is 4 years squared. Most people find it hard to relate to the variance because the measurement units are squared. What does "years squared" really mean?

Sample standard deviation (s)—The standard deviation is an easier-to-understand measure of the average distance between each value and the mean. It is the square root of the sample variance.

$$s = \sqrt{s^2}$$

Thus, the sample standard deviation of our previous example is 2 years. The larger the variance and standard deviation, the more the projects differ from one another.

Perhaps you are wondering why we go through the bother of squaring the differences and then taking their square root. Why not just use the actual differences in the calculation? Well, the reason why the differences are squared is so that the positive and negative differences do not cancel each

---

2. One is subtracted as a corrective measure. Statisticians have found that the variance is underestimated for small samples if we just divide by n.

other out. However, it is true that this could also be achieved by taking the absolute value of the differences. So why don't we do that? The reason is because certain mathematical operations necessary for the development of advanced statistical techniques cannot be carried out on absolute values. What is an absolute value? It is the positive value of a number. For example, 3 is the absolute value of both positive 3 and negative 3. This is expressed mathematically as $|3| = 3$ and $|-3| = 3$.

Unfortunately, we cannot calculate these six measures for all variable types. Table 6.3 shows which measures are authorized for each variable type.

Now, let's look at an example of how to determine these measures for a hypothetical sample of seven projects in which all variables are already ordered from lowest to highest (Table 6.4). In this example, application type is a nominal-scale variable. There are two values for application type: customer service and MIS. Risk level is an ordinal-scale variable measured using a scale of 1-5. We know that some applications are riskier than others, but that is all. Quality requirements, a quasi-interval scale variable, is carefully measured using a Likert scale with 1, 2, 3, 4, and 5 representing very low, low, average, high, and very high. Effort is a ratio-scale variable; it is measured in hours.

First, let's describe a typical project using the mean, median, and mode. In Table 6.4, we can see that the most frequent application type is customer service. The mode is the only central tendency measure authorized for nominal variables. For ordinal variables, we can calculate the median and mode. Observation 4 is the middle observation. There are three observations above it and three observations below it. Thus, the median risk level is 2. There are two modes: 2 and 4. Therefore, there is no single typical risk level.

TABLE 6.3
Authorized Operations by Variable Type

Variable Type	Nominal	Ordinal	Interval	Ratio
Mean			X	X
Median		X	X	X
Mode	X	X	X	X
Range		X	X	X
Variance and Standard Deviation			X	X

TABLE 6.4
Examples of Central Tendency and Variability Measures for Each Variable Type

Variable Type	Nominal Application Type	Ordinal Risk Level	Interval Quality Requirements	Ratio Effort
Observation 1	Customer Service	1	1	300
2	Customer Service	2	2	400
3	Customer Service	2	3	500
4	Customer Service	2	3	600
5	MIS	4	3	1000
6	MIS	4	4	5000
7	MIS	4	5	30,000
Mean			3	5,400 hours
Median		2	3	600 hours
Mode	Customer Service	2 and 4	3	none
Range		1 to 4	1 to 5	300 to 30,000 hours
Sample Variance			1.67	120,456,667 hours^2
Sample Standard Deviation			1.29	10,975.3 hours

For interval and ratio variables, we can also calculate the mean in addition to the median and mode. The mean value of quality requirements is 3. The median value is 3, and 3 is the most frequent value. It looks like we can safely say that a typical project has average quality requirements.

For effort, the mean is 5400 hours, the median is 600 hours, and there is no mode as no number appears more than once. In this case, we have two different numbers describing a typical project's effort. The advantages and disadvantages of each of these measures are summarized in Table 6.5. For example, one of the disadvantages of the mean is that it is very sensitive to extreme values. As you can see, the one effort of 30,000 hours has a very big impact on the mean value. Most projects actually have efforts below the mean value. The median is insensitive to extreme values. Even if the effort of the last project was 90,000 hours, the median would remain unchanged.

TABLE 6.5
Relative Merits of Mean, Median, and Mode

	Advantages	Disadvantages
Mean	– Located by simple process of addition and division – Affected by every item in group	– Affected by the exceptional and the unusual – Calculated value may not actually exist
Median	– Not affected by items having extreme deviation from the normal – Unlike the mode, not overly affected by small number of items	– Not as easy to calculate (by hand) as the mean – Not useful when extreme variations should be given weight – Insensitive to changes in minimum and maximum values – Calculated value may not actually exist (when there is even number of observations)
Mode	– Not affected by extreme values – Only way to represent nominal variable	– No single, well-defined type may exist – Difficult to determine accurately – Ignores extreme variations – May be determined by small number of items

Now, let's consider the three variability measures: range, sample variance, and sample standard deviation. The range can be described for all variable types except nominal. The sample variance and sample standard deviation can only be calculated for interval and ratio variables as they depend on the mean. Like the mean, they are also sensitive to extreme values. The one project with a 30,000-hour effort has a big impact on all three variability measures.

Frequency Distributions   Data can also be described with frequency distributions. A frequency distribution refers to the number or percentage of observations in a group. The group can be either a category or a numerical interval. For example, Table 6.6 shows the frequency distribution of the categorical variable application type (*app*) from Chapter 1. We can see in Table 6.6 that we have 20 transaction processing (*TransPro*) applications. This is the number under *Frequency*. This corresponds to approximately 59% of all applications in our sample (*Percent*). The cumulative frequency (*Cumulative*) is more applicable to numerical intervals, for example, if you want to know

TABLE 6.6
Application Type Frequency Distribution

Application Type	Frequency	Percent	Cumulative
CustServ	6	17.65	17.65
MIS	3	8.82	26.47
TransPro	20	58.82	85.29
InfServ	5	14.71	100.00
Total	34	100.00	

the total number of projects less than a certain size. Here it just means that 85% of the applications were customer service (*CustServ*), management information system (*MIS*), or transaction processing (*TransPro*) applications. While this table provides valuable information to data analysts, it is a bit boring to show upper management.

Frequency distribution tables can be used to make attractive graphs for your presentations (see Figure 6.1). You have probably been making pie charts like this most of your professional life without realizing you were calculating frequency distributions.

Now let's look at the frequency distribution of a numerical variable. If I wanted to make a frequency distribution for the size variable (*size*) in Chapter 1, I would first separate the data into meaningful groups of increasing size, say 0-999 function points, 1000-1999 function points, and so on. Then I would count how many applications fell into each interval (see Table 6.7).

With numerical data, we are usually interested in knowing the shape of the distribution. We can see the shape by making a histogram. A histogram is a

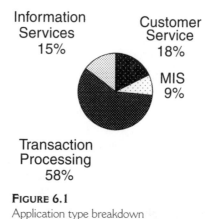

FIGURE 6.1
Application type breakdown

TABLE 6.7
Size Frequency Distribution

Size in Function Points	Frequency	Percent	Cumulative
0 – 999	29	85.30	85.30
1000 – 1999	3	8.82	94.12
2000 – 2999	1	2.94	97.06
3000 – 3999	1	2.94	100.00
Total	63	100.00	

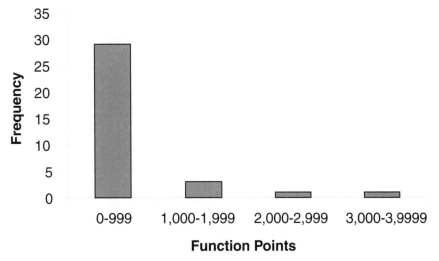

FIGURE 6.2
Distribution of size

chart with a bar for each class. Figure 6.2 shows the histogram of size using the percentage of projects in each class. We can easily see from this graph that most projects have a size of less than 1000 function points. Often we make histograms to determine if the data is normally distributed.

The Normal Distribution

One very important frequency distribution is the normal distribution. Figure 6.3 shows the fundamental features of a normal curve. It is bell-shaped, with tails extending indefinitely above and below the center. A normal distribution

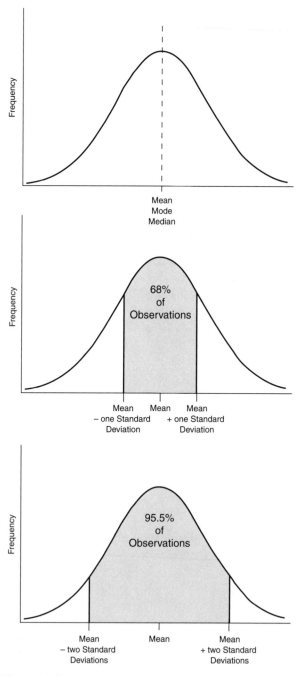

FIGURE 6.3

Example of normal distribution

is symmetrical about the average. In a normal distribution, the mean, median, and mode all have the same value and thus all describe a typical project. A normal curve can be described mathematically in terms of just two parameters, the mean and standard deviation. The width of a normal distribution is a function of the standard deviation of the data. The larger the standard deviation, the wider the distribution. If our numerical data follow a normal distribution, we know that about 68% of all observations fall within plus or minus one standard deviation of the mean. About 95.5% of the observations lie within plus or minus two standard deviations of the mean, and 99.7% fall within plus or minus three standard deviations.

Overview of Sampling Theory

Now that you know how to describe and summarize individual variables, there is another key concept to understand before we can proceed to identifying relationships in data: the difference between samples and populations. This is important because you probably haven't been able to collect valid data for every software project your company has ever undertaken. So, if we consider that the population of software project data is data for all projects in your company, what you have is a sample of that data. How, then, can you be sure that what you find in your sample is true for all projects in your company?

Imagine that you are able to select different samples (groups of projects) at random[3] from the population of all software projects in your company (see Figure 6.4). As an example, let's consider the variable *effort*.[4] For each sample, we can compute the mean value of effort. The mean value of effort in each sample will not always be the same. In one sample, it might be 600 hours ($\bar{x}_1$), in a second sample, 620 hours ($\bar{x}_2$), in a third sample, 617 hours ($\bar{x}_3$), and so on. We can make a frequency distribution of the mean efforts of each sample. This distribution is called the sampling distribution of the sample means. The mean value of an infinite number of sample means is equal to the population mean (see Figure 6.5).

If the sample size is large (≥ 30), the sampling distribution of the sample means is approximately a normal distribution. The larger the sample, the better the approximation. This is true even if the *effort* variable in the population

---

3. As all inferential (i.e., predictive) techniques assume that you have a random sample, you should not violate that assumption by removing projects just because they do not fit your model!

4. To simplify this complicated discussion, the effort in my example is normally distributed. In practice, this is not the case.

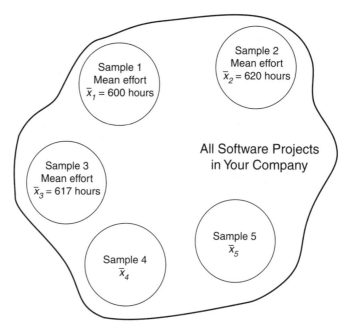

FIGURE 6.4
Sampling from a population

is not normally distributed. This tendency to normality of sampling distributions is known as the Central Limit Theorem.[5] This theorem has great practical importance. It means that it doesn't matter that we don't know the distribution of effort in the population. (This is handy because in practice, all we have is one sample.) If we have a sample of at least 30 projects, we can use a normal distribution to determine the probability that the mean effort of the population is within a certain distance of the mean effort of our one sample.

As you can see in Figure 6.5, the sampling distribution of all sample mean efforts is not as wide as the distribution of all software projects' efforts. In fact, one of the most important properties of the sample mean is that it is a very stable measure of central tendency. We can estimate the hypothetical standard deviation of the sampling distribution of sample means from the variation of effort in our one sample. This is known as the standard error of the mean. Note that "error" does not mean "mistake" in this context. It really means deviation. The term "error" is used to distinguish the standard deviation of the sampling distribution (the standard error) from the standard deviation of our sample.

_____

5. In addition, it has also been shown that if a variable is normally distributed in the population, the sampling distribution of the sample mean is exactly normal no matter what the size of the sample.

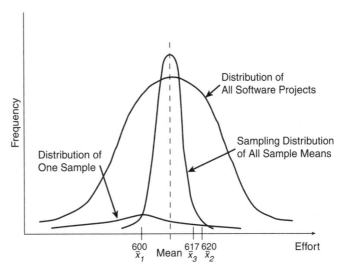

FIGURE 6.5
Distributions of one sample, means of all samples, and the population

Otherwise, it is not clear just what standard deviation we are talking about. The standard error is expressed mathematically as:

$$s_{\bar{x}} = \frac{s}{\sqrt{n}}$$

where $s_{\bar{x}}$ is the estimated standard error of the mean, s is the standard deviation of our one sample, and n is the size of our one sample. You can see that if s is very small and n is very large, the standard error of the mean will be small. That is, the less variation there is in the variable *effort* in our sample, and the more projects we have in our sample, the smaller the standard error of the mean (and the narrower the sampling distribution of the sample means). The narrower the sampling distribution of the sample means, the more certain we are that the population's mean effort is near our one-sample mean effort. This is because in a very narrow distribution, the population mean is near every sample mean.

The standard error of the mean is important because we can use it to calculate the limits around our one-sample mean which probably contain the population mean—probably, because we specify these limits with a certain degree of confidence. Typically, we are interested in 95% confidence intervals. The 95% confidence interval estimate of the mean states that the population mean is equal to the sample mean plus or minus 1.96 multiplied by the standard error of the mean. That is:

population mean $= \bar{x} \pm 1.96s_{\bar{x}}$

The value 1.96 is related to the normal curve. Recall that approximately 95.5% of the observations lie within plus or minus two standard deviations of the mean (see Figure 6.3). If 95% confidence intervals were constructed for many samples, about 95% of the intervals would contain the true population mean. Thus, there is still a 5% probability that the true population mean effort lies outside the 95% confidence interval of our one sample. The accuracy of this probability increases with larger sample sizes. You can find a detailed example of 95% confidence intervals for predictive models in Chapter 4.

Other Probability Distributions

Three additional common probability distributions are used by the statistical methods described in this book. You don't need to worry about which distribution to use in which circumstance, what they actually look like, or how to read probabilities from the complicated tables that you find in the appendices of many statistics books. Your statistical analysis package automatically applies the correct distribution. All you need to know is how to read the probability from the statistical output.

- Student t-distribution—If the sample size is less than 30 projects, then the t-distribution must be used instead of the normal distribution. The Student t-distribution assumes that the population from which we are drawing our sample is normally distributed. (i.e., the Central Limit Theorem does not apply). The Student t-distribution tends to coincide with the normal distribution for large sample sizes. Because it is appropriate for either large or small samples, the t-distribution is used in place of the normal distribution when inferences must be made from accessible samples to unmeasurable populations. Think of it as a modified normal distribution. You will see the t-distribution referred to in correlation and regression analysis output.
- Chi-square distribution—If a population is normally distributed, the sample distribution of the sample variance is approximated by the chi-square distribution. The chi-square distribution is used in this book in the chi-square test of independence. This test is explained in detail later in this chapter.
- Fisher F-distribution—If samples taken from two different normally distributed populations are independent, the F-distribution can be used to compare two variances. The F-distribution is used in this book to test the reliability of regression models, and to compare several means in the analysis of variance method. The calculation of the F-ratio is explained in detail in the "Analysis of Variance (ANOVA)" section of this chapter.

Each of these probability distributions assumes that the underlying data is normally distributed. You can now appreciate why the normal distribution is so important in statistics, and why we must check if the numerical variables in our software project database are normally distributed—it is even more important when we don't have very many projects in our sample.

Identifying Relationships in the Data_____

Now that you have learned the basics, you are ready to identify relationships between variables. Table 6.8 shows which statistical methods can be used in which circumstances. It is important to know what types of variables you have to apply the correct method. Choosing the correct statistical method is extremely important. Your statistical analysis package does not automatically decide what method to use—**you do.**

TABLE 6.8
Mappings of Statistical Methods Covered in this Book to Variable Types

Variable Type	Independent Variable			
Dependent Variable	**Nominal**	**Ordinal**	**Interval**	**Ratio**
Nominal	Chi-square test for independence	Chi-square test for independence		
Ordinal	Chi-square test for independence	Spearman's correlation, Chi-square test for independence	Spearman's correlation	Spearman's correlation
Interval	ANOVA	Spearman's correlation, ANOVA	Spearman's correlation, Pearson's correlation, Regression	Spearman's correlation, Pearson's correlation, Regression
Ratio	ANOVA	Spearman's correlation, ANOVA	Spearman's correlation, Pearson's correlation, Regression	Spearman's correlation, Pearson's correlation, Regression

The concept of dependent and independent variables does not apply to the chi-square test for independence, nor does it apply to Spearman's and Pearson's correlation coefficients. However, to use the analysis of variance method (ANOVA), you need to pay attention to which variable is the dependent variable. The dependent variable is the variable you want to predict. For example, if you have a ratio-type variable (effort) and an ordinal-type variable (risk level) as in Table 6.4, you can calculate Spearman's correlation coefficient between these two variables. You can also run an ANOVA procedure to determine how much of the variation in effort (dependent variable) is explained by the variation in the risk level (independent variable). However, you cannot run an ANOVA procedure with risk level as the dependent variable.

Chi-Square Test for Independence

Two events are independent whenever the probability of one happening is unaffected by the occurrence of the other. This concept can be extended to categorical variables. The chi-square test for independence compares the actual and expected frequencies of occurrence to determine whether or not two categorical variables are independent. For example, let's consider two nominal variables, Telon use (*telonuse*) and application type (*subapp*), from Chapter 2. We want to know if Telon use is independent of application type in the bank. We will base our conclusion on data from 62 projects collected by the bank. This is our sample size. Table 6.9 summarizes the actual frequencies found in our sample. This table is called a contingency table because it shows the frequency for every combination of attributes (i.e., every possible contingency).

If two variables are independent, the proportion of observations in any category should be the same regardless of what attribute applies to the other variable. So, if Telon use and application type are independent, we would

TABLE 6.9
Contingency Table—Actual Frequencies

Application Type	Telon Use		
	No	Yes	Total
CustServ	12	6	18
MIS	4	0	4
TransPro	24	5	29
InfServ	8	3	11
Total	48	14	62

TABLE 6.10

Percentage of Applications that Did/Did Not Use Telon

Application Type	Telon Use		Total
	No	Yes	
CustServ	66.67	33.33	100.00
MIS	100.00	0.00	100.00
TransPro	82.76	17.24	100.00
InfServ	72.73	27.27	100.00
Total	77.42	22.58	100.00

expect the percentage of Telon use to be the same for all four application types. It is easy to see in Table 6.10 that the percentages are not exactly the same.

The frequencies we would expect if the percentages were the same are computed in the following way: The overall proportion of projects in our sample that did not use Telon is approximately 0.77 (=48/62); the proportion that used Telon is approximately 0.23 (=14/62). This proportion can be used to compute the expected number of Telon projects for each application type. There were 18 customer service (*CustServ*) applications. If approximately 23% used Telon this makes 4.1 expected Telon/customer service projects.[6] Out of a total of four *MIS* applications, we would expect 4*(14/62) = .9 to use Telon. For transaction processing (*TransPro*) applications, 29*(14/62) = 6.5 is the expected number of Telon projects. For information service (*InfServ*) applications, 11*(14/62) = 2.5 is the expected number of Telon projects. Then for each application type, the expected number of projects that did not use Telon is simply the total number for each application type minus the number that did use Telon. The expected frequencies are presented in Table 6.11.

Our null hypothesis is that there is no relationship between Telon use and application type. If we demonstrate that:

1. The actual frequencies differ from the frequencies expected if there was no relationship, and
2. The difference is larger than we would be likely to get through sampling error,

then we can reject the null hypothesis and conclude that there is a relationship between Telon use and application type. So far in our example, we have

---

6. Obviously, a fraction of a project does not exist; however, it is necessary to keep the decimal places for the calculations.

TABLE 6.11
Contingency Table-Expected Frequencies

Application Type	Telon Use		Total
	No	**Yes**	**Total**
CustServ	13.9	4.1	18
MIS	3.1	0.9	4
TransPro	22.5	6.5	29
InfServ	8.5	2.5	11
Total	48	14	62

seen that the actual and expected frequencies are not exactly the same (Condition 1). Now we need to see if the difference is significant (Condition 2). We compare the difference between the actual and expected frequencies with the chi-square statistic.

The chi-square statistic is calculated with the following expression:

$$\chi^2 = \Sigma \frac{(actual_{ij} - expected_{ij})^2}{expected_{ij}}$$

where $actual_{ij}$ is the actual frequency for the combination at the ith row and jth column (Table 6.9), and $expected_{ij}$ is the expected frequency for the combination at the ith row and jth column (Table 6.11). For example, $actual_{11}$ refers to the actual frequency of customer service (CustServ) applications that did not use Telon; $expected_{42}$ refers to the expected frequency of information service (InfServ) applications that used Telon.

Table 6.12 shows the calculation of the chi-square statistic for our example. First we subtract the expected value (exp) from the actual value (act) for each attribute combination. The farther the expected value is from the actual value, the bigger the difference. Then we square this value. This allows negative differences to increase rather than reduce the total. Next, we divide by the expected value. Finally, we sum up (Σ) the values in the last column to arrive at the chi-square statistic.

The chi-square distribution provides probabilities for different values of χ^2. There is a separate distribution for each number of degrees of freedom. The number of degrees of freedom refers to the number of independent comparisons. In our example, the number of degrees of freedom is 3 because once we have calculated frequencies for Telon use for three application types in Table 6.11, the remaining five cells can be filled in without any further calculation of frequencies. For example, the expected frequency for information service

TABLE 6.12
Example of Chi-Square Statistic Calculation

(i,j)	act	exp	act – exp	(act – exp)²	(act – exp)²/ exp
(1,1)	12	13.9	–1.9	3.61	0.260
(1,2)	6	4.1	1.9	3.61	0.880
(2,1)	4	3.1	0.9	0.81	0.261
(2,2)	0	0.9	–0.9	0.81	0.900
(3,1)	24	22.5	1.5	2.25	0.100
(3,2)	5	6.5	–1.5	2.25	0.346
(4,1)	8	8.5	–0.5	0.25	0.029
(4,2)	3	2.5	0.5	0.25	0.100
sum	62	62	0		**chi-square = 2.877**

(*InfServ*) applications that used Telon is the total number of applications that used Telon minus the expected frequencies of the three other application types that used Telon (14 – 4.1 – 0.9 – 6.5 = 2.5). We don't need to calculate its frequency because we can derive it from the information we already have. The number of degrees of freedom for the chi-square test is always the number of rows minus one multiplied by the number of columns minus one. Here, $(4 – 1)$ $(2 – 1) = 3$. (Ignore the "total" values.)

Once we have our chi-square value and the number of degrees of freedom, we can see if the difference between actual and expected frequencies is significant using a chi-square distribution table. However, in practice, you will not be undertaking these calculations yourself and you do not need to learn how to use the chi-square distribution tables. A computer will calculate everything for you (Example 6.1).

Example 6.1

```
.  tabulate app telonuse, chi2

Application          Telon Use
Type                 No              Yes         Total
CustServ             12              6            18
MIS                  4               0            4
TransPro             24              5            29
InfServ              8               3            11
Total                48              14           62
        Pearson chi2(3)  = 2.9686  Pr = 0.396
```

My statistical analysis package informs me that the chi-square statistic (*Pearson chi2*) associated with this table has 3 degrees of freedom and a value of 2.9686. There is a small difference between the computer's value and my value because of rounding errors. The computer's value is more precise. The significance level is 0.396 (approximately 40%). The significance level states the probability (*Pr*) that we are making an error when we reject the null hypothesis. Only if the *Pr* is less than or equal to 0.05 can we reject the hypothesis that application type and Telon use are independent at the 5% significance level. Thus, our null hypothesis that there is no relationship between Telon use and application type cannot be rejected.

Correlation Analysis

A correlation coefficient measures the strength and direction of the relationship between two numerical variables. The correlation coefficient can have any value between −1 and +1 (see Figure 6.6).

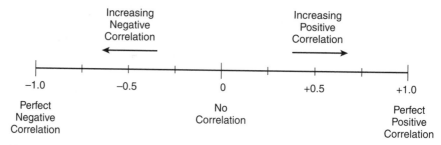

FIGURE 6.6
Interpreting the correlation coefficient

If the correlation coefficient is −1, this means that the two variables are perfectly negatively correlated. High values of one are associated with low values of the other, and vice versa (see Figure 6.7).

If the correlation coefficient is +1, this means that the two variables are perfectly positively correlated. High values of one are associated with high values of the other, and vice versa (see Figure 6.8).

If the correlation coefficient is 0, this means that the two variables are not correlated at all (see Figure 6.9).

In practice, we rarely see perfect correlation or complete non-correlation. Figure 6.10 shows a more typical relationship.

We can see that development effort and software size are positively correlated because the relationship looks linear and the slope of the line is increasing. But how strong is the relationship? How can we measure the correlation?

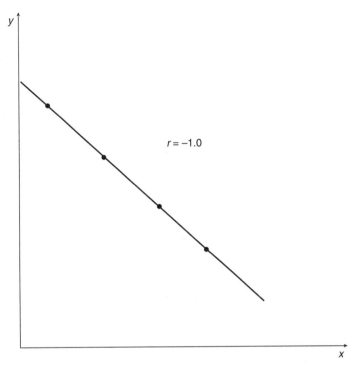

FIGURE 6.7
Perfect negative correlation

Two measures of correlation are commonly used when analyzing software project data. Spearman's rank correlation coefficient must be used when the data is ordinal,[7] or when the data is far from normally distributed. Pearson's correlation coefficient can be used when the data is of an interval or ratio type. Pearson's correlation coefficient is based on two key assumptions: (1) the data is normally distributed, and (2) the relationship is linear.

Spearman's Rank Correlation   Spearman's rank correlation coefficient compares the differences in two variables' rank for the same observation. A variable's rank refers to its placement in an ordered list. For example, consider the following five software development projects from Chapter 1, which are shown in Table 6.13.

We are interested in the relationship between size and effort. First we have to rank the projects' size. There are five projects, so the rank of each project will be a number between 1 and 5. The smallest size project is given rank 1, the second smallest 2, and so on. I do the same thing for project effort.

---

7. I also prefer the Spearman's rank correlation coefficient for quasi-interval variables.

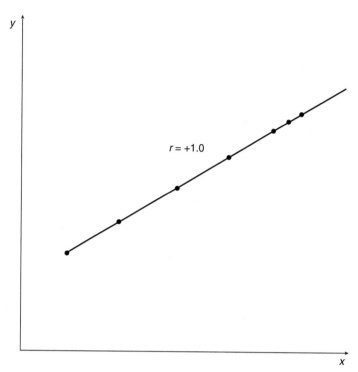

Figure 6.8
Perfect positive correlation

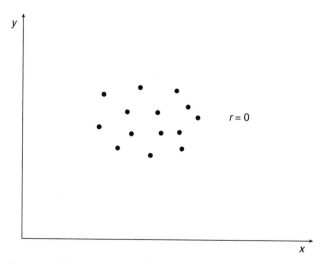

Figure 6.9
No correlation

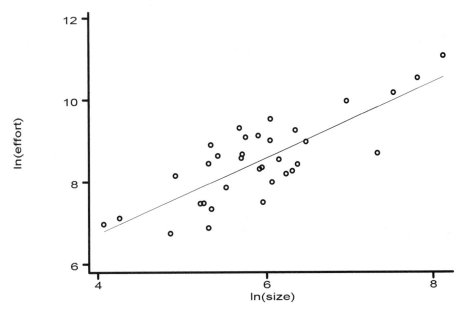

FIGURE 6.10
Typical relationship between *ln(effort)* and *ln(size)*

I now have two new variables, *sizerank* and *effrank*, which are the respective ranks of the variables *size* and *effort*.

I can easily calculate Spearman's rank correlation coefficient, ρ, using the following equation:

$$\rho = 1 - \frac{6\Sigma D^2}{n(n^2 - 1)}$$

where D is the difference between the two variables' rank for the same project, and n is the number of projects.

TABLE 6.13
Data for Five Software Development Projects

id	size	sizerank	effort	effrank
2	647	4	7871	4
3	130	1	845	1
5	1056	5	21272	5
6	383	3	4224	3
15	249	2	2565	2

TABLE 6.14
Calculation of Sum of Squared Differences

Project id	Rank of size	Rank of effort	Difference Between Ranks, D	Square of Difference, D^2
2	4	4	$4 - 4 = 0$	0
3	1	1	$1 - 1 = 0$	0
5	5	5	$5 - 5 = 0$	0
6	3	3	$3 - 3 = 0$	0
15	2	2	$2 - 2 = 0$	0
n = 5				$\Sigma D^2 = 0$

How strong is the relationship between effort and size? Some calculation steps are shown in Table 6.14.

The sum of the squared differences is 0. This results in a Spearman's rank correlation coefficient of 1. This is an example of perfect positive correlation.

$$\rho = 1 - \frac{6(0)}{5(5^2 - 1)} = 1$$

The second example compares the quality requirements and development time constraints of five hypothetical projects. Quality requirements and development time constraints are quasi-interval variables measured using a Likert scale from 1 (very low) to 5 (very high). We see that very low quality requirements are associated with very high development time constraints, low quality requirements are associated with high development time constraints, and so on. Table 6.15 shows how the sum of the squared differences was calculated for this example.

The sum of the squared differences is 40. Plugging this into Spearman's equation results in a correlation coefficient of –1. This is an example of perfect negative correlation.

$$\rho = 1 - \frac{6(40)}{5(5^2 - 1)} = -1$$

These calculations are slightly more complicated when there are ties in the ranks. However, as your statistical analysis package will automatically calculate the correlation coefficient, you do not need to be concerned about this.

Pearson's Correlation Pearson's correlation coefficient uses the actual values of the variables instead of the ranks. So, it takes into account not only the

TABLE 6.15
Calculation of Sum of Squared Differences

Project id	Rank of Quality Requirements	Rank of Development Time Constraints	Difference Between Ranks, D	Square of Difference, D^2
P01	1 (very low)	5 (very high)	$1 - 5 = -4$	16
P22	2 (low)	4 (high)	$2 - 4 = -2$	4
P33	3 (average)	3 (average)	$3 - 3 = 0$	0
P54	4 (high)	2 (low)	$4 - 2 = 2$	4
P65	5 (very high)	1 (very low)	$5 - 1 = 4$	16
n = 5				$\Sigma D^2 = 40$

fact that one value is higher than another, but also the size of the quantitative difference between two values. It can be calculated with the following formula:

$$r = \frac{\Sigma(x_i - \bar{x})(y_i - \bar{y})}{(n-1)s_x s_y}$$

where $x_i - \bar{x}$ is the difference between a project's value on the x variable from the mean of that variable, $y_i - \bar{y}$ is the difference between a project's value on the y variable from the mean of that variable, s_x and s_y are the sample standard deviations of the x and y variables, respectively, and n is the number of observation pairs.

There is no better way to understand an equation than to try out the calculation with some real data. So let's return to our software project data in Table 6.13. In Example 6.2, we have the mean and standard deviation of effort and size for the five projects in our sample.

Example 6.2

```
                . summarize effort size

    Variable      Obs        Mean     Std. Dev.       Min        Max
    effort          5      7355.4     8201.776        845      21272
    size            5         493     368.8123        130       1056
```

For our sample of five projects, the mean of the effort is 7355.4 hours and its standard deviation is 8201.776 hours. The mean of the size is 493 function points and its standard deviation is 368.8123 function points. Table 6.16 demonstrates some steps for the calculation of Pearson's correlation coefficient between effort and size for these projects.

TABLE 6.16
Calculation of Pearson's Correlation Coefficient Numerator

Project id	x, size	y, effort	$x_i - \bar{x}$	$y_i - \bar{y}$	$(x_i - \bar{x})(y_i - \bar{y})$
2	647	7871	154	515.6	79402.4
3	130	845	−363	−6510.4	2363275.2
5	1056	21272	563	13916.6	7835045.8
6	383	4224	−110	−3131.4	344454.0
15	249	2565	−244	−4790.4	1168857.6
					$\Sigma = 11791035$

Plugging these numbers into our formula gives us the following result:

$$r = \frac{11791035}{(5-1) \times 368.8123 \times 8201.776} = 0.9745$$

Pearson's correlation coefficient is 0.9745. Recall that we calculated a Spearman's rank correlation coefficient of 1 for this data in the previous section. Pearson's correlation coefficient is a more accurate measurement of the association between interval- or ratio-scale variables than Spearman's coefficient, as long as its underlying assumptions have been met. This is because some information is lost when we convert interval- or ratio-scale variables into rank orders.

One of the assumptions underlying Pearson's correlation coefficient is that the relationship between the two variables is linear. Let's look at the data and see if this is the case. We can see in Figure 6.11 that although it is possible to fit a straight line close to the five data points, the relationship is really a bit curved.

Taking the natural log of the variables *effort* and *size* results in a more linear relationship (Figure 6.12).

Pearson's correlation coefficient between *ln(size)* and *ln(effort)* is shown in Example 6.3.

Example 6.3

```
.corr lsize leffort
       (obs=5)

              lsize     leffort

 lsize        1.0000
 leffort      0.9953     1.0000
```

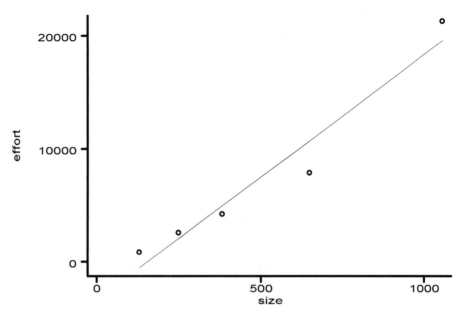

FIGURE 6.11
effort vs. *size* for correlation example

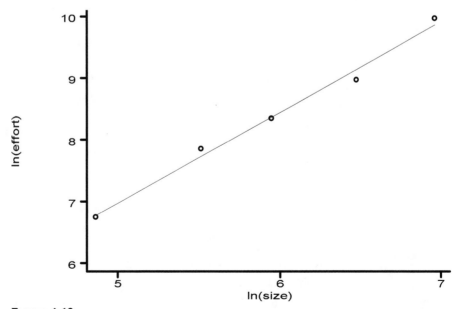

FIGURE 6.12
ln(effort) vs. *ln(size)* for correlation example

Thus, the linear association is stronger between the natural log of size and the natural log of effort (0.9953) than it is between size and effort (0.9745). As you can see in Example 6.4, the natural log transformation has no effect on Spearman's rank correlation coefficient because although the actual values of the variables change, their relative positions do not. Thus, the ranking of the variables stays the same.

Example 6.4

```
. spearman lsize leffort

 Number of obs = 5
Spearman's rho = 1.0000
```

Regression Analysis

Whereas a correlation coefficient measures only the strength and direction of the relationship between two variables, regression analysis provides us with an equation describing the nature of their relationship. Furthermore, regression analysis allows us to assess the accuracy of our model.

In simple regression analysis, we are interested in predicting the dependent variable's value based on the value of only one independent variable. For example, we would like to predict the effort needed to complete a software project based only on knowledge of its size. In this case, effort is the dependent variable and size is the independent variable. In multiple regression analysis, we are interested in predicting the value of the dependent variable based on several independent variables. For example, we would like to predict the effort needed to complete a software project based on knowledge about its size, required reliability, duration, team size, and other factors. All of the case studies in this book use multiple regression analysis. However, because it is easier to grasp multiple regression analysis if you understand simple regression analysis, we'll start with that.

Simple Regression   The least-squares method fits a straight line through the data that minimizes the sum of the squared errors. The errors are the differences between the actual values and the predicted (i.e., estimated) values. These errors are also often referred to as the residuals.

In Figure 6.13, the three points, (x_1, y_1), (x_2, y_2), and (x_3, y_3), represent the actual values. The predicted values, $(x_1, \hat{y}_1)$, $(x_2, \hat{y}_2)$, and $(x_3, \hat{y}_3)$, are on the line. The errors are the differences between y and $\hat{y}$ for each observation. We want to find the straight line that minimizes $error_1^2 + error_2^2 + error_3^2$.

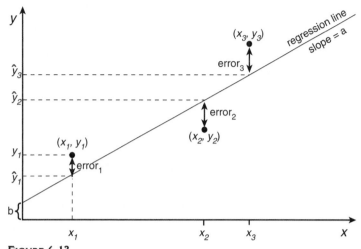

FIGURE 6.13
Illustration of regression errors

You may recall from algebra that the equation for a straight line is of the form:

$$\hat{y} = a + bx$$

where is $\hat{y}$ the predicted value of the dependent variable, y, given the value of the independent variable, x. The constant a represents the value of $\hat{y}$ when x is zero. This is also known as the y-intercept. The constant b represents the slope of the line. It will be positive when there is a positive relationship and negative when there is a negative relationship.

To find the a and b values of a straight line fitted by the least-squares method, the following two equations must be solved simultaneously:

$$\Sigma y = na + b\Sigma x$$

$$\Sigma xy = a\Sigma x + b\Sigma x^2$$

where n is the number of observations. By plugging in the known values of x and y, a and b can be calculated. Table 6.17 demonstrates some steps in the calculation of the regression line for the five projects from our correlation example (Figure 6.11).

We can now solve these two equations for a and b:

$$36777 = 5a + 2465b$$

$$29922096 = 2465a + 1759335b$$

This results in the following regression line:

$$\textit{predicted effort} = -3328.46 + 21.67 \times \textit{size}$$

TABLE 6.17
Calculation of Sums Needed to Solve Regression Equations

Project id	x, size	y, effort	x^2	xy
2	647	7871	418609	5092537
3	130	845	16900	109850
5	1056	21272	1115136	22463232
6	383	4224	146689	1617792
15	249	2565	62001	638685
$n = 5$	$\Sigma x = 2465$	$\Sigma y = 36777$	$\Sigma x^2 = 1759335$	$\Sigma xy = 29922096$

This is what your statistical analysis package is doing when you ask it to regress two variables.

Regression Accuracy   A regression line is only a measure of the average relationship between the dependent and independent variable. Unless there is perfect correlation, in which all the observations lie on a straight line, there will be errors in the estimates. The farther the actual values are from the regression line, the greater the estimation error. How can we translate this into a measure that will tell us if the fit of the regression line is any good?

Imagine that you join a company and you need to estimate a project's effort. The only data available is the effort of past projects. You don't even know if there were any similar projects in the past or what the projects' sizes were. How can you use this data? Well, the simplest thing to do would be to use the average effort of past projects as an estimate for the new project. You are not happy with the result and convince your company that you could improve future effort estimation if you also knew the sizes of past projects. Obviously, if you then collected and used this size data to develop a regression model to estimate effort, you would expect your model to perform better than just taking the average of past efforts. Otherwise, you would have wasted a great deal of your company's time and money counting function points. Similarly, comparing the results obtained by the regression equation with the results of using averages is how the accuracy of the regression model is determined.

Figure 6.14 shows an example using three projects. Let's pretend that y is the project effort and x is the size. We can see that for Project 1, the mean value of effort, $\bar{y}$, overestimates the actual value of effort, y_1. The predicted value of effort, $\hat{y}$, underestimates the actual effort. For Project 2, both the mean value of effort and the predicted value of effort, $\hat{y}_2$, overestimate the

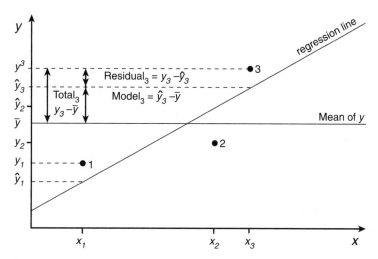

FIGURE 6.14
Illustration of regression accuracy

actual effort, y_2. For Project 3, both the mean value of effort and the predicted value of effort, $\hat{y}_3$, underestimate the actual effort, y_3. We need to compare the differences between the actual values, the predicted values, and the mean for each project to calculate the overall accuracy of our model.

The total squared error between the actual value of effort and the mean value of effort for each project is:

$$Total\ SS = \Sigma(y_i - \bar{y})^2$$

This is the total variation of the data.[8] If effort really does depend on size, then the errors (residuals) should be small compared to the total variation of the data. The error (*Residual SS*) is the sum of the squared differences between the actual value of effort and the predicted value of effort for each project.

$$Residual\ SS = \Sigma(y_i - \hat{y}_i)^2$$

This can also be thought of as the total variation in the data not explained by our model. The total variation of the data equals the variation explained by the model plus the variation not explained by the model, that is, *Total SS = Model SS + Residual SS*. The variation in the data explained by our model is:

$$Model\ SS = \Sigma(\hat{y}_i - \bar{y})^2$$

8. The statistical term "variance" is defined as the sum of squared deviations divided by the number of observations minus one. It is a measure of the average variation of the data. Here I am referring to the total variation of the data (i.e., we don't divide by the number of observations).

Thus, if effort really does depend on size, the *Residual SS* will be small and the differences between the predicted values of effort and the mean value of effort (*Model SS*) will be close to the *Total SS*.

This is the logic that underlies the accuracy measure of the regression model, r^2.

$$r^2 = \frac{Model\ SS}{Total\ SS}$$

This is the R-squared (r^2) value. It is the fraction of the variation in the data that can be explained by the model. It can vary between 0 and 1 and measures the fit of the regression equation. If the model is no better than just taking averages, the *Model SS* will be small compared to the *Total SS* and r^2 will approach zero. This means that the linear model is bad. If the *Model SS* is almost the same as the *Total SS*, then r^2 will be very close to 1. An r^2 value close to 1 indicates that the regression line fits the data well. Our effort example has an r^2 value of 0.95. This means that 95% of the variation in effort is explained by variations in size. In simple regression, r^2 is also the square of Pearson's correlation coefficient, r, between two variables.

You may wonder how high of a r^2 value is needed for a regression model to be useful? The answer is that it depends. If I didn't know anything about the relationship between quality requirements and productivity, I would find any r^2 to be useful. Before I knew nothing, but now I know something. If the r^2 is very small, then I know there is no linear relationship. If the r^2 of productivity as a function of quality requirements is .25, I would find it useful to know that quality requirements explain 25% of the variation in productivity. This is quite a high percentage of productivity for one variable to explain. However, .25 is too small for a good predictive model. In this case, an r^2 over 0.90 would be great. But, I would also need to check for influential observations and consider the 95% confidence intervals before I got too excited. A very high r^2 is sometimes due to an extreme value. Be sure and read the "Checking the Model" sections of Chapters 1 through 5 to see how I detected influential observations.

Multiple Regression   Multiple regression is basically the same as simple regression except that instead of the model being a simple straight line, it is an equation with more than one independent variable. As a result, the calculations are more complex. In addition, once we get beyond three dimensions (two independent variables), we can no longer visualize the relationship. For example, at the most, we can draw a three-dimensional graph of effort as a function of application size and team size. The three-dimensional model is the plane that minimizes the sum of the squared deviations between each project and the plane. However, it is impossible to draw a four-dimensional diagram of effort as a function of application size, team size, and reliability requirements. In multiple regression, the r^2 is capitalized, R^2, and is called the coefficient of multiple determination.

Significance of Results In both simple and multiple regression, the final step is to determine if our result is significant. Is our model significant? Are the coefficients of each variable and the constant significant? What does "significant" mean? Significance is best explained as follows: The lower the probability that our results are due to chance, the higher their significance. The probability is related to our sample size (i.e., the number of projects) and the number of variables we used to model the dependent variable. Different distributions, namely the F-distribution and the t-distribution, are used to determine these probabilities. Our statistical analysis package knows which distributions to use and will calculate the probability of our results being due to chance. We usually consider significant a probability value lower than or equal to 0.05. In research papers, it is common to read that results are significant at the 5% level (for a probability value lower than or equal to 0.05) or the 1% level (for a probability value lower than or equal to 0.01).

How to Interpret Regression Output Now that you know some basics of regression analysis, you will be able to better understand the regression output in Example 6.5 below. This is an example of the regression model $ln(effort)$ as a function of $ln(size)$ using the software project data from Chapter 1. (Figure 6.10 shows the regression line fit to the data.)

Example 6.5

```
                    . regress leffort lsize
```

Source	SS	df	MS		
Model	22.6919055	1	22.6919055	Number of obs =	34
Residual	12.1687291	32	.380272786	F(1, 32) =	59.67
				Prob > F =	0.0000
Total	34.8606346	33	1.05638287	R-squared =	0.6509
				Adj R-squared =	0.6400
				Root MSE =	.61666

leffort	Coef.	Std. Err.	t	P>|t|	[95% Conf. Interval]	
lsize	.9297666	.1203611	7.725	0.000	.6845991	1.174934
_cons	3.007431	.7201766	4.176	0.000	1.54048	4.474383

In the upper left corner of the output, we have a table. This is known as the analysis of variance (ANOVA) table. The column headings are defined as follows: SS = sum of squares, df = degrees of freedom, and MS = mean square. In this example, the total sum of squares (*Total SS*) is 34.86. The sum of squares accounted for by the model is 22.69 (*Model SS*), and *12.17* is left unexplained (*Residual SS*). There are 33 total degrees of freedom (34 observations –1 for mean removal), of which 1 is used by the model (one variable, *lsize*), leaving 32 for the residual. The mean square error (*Residual MS*) is defined as the sum of squares (*Residual SS*) divided by the corresponding degrees of freedom (*Residual df*). Here, $12.17/32 = 0.38$.

In the upper right corner of the output, we have other summary statistics. The number of observations is 34. The *F* statistic associated with the ANOVA table (1 and 32 refer to the degrees of freedom of the model and the residual, respectively) is 59.67. The *F* statistic is calculated with the following equation:

$$F = \frac{Model\ SS/Model\ df}{Residual\ SS/Residual\ df} = \frac{22.6919/1}{12.1687/32} = 59.67$$

The *F* statistic tests the null hypothesis that all coefficients excluding the constant are zero. *Prob* > *F* = 0.0000 means that the probability of observing an *F* statistic of 59.67 or greater is 0.0000, which is my statistical analysis package's way of indicating a number smaller than 0.00005. Thus, we can reject the null hypothesis as there is only a .005% probability that all the coefficients are zero. This means that there is a 99.995% probability that at least one of them is not zero. In this case, we only have one independent variable, so its coefficient is definitely not zero. The R^2 (*R-squared*) for the regression is 0.6509, and the R^2 adjusted for the degrees of freedom (*Adj R-squared*) is 0.6400. The root mean square error (*Root MSE*) is 0.61666. This is the same as the square root of *MS Residual* in the ANOVA table.

When you interpret the R^2 in the statistical output, you should use the Adjusted R-squared. This is because it is always possible to increase the value of R^2 just by adding more independent variables to the model. This is true even when they are not related to the dependent variable. The number of observations must be significantly greater than the number of variables for the results to be reliable. The Adjusted R-squared is calculated by the following equation:

$$Adjusted\ R^2 = 1 - \frac{(1 - R^2)(Total\ df)}{(Residual\ df)}$$

The total and residual degrees of freedom (*df*) can be read directly from the statistical output. In regression analysis, the total degrees of freedom is $n - 1$ and the residual degrees of freedom is $n - k$, where *n* is the number of observations and *k* is the number of independent variables + 1 (for the constant term).

At the bottom of the output, we have a table of the estimated coefficients (*Coef.*). The first line of the table tells us that the dependent variable is *leffort*. The estimated model is:

$$leffort = 3.0074 + 0.9298 \times lsize$$

At the right of the coefficients in the output are their standard errors (*Std. Err.*), t statistics (*t*), significance of the t statistics ($P > |t|$), and 95% confidence intervals (*95% Conf. Interval*). In this example, the standard error for the coefficient of *lsize* is 0.1203611. The corresponding t statistic is 7.725 ($t = $ *Coef.*/*Std.Err.*), which has a significance level of 0.000. This is my statistical analysis package's way of indicating a number less than 0.0005. Thus, we can be 99.95% sure that the coefficient of *lsize* is not really 0. That is, we can be confident that there really is a relationship between *leffort* and *lsize*. The 95% confidence interval for the coefficient is [–0.6846, 1.1749]. This means that we are 95% confident that the true coefficient of *lsize* in the population lies between –0.6846 and 1.1749. Confidence intervals are explained in the "Overview of Sampling Theory" section of this chapter and in Chapter 4.

Analysis of Residual Errors   If the assumptions of the regression model are met, then the plot of the residuals vs. fitted values (predicted values) should look like a random array of dots. If there is a pattern, this indicates that we have a problem. Figure 6.15 shows this plot for our regression output.

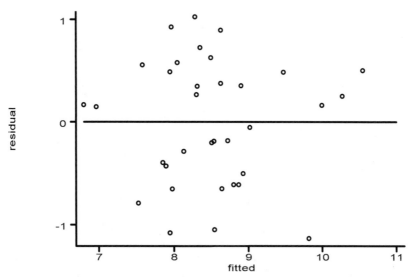

FIGURE 6.15
Plot of residuals vs. fitted values

The assumptions of regression are:

1. A linear relationship exists.
2. The residuals have a constant variance. (This is called homoscedasticity.)
3. The residuals are independent.
4. The residuals are normally distributed.

We can check Assumptions 1–3 by looking out for the following patterns in the residuals (Figures 6.16 through 6.18):

The residuals in Figure 6.16 indicate that the relationship is not linear (violation of Assumption 1). Figure 6.17 shows an example where the errors increase with increasing values of x. This is a violation of Assumption 2. A residual pattern like Figure 6.18 could mean that Assumption 3 has been violated. Assumption 4 is the easiest to check. We simply plot the distribution of the residuals. Figure 6.19 shows the residual distribution for our example.

This distribution of residuals is not too far from a normal distribution. If the assumption of a normal distribution is not met, the tests of significance and the confidence intervals developed from them may be incorrect.

Analysis of Variance (ANOVA)

When many of the independent variables are qualitative, we cannot use regression analysis. We need a different method. Analysis of variance techniques can be used to identify and measure the impact of qualitative vari-

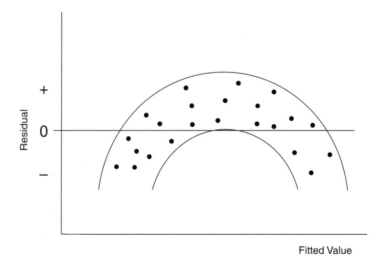

FIGURE 6.16
Violation of Assumption 1

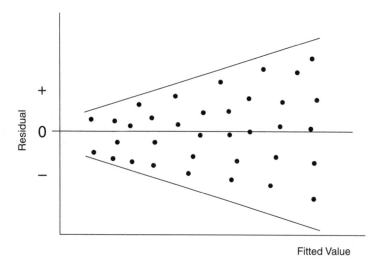

FIGURE 6.17
Violation of Assumption 2

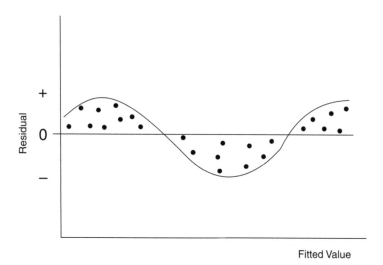

FIGURE 6.18
Possible violation of Assumption 3

ables (business sector, application language, hardware platform, etc.) on a dependent variable (effort, productivity, duration, etc.). Like regression analysis, these techniques break down the total variation of the data into its various parts using a set of well-defined procedures. As with regression analysis, entire books have been written about ANOVA methods. I've summarized the fundamental concepts in this short section.

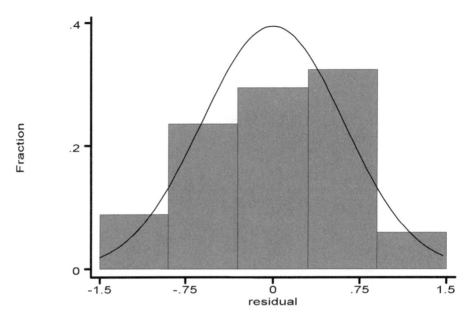

FIGURE 6.19
Checking Assumption 4: distribution of the residuals

Simple ANOVA   Let's say that we want to know if the percentage of
JCL used is related to application type. We will study this relationship using
some of the maintenance data from Chapter 5. I have chosen to illustrate the
ANOVA method with a subset of the data that contains an equal number of
observations in each category. In practice, the number of observations in
each category will not be the same because software project data is inher-
ently unbalanced. However, although the calculations are more complicated,
the principal remains the same. If you understand this example, you will
understand the basics of ANOVA.

One important assumption of ANOVA is that the sample is selected from
a normally distributed parent population. As we can see in Figure 5.11 in
Chapter 5, the percentage of JCL use is approximately normally distributed.

Is there a difference in the percentage of JCL use among the three application types? Let's look at Table 6.18. At first glance, I would say no. It looks
like the percentage of JCL use varies quite a lot within each application type.
It is not as if we see values around 30% for all backoffice database applications, around 50% for all customer interconnection service applications, and
around 70% for all core banking business system applications. However, it is
impossible to make any conclusion by just looking at the data.

TABLE 6.18
% JCL Use Data and Some ANOVA Calculations

	Backoffice Database	Customer Interconnection Service	Core Banking Business System	
	38	54	12	
	24	0	52	
	2	90	90	
	43	0	74	
	60	30	64	
	100	33	55	
	63	21	13	
	55	68	49	
	9	58	12	
	62	56	31	
	55	89	39	
	37	84	49	
	37	96	31	
	35	79	35	
	95	31	53	
Group Means	47.67	52.60	43.93	**Sample Mean = 48.07**
Group Variances	737.38	1033.11	513.21	**Mean of Group Variances = 761.23**

Our ANOVA example will test the following null hypothesis:

The mean percentage of JCL use is the same (in the population) for each of the three application types.

Of course, we do not know what the means in the population are. But, we can use our sample to estimate the means. If the means of percentage of JCL use for each application type in our sample are very close together, we will be more willing to accept that the null hypothesis is true. Our group means are 47.67%, 52.60%, and 43.93%. These group means do not seem that close to me. But are they significantly different given the size of our sample?[9]

We can get a better idea of any relationship that exists by calculating two variances, the variance between the groups and the variance within the groups, and comparing them. Both of these are estimates of the population variance. We can use their ratio to accept or reject the null hypothesis. The larger the variance in JCL use between application types and the smaller the variance within the application types, the more likely it is that percentage of JCL use really does differ among application types.

Between Groups Variance   The between groups variance calculates the variation between the mean percentage of JCL use of the three application types (47.67, 52.60, 43.93) measured about the mean JCL use of all 45 applications in our sample (48.07). The sample variance of the group means is a function of the squared differences of each group mean and the overall sample mean divided by the number of groups (application types) minus one.

$$s_{\bar{x}}^2 = \frac{(47.67 - 48.07)^2 + (52.60 - 48.07)^2 + (43.93 - 48.07)^2}{2} = 18.91$$

As this is the sample variance of the group mean, we must multiply it by the number of observations in the group (15) to calculate the between groups variance.

$$s_{bg}^2 = ns_{\bar{x}}^2 = 15(18.91) = 283.65$$

Within Groups Variance   The group variance for each application type tells us how close the actual values of JCL use are to the mean values for that application type, that is, how much the data varies within each group. This is known as the within groups variance. For example, the variance of JCL use for backoffice database applications is:

$$s_{backoffice}^2 = \frac{(38 - 47.67)^2 + (24 - 47.67)^2 + (2 - 47.67)^2 + \cdots + (95 - 47.67)^2}{14} = 737.38$$

We have three application types and thus three estimates of population variance (737.38, 1033.11, and 513.21). Since none of these estimates is any better than the others, we combine them to create a single estimate of the population variance based on the average "within" groups variation.

---

9. In practice, a software manager would probably not consider a 9% difference in percentage of JCL use to be that important, even if it was significant.

$$s_{wg}^2 = \frac{737.38 + 1033.11 + 513.21}{3} = 761.23$$

F Ratio

Now we can calculate the ratio of the between groups variance and the within groups variance. This is known as the *F* ratio.

$$F = \frac{s_{bg}^2}{s_{wg}^2} = \frac{283.65}{761.23} = 0.37$$

The within groups variance can be thought of as the variance due to random differences among applications. The between groups variance can be thought of as the variance due to random differences among applications plus differences in application type. Thus, the extent to which *F* exceeds 1 is indicative of a possible real effect of application type on JCL use. However, even if *F* exceeds 1, it is possible that it could be by chance alone. The probability of this occurring by chance is given by the F-distribution and is calculated automatically by your statistical analysis package. In our example, *F* is less than 1, and we can conclude that there is no relationship between application type and the percentage of JCL use.

How to Interpret ANOVA Output   Now that you know some basics of ANOVA, you will be able to better understand the ANOVA output in Example 6.6. This is the output from my statistical analysis package for our ANOVA example: percentage of JCL use as a function of application type. To simplify the example, I multiplied the *pjcl* variable in Chapter 5 by 100 and rounded it to the nearest integer to create the percentage of JCL use variable in Table 6.18, *rperjcl*. In practice, I would not alter *pjcl* and the computer would carry out the calculations using all significant digits.

Example 6.6

```
                    . anova rperjcl apptype

          Number of obs =      45      R-squared     = 0.0174
          Root MSE      = 27.5905      Adj R-squared = -0.0294
```

Source	Partial SS	df	MS	F	Prob > F
Model	566.933333	2	283.466667	0.37	0.6913
apptype	566.933333	2	283.466667	0.37	0.6913
Residual	31971.8667	42	761.234921		
Total	32835.80	44	739.518182		

At the top of the ANOVA output is a summary of the underlying regression. The model was estimated using 45 observations, and the root mean square error (*Root MSE*) is 27.59. The *R-squared* for the model is 0.0174, and the R-squared adjusted for the number of degrees of freedom (*Adj R-squared*) is –0.0294. (See the regression output in the previous section for a discussion of Adjusted R-squared.) Obviously, this model is pretty bad.

The first line of the table summarizes the model. The sum of squares (*Model SS*) for the model is 566.9 with 2 degrees of freedom (*Model df*). This results in a mean square (*Model MS*) of 566.9/2 ≃ 283.5. This is our between groups variance, s_{bg}^2. (Once again, there is a small difference between the computer's between groups variance and my calculation due to rounding errors.)

$$F = \frac{Model\ SS/Model\ df}{Residual\ SS/Residual\ df} = \frac{s_{bg}^2}{s_{wg}^2}$$

The corresponding *F* ratio has a value of 0.37 and a significance level of 0.6913. Thus, the model is not significant. We cannot reject the null hypothesis and say that there is no difference in the mean percentage of JCL use of different application types.[10]

The next line summarizes the first (and only) term in the model, *apptype*. Since there is only one variable, this line is the same as the previous line.

The third line summarizes the residual. The residual sum of squares (*Residual SS*) is 31971.87, with 42 degrees of freedom (*Residual df*), resulting in a mean square error of 761.23 (*Residual MS*). This is our within groups variance, s_{wg}^2. The *Root MSE* is the square root of this number.

The *Model SS* plus the *Residual SS* equals the *Total SS*. The *Model df* plus the *Residual df* equals the *Total df*, 44. As there are 45 observations, and we must subtract one degree of freedom for the mean, we are left with 44 total degrees of freedom.

Multi-Variable ANOVA   ANOVA can also be used to produce regression estimates for models with numerous quantitative and qualitative variables. ANOVA uses the method of least squares to fit linear models to the quantitative data. Thus, you can think of it as a combination of multiple regression analysis and the simple ANOVA I just explained. This is not so strange as you can see that the underlying principal in both methods is that we compare values to a mean value. In both methods, we also compare the variation explained by the model with the total variation of the data to measure its accu-

---

10. Had we been able to reject the null hypothesis in this example, it might not have been because of the differences in the population means, but because of the differences in their variances. When the sample variances for the different groups are very different, as they are in this example, then reject with caution. The ANOVA approach assumes that the population variances are similar.

racy. To learn how to interpret the regression output of categorical variables, read the "Choosing Baseline Categorical Variables" section of Chapter 5.

Comparing Two Estimation Models

I recommend that non-statistical experts use the Wilcoxon signed-rank test with matched pairs to determine if there is a statistically significant difference between two estimation models. This is a non-parametric statistic. As such, it is free from the often unrealistic assumptions underlying parametric statistics.[11] For example, one of the assumptions of the parametric paired t-test is that the paired data have equal variances. This may not be the case with your data and you do not want to have to worry about it. Non-parametric tests can always be used instead of parametric tests; however, the opposite is not true. Read the "Measuring Estimation Accuracy" section of Chapter 4 for an overview of the different accuracy measures.

The Wilcoxon Signed-Rank Test Applied to Matched Pairs

The Wilcoxon signed-rank test is based on the sign and rank of the absolute values of pair differences and is done automatically by most statistical analysis packages. What does this actually mean and how can we apply it to effort estimation models? Table 6.19 shows the *estimation error* (i.e., *actual – estimate*) and the *absolute estimation error* (i.e., |*actual – estimate*|) of two hypothetical effort estimation models used on three projects. We use the *absolute estimation error* in our calculations because we are interested only in the magnitude of the estimation error and not if it is over or under the estimate. The *pair difference*, then, is then the difference in the absolute values of the estimation errors of the two models, C and D, for each project. The *sign* is negative if Model D's error is greater than Model C's for that project. The *sign* is positive if Model C's error is greater than Model D's for that project. The *rank* is based on the comparison of absolute values of the pair differences for each project. The smallest absolute pair difference of all three projects gets a rank of 1, the second smallest gets a rank of 2, and so on. The computer uses the information in the last two columns to compute the Wilcoxon signed-rank test statistic. From this test, we can determine if either Model C or Model D has consistently smaller errors.

---

11. Parametric statistics are only suitable for data measured on interval and ratio scales, where parameters such as the mean of the distribution can be defined.

TABLE 6.19

How to Rank Differences for Wilcoxon Signed-Rank Tests on Matched Pairs

id	Estimation Error (hours) Model C	Estimation Error (hours) Model D	Absolute Estimation Error (hours) Model C	Absolute Estimation Error (hours) Model D	Pair Difference	Sign	Rank of Absolute Difference
OB1	−200	300	200	300	−100	−	2
OB2	50	100	50	100	−50	−	1
OB3	150	−20	150	20	130	+	3

Let's look at the statistical output for this test (Example 6.7) to try to understand what is going on. This example is from the comparison of two effort estimation models, Model A and Model B, in Example A of Chapter 4.

Example 6.7

```
          . signrank aModel_A=aModel_B
Wilcoxon signed-rank test

sign          obs      sum ranks      expected
positive       26           798         976.5
negative       36          1155         976.5
zero            0             0             0
all            62          1953          1953

unadjusted variance        20343.75
adjustment for ties            0.00
adjustment for zeros           0.00
adjusted variance          20343.75

Ho: aModel_A = aModel_B
          z = -1.251
  Prob > |z| = 0.2108
```

In the statistical output, *aModel_A* refers to Model A's absolute errors and *aModel_B* refers to Model B's absolute errors. The null hypothesis is that the distribution of the paired differences has a median of 0 and is symmetric. This implies that for approximately half the projects, Model A has a smaller error, and for half the projects, Model B has a smaller error. Thus neither model is better. If this were the case, then we would expect the sum of the ranks to be the same for positive and negative differences. These are the *expected* values, 976.5, in the statistical output. What we find, however, is that the rank sum of the *positive* differences is 798 and the rank sum of the *negative* differences is 1155. This means that Model B's absolute error is ranked higher than Model A's absolute error for more projects (remember that the difference = Model A – Model B). However, we only have a sample and this may have happened by chance. So, we need to check the probability that this happened by chance. The statistic computed by the Wilcoxon test, the z value, is –1.251. If –1.96 > z > 1.96, there is no difference between the models. If z is less than –1.96, then Model A has a significantly lower absolute error. If z is greater than 1.96, then Model A has a significantly higher absolute error. As –1.251 is between –1.96 and 1.96, this means that there is no statistically significant difference between the models. Our significance level is 21% (Pr > $|z|$ = 0.2108). This means that if we reject the null hypothesis, there is a 21% probability of being wrong (i.e., rejecting the null hypothesis when it is in fact true). It is typical in statistical studies to accept only a 5% chance of being wrong. Thus, there is no statistically significant difference between the two models.

Does this z value, 1.96, seem familiar? In fact, it comes from the 95% confidence interval of the normal curve. There is a 5% chance of getting a value higher than $|1.96|$. This means there is a 2.5% chance of getting a value lower than –1.96 and a 2.5% chance of getting a value higher than 1.96. This is what is meant by a two-sided (or two-tailed) test. A one-sided test checks only the chance of a value being lower **or** higher.

Final Comments

In this chapter, you learned some of the basic concepts of statistics and developed a deeper understanding of multivariate statistical analysis. In the previous chapters, you learned how to apply these methods to real software project data. You're now ready to analyze your own data. I'll end with one final word of advice: Remember to be reasonable with your inferences. If you find some interesting results based on 30 projects in your company, you can say something about what is going on in your company. This does not mean that this is true for all software projects in the world. Only if people in different companies keep finding the same results can you start to believe that you have found a fundamental truth. For example, enough studies have now been published that we can be certain that there is a real relationship between software effort and size. However, the exact equation describing the relationship varies by study. This is why it is often necessary to calibrate software cost estimation tools using your company's data.

Appendix A
Raw Software Development Project Data

id	size	effort	duration	start	app	har	dba	source	ifc	lan1	lan2	lan3	lan4	t01
1	562	1062	14	10/15/91	408	1003	1602	7004	2001	2621				5
2	647	7871	16	3/1/92	406	1002	1602	7001	2002	2617	2622	2654		4
3	130	845	5	6/1/93	406	1002	1602	7001	2002	2617	2622	2654		2
4	254	2330	8	11/1/90	408	1002	1602	7001	2002	2624	2654			3
5	1056	21272	16	6/1/86	401	1002	1602	7001	2002	2601	2617	2636		2
6	383	4224	12	10/15/88	406	1002	1602	7001	2002	2617	2654			3
7	345	2826	12	3/15/92	406	1005	1602	7001	2002	2617	2622	2654	2660	2
8	209	7320	27	12/1/87	406	1002	1602	7001	2002	2617	2654			4
9	366	9125	24	4/15/86	406	1002	1602	7001	2002	2617				2
10	1181	11900	54	1/1/87	406	1004	1605	7004	2002	2616	2668			4
11	181	4300	13	5/1/87	408	1002	1602	7001	2002	2624	2648			2
12	739	4150	21	1/1/90	406	1001	1602	7004	2002		2655			5
13	108	900	7	2/6/91	401	1003		7001	2002	2617	2636			2
14	48	583	10	1/5/90	401	1001		7001	2002	2601	2617	2636		2
15	249	2565	19	1/2/91	408	1002	1602	7001	2002	2617	2648			2
16	371	4047	11	3/1/92	406	1002	1602	7001	2002	2617	2648			3
17	211	1520	13	2/1/87	406	1002	1602	7001	2002	2617				2
18	1849	25910	32	10/15/91	406	1002	1602	7001	2002	2617	2660	2654	2622	4
19	2482	37286	38	6/1/89	406	1002	1602	7001	2002	2617	2622	2660	2654	4
20	434	15052	40	12/1/85	401	1005	1602	7001	2002	2601	2617	2636	2654	3
21	292	11039	29	12/1/87	406	1002	1602	7001	2002	2617	2622	2654		4
22	2954	18500	14	9/1/90	401	1005	1602	7001	2002	2601	2617	2622	2654	4
23	304	9369	14	3/1/91	406	1005	1602	7001	2002	2617				4
24	353	7184	28	10/15/89	406	1001	1602	7004	2002	2670				4
25	567	10447	16	2/1/92	406	1002	1602	7001	2002	2611	2617	2622	2660	2
26	467	5100	13	11/15/91	406	1002	1602	7001	2002	2617	2654	2660		4
27	3368	63694	45	4/15/87	406	1002	1602	7001	2002	2617	2622	2654		4
28	253	1651	4	7/1/92	401	1002	1602	7001	2002	2660	2622			3
29	196	1450	10	4/15/91	407	1005	1602	7001	2002	2614	2617	2660		1
30	185	1745	12	4/1/92	408	1002	1602	7001	2002	2617	2622	2624	2654	3
31	387	1798	6	8/15/88	401	1002	1602	7001	2002	2617	2654			2
32	430	2957	28	10/1/88	402	1002	1602	7001	2002	2617	2654			1
33	204	963	6	9/15/89	406	1002	1602	7001	2002	2617	2654			3
34	71	1233	6	1/2/88	406	1002	1602	7001	2002	2617				3
35	840	3240	6	11/1/91	408	1005	1602	7004	2001	2614	2617	2629		4
36	1648	10000	11	9/1/90	406	1005	1602	7004	2001	2614	2617	2629	2654	4
37	1035	6800	8	4/8/91	406	1005	1602	7004	2001	2614	2617	2629	2654	4
38	548	3850	22	12/1/85	401	1002	1602	7001	2002	2617				3
39	2054	14000	31	2/1/91	401	1005	1602	7001	2002	2617	2660	2654		4
40	302	5787	26	4/15/88	402	1002	1602	7001	2002	2617	2624			2
41	1172	9700	22	2/1/93	401	1005	1602	7001	2002	2660	2622	2617		4
42	253	1100	7	7/15/91	408	1001	1602	7001	2001	2614				3
43	227	5578	14	2/1/92	406	1002	1602	7001	2002	2617	2654			3
44	59	1060	6	9/1/92	406	1002	1602	7001	2002	2617	2622	2654		4
45	299	5279	6	9/15/91	408	1002	1602	7001	2002	2617	2622	2648	2660	3
46	422	8117	15	11/1/89	401	1002	1602	7001	2002	2617				3
47	1058	8710	9	4/1/90	406	1001	1602	7004	2002	2614	2617	2654		4
48	65	796	9	2/1/90	408	1001	1604	7001	2002	2601	2617	2636		4
49	390	11023	26	9/1/88	401	1005	1602	7001	2002	2617	2601	2636		5
50	193	1755	13	10/1/90	406	1002	1602	7001	2002	2617	2654			4
51	1526	5931	28	2/1/91	408	1002	1602	7001	2002	2617	2668	2660	2648	4
52	575	4456	13	11/1/93	401	1005	1602	7001	2002	2617	2660			2
53	509	3600	13	2/1/87	406	1002	1602	7001	2002	2617				2
54	583	4557	12	12/1/88	402	1002	1602	7001	2002	2617	2622	2654		1
55	315	8752	14	3/1/88	401	1002	1602	7001	2002	2617	2654			4
56	138	3440	12	5/1/89	401	1002	1602	7001	2002	2617	2654			3
57	257	1981	9	7/25/88	406	1005	1602	7001	2002	2617	2636	2654		3
58	423	13700	30	10/1/85	406	1002	1602	7001	2002	2617				2
59	495	7105	20	1/1/91	402	1001	1602	7004	2002	2614	2643	2654		4
60	622	6816	16	9/15/90	401	1005	1602	7001	2002	2617	2622	2654	2660	2
61	204	4620	12	11/16/92	408	1002	1602	7001	2002	2617	2660			3
62	616	7451	15	9/1/90	401	1005	1602	7001	2002	2606	2617	2654	2660	2
63	3634	39479	33	8/19/91	401	1005	1602	7001	2002	2617	2622	2654		2

t02	t03	t04	t05	t06	t07	t08	t09	t10	t11	t12	t13	t14	t15
3	3	2	3	4	4	4	3	3	2	4	3	5	3
3	5	3	3	3	4	5	4	5	4	4	4	4	5
3	3	3	3	3	2	2	4	3	4	4	4	4	4
3	2	3	3	4	2	3	4	5	4	3	2	3	3
2	4	2	2	1	3	5	4	4	5	4	3	2	3
3	3	4	3	3	4	3	4	4	3	4	5	4	4
3	5	4	3	2	3	5	5	5	3	4	4	2	3
3	3	2	2	2	4	5	4	3	3	3	3	2	3
3	3	2	1	2	4	5	3	2	2	2	3	4	2
3	2	3	3	2	2	5	3	4	2	3	2	3	3
3	4	2	3	1	3	3	3	2	2	2	1	1	2
2	2	4	3	3	1	4	4	3	4	4	1	5	1
3	3	4	2	2	2	4	4	3	5	3	3	4	2
3	2	4	3	3	3	5	4	3	3	4	2	4	3
4	3	3	3	3	3	3	5	5	2	3	3	3	3
3	2	4	3	3	4	4	4	3	2	4	3	3	3
1	3	3	3	4	4	5	4	4	4	4	3	3	4
3	4	3	4	4	5	4	5	4	5	5	3	1	4
2	3	3	3	2	4	5	4	4	4	4	4	2	3
3	4	4	4	2	3	4	5	5	3	4	4	2	3
4	2	3	3	3	4	3	4	4	5	3	2	3	3
3	2	4	3	3	4	4	5	4	3	4	2	4	3
3	2	3	2	3	2	4	4	4	2	2	3	3	3
2	2	4	3	3	4	4	5	5	5	4	2	2	4
3	4	3	3	3	3	3	4	4	3	3	2	3	3
3	3	4	3	3	4	5	4	4	4	4	4	2	4
3	3	4	3	4	2	4	4	3	2	4	4	2	4
4	2	3	3	4	2	3	2	3	2	4	2	4	3
4	2	3	3	4	3	5	3	3	3	4	4	5	3
4	3	2	2	2	3	4	5	4	4	4	3	3	4
3	3	3	3	2	4	5	3	2	3	3	3	4	3
4	2	3	3	3	4	3	4	4	2	4	3	3	3
3	3	4	3	3	2	3	4	2	3	4	2	4	3
2	4	3	5	3	4	5	5	4	3	5	4	4	5
2	4	3	5	3	5	3	5	5	4	5	3	4	5
2	4	3	5	3	5	3	5	5	4	5	3	4	5
3	4	2	3	2	3	4	3	3	3	4	4	3	3
3	4	4	4	3	3	4	4	4	5	5	4	3	4
3	2	4	3	3	3	4	3	3	3	3	2	4	3
2	2	3	4	4	4	2	4	2	4	3	4	3	4
3	3	2	2	3	3	3	4	3	3	4	4	4	3
4	2	4	3	3	3	3	5	5	3	3	2	3	3
3	3	3	3	3	2	3	4	3	3	4	3	3	3
3	4	4	4	4	3	4	4	3	5	4	3	2	3
3	3	4	3	3	3	3	5	3	4	4	3	2	4
4	3	5	4	4	5	3	4	4	3	5	2	4	4
2	2	3	3	2	4	4	4	4	3	4	4	5	3
5	3	3	2	3	4	5	5	4	4	4	3	4	4
4	2	3	4	3	2	2	3	3	3	3	2	4	4
3	2	3	3	3	3	3	4	3	4	4	4	3	3
3	3	3	3	3	4	2	4	3	4	4	2	3	3
3	3	4	3	3	3	4	4	3	2	4	2	2	3
4	4	2	3	3	2	3	2	2	2	4	5	3	3
3	5	3	3	3	4	5	4	3	3	4	3	3	3
4	5	3	3	3	3	3	4	4	2	4	4	3	3
4	3	3	3	3	3	4	4	4	4	4	4	4	3
3	3	2	2	2	4	5	4	3	3	4	4	2	3
2	4	3	3	3	3	3	5	3	3	4	3	4	4
3	3	4	3	3	4	4	4	3	4	3	2	4	3
3	3	3	3	4	4	5	5	5	5	4	3	2	3
3	2	3	3	2	3	5	5	4	5	5	1	5	4
4	3	3	3	3	4	3	5	5	5	4	4	5	4

Appendix B
Validated Software
Development Project Data

id	size	effort	duration	syear	app	har	dba	ifc	source	lan1	lan2	lan3	lan4	nlan	telonuse	t01
1	562	1062	14	1991	InfServ	PC	Relatnl	GUI	Outsrced	Dbase				1	No	5
2	647	7871	16	1992	TransPro	Mainfrm	Relatnl	TextUI	Inhouse	Cobol	Easytrv	SQL		3	No	4
3	130	845	5	1993	TransPro	Mainfrm	Relatnl	TextUI	Inhouse	Cobol	Easytrv	SQL		3	No	2
4	254	2330	8	1990	InfServ	Mainfrm	Relatnl	TextUI	Inhouse	Focus	SQL			2	No	3
5	1056	21272	16	1986	CustServ	Mainfrm	Relatnl	TextUI	Inhouse	Ada	Cobol	Mps-frms		3	No	2
6	383	4224	12	1988	TransPro	Mainfrm	Relatnl	TextUI	Inhouse	Cobol	SQL			2	No	3
7	345	2826	12	1992	TransPro	Multi	Relatnl	TextUI	Inhouse	Cobol	Easytrv	SQL	Telon	4	Yes	2
8	209	7320	27	1987	TransPro	Mainfrm	Relatnl	TextUI	Inhouse	Cobol	SQL			2	No	4
9	366	9125	24	1986	TransPro	Mainfrm	Relatnl	TextUI	Inhouse	Cobol				1	No	2
10	1181	11900	54	1987	TransPro	Mini	Sequentl	TextUI	Outsrced	CI	RPG			2	No	4
11	181	4300	13	1987	InfServ	Mainfrm	Relatnl	TextUI	Inhouse	Focus	Qmf			2	No	2
12	739	4150	21	1990	TransPro	Network	Relatnl	TextUI	Outsrced		Sql-srvr			1	No	5
13	108	900	7	1991	CustServ	PC	None	TextUI	Inhouse	Cobol	Mps-frms			2	No	2
14	48	583	10	1990	TransPro	Network	None	TextUI	Inhouse	Ada	Cobol	Mps-frms		3	No	2
15	249	2565	19	1991	InfServ	Mainfrm	Relatnl	TextUI	Inhouse	Cobol	Qmf			2	No	2
16	371	4047	11	1992	TransPro	Mainfrm	Relatnl	TextUI	Inhouse	Cobol	Qmf			2	No	3
17	211	1520	13	1987	TransPro	Mainfrm	Relatnl	TextUI	Inhouse	Cobol				1	No	2
18	1849	25910	32	1991	TransPro	Mainfrm	Relatnl	TextUI	Inhouse	Cobol	Telon	SQL	Easytrv	4	Yes	4
19	2482	37286	38	1989	TransPro	Mainfrm	Relatnl	TextUI	Inhouse	Cobol	Easytrv	SQL		4	Yes	4
20	434	15052	40	1985	CustServ	Multi	Relatnl	TextUI	Inhouse	Ada	Cobol	Mps-frms	SQL	4	No	3
21	292	11039	29	1987	TransPro	Mainfrm	Relatnl	TextUI	Inhouse	Cobol	Easytrv	SQL		3	No	4
22	2954	18500	14	1990	CustServ	Multi	Relatnl	TextUI	Inhouse	Ada	Cobol	Easytrv	SQL	4	No	4
23	304	9369	14	1991	TransPro	Multi	Relatnl	TextUI	Inhouse	Cobol				1	No	4
24	353	7184	28	1989	TransPro	Network	Relatnl	TextUI	Outsrced	Clipper				1	No	4
25	567	10447	16	1992	TransPro	Mainfrm	Relatnl	TextUI	Inhouse	Assemblr	Cobol	Easytrv	Telon	4	Yes	2
26	467	5100	13	1991	TransPro	Mainfrm	Relatnl	TextUI	Inhouse	Cobol	SQL	Telon		3	Yes	4
27	3368	63694	45	1987	TransPro	Mainfrm	Relatnl	TextUI	Inhouse	Cobol	Easytrv	SQL		3	No	4
28	253	1651	4	1992	CustServ	Mainfrm	Relatnl	TextUI	Inhouse	Telon	Easytrv			2	Yes	3
29	196	1450	10	1991	ProdCont	Multi	Relatnl	TextUI	Inhouse	C-def	Cobol	Telon		3	Yes	1
30	185	1745	12	1992	InfServ	Mainfrm	Relatnl	TextUI	Inhouse	Cobol	Easytrv	Focus	SQL	4	No	3
31	387	1798	6	1988	TransPro	Mainfrm	Relatnl	TextUI	Inhouse	Cobol	SQL			2	No	2
32	430	2957	28	1988	MIS	Mainfrm	Relatnl	TextUI	Inhouse	Cobol	SQL			2	No	1
33	204	963	6	1989	TransPro	Mainfrm	Relatnl	TextUI	Inhouse	Cobol	SQL			2	No	3
34	71	1233	6	1988	TransPro	Mainfrm	Relatnl	TextUI	Inhouse	Cobol				1	No	3
35	840	3240	6	1991	InfServ	Multi	Relatnl	GUI	Outsrced	C-def	Cobol	Ingres		3	No	4
36	1648	10000	11	1990	TransPro	Multi	Relatnl	GUI	Outsrced	C-def	Cobol	Ingres	SQL	4	No	4
37	1035	6800	8	1991	TransPro	Multi	Relatnl	GUI	Outsrced	C-def	Cobol	Ingres	SQL	4	No	4
38	548	3850	22	1985	CustServ	Mainfrm	Relatnl	TextUI	Inhouse	Cobol				1	No	3
39	2054	14000	31	1991	CustServ	Multi	Relatnl	TextUI	Inhouse	Cobol	Telon	SQL		3	Yes	4
40	302	5787	26	1988	MIS	Mainfrm	Relatnl	TextUI	Inhouse	Cobol	Focus			2	No	2
41	1172	9700	22	1993	CustServ	Multi	Relatnl	TextUI	Inhouse	Telon	Easytrv	Cobol		3	Yes	4
42	253	1100	7	1991	InfServ	Network	Relatnl	GUI	Inhouse	C-def				1	No	3
43	227	5578	14	1992	TransPro	Mainfrm	Relatnl	TextUI	Inhouse	Cobol	SQL			2	No	3
44	59	1060	6	1992	TransPro	Mainfrm	Relatnl	TextUI	Inhouse	Cobol	Easytrv	SQL		3	No	4
45	299	5279	6	1991	InfServ	Mainfrm	Relatnl	TextUI	Inhouse	Cobol	Easytrv	Qmf	Telon	4	Yes	3
46	422	8117	15	1989	CustServ	Mainfrm	Relatnl	TextUI	Inhouse	Cobol				1	No	3
47	1058	8710	9	1990	TransPro	Network	Relatnl	TextUI	Outsrced	C-def	Cobol	SQL		3	No	4
48	65	796	9	1990	InfServ	Network	Other	TextUI	Inhouse	Ada	Cobol	Mps-frms		3	No	4
49	390	11023	26	1988	CustServ	Multi	Relatnl	TextUI	Inhouse	Cobol	Ada	Mps-frms		3	No	5
50	193	1755	13	1990	TransPro	Mainfrm	Relatnl	TextUI	Inhouse	Cobol	SQL			2	No	4
51	1526	5931	28	1991	InfServ	Mainfrm	Relatnl	TextUI	Inhouse	Cobol	RPG	Telon	Qmf	4	Yes	4
52	575	4456	13	1993	CustServ	Multi	Relatnl	TextUI	Inhouse	Cobol	Telon			2	Yes	2
53	509	3600	13	1987	TransPro	Mainfrm	Relatnl	TextUI	Inhouse	Cobol				1	No	2
54	583	4557	12	1988	MIS	Mainfrm	Relatnl	TextUI	Inhouse	Cobol	Easytrv	SQL		3	No	1
55	315	8752	14	1988	CustServ	Mainfrm	Relatnl	TextUI	Inhouse	Cobol	SQL			2	No	4
56	138	3440	12	1989	CustServ	Mainfrm	Relatnl	TextUI	Inhouse	Cobol	SQL			2	No	3
57	257	1981	9	1988	TransPro	Multi	Relatnl	TextUI	Inhouse	Cobol	Mps-frms	SQL		3	No	3
58	423	13700	30	1985	TransPro	Mainfrm	Relatnl	TextUI	Inhouse	Cobol				1	No	2
59	495	7105	20	1991	MIS	Network	Relatnl	TextUI	Outsrced	C-def	Oracle	SQL		3	No	4
60	622	6816	16	1990	CustServ	Multi	Relatnl	TextUI	Inhouse	Cobol	Easytrv	SQL	Telon	4	Yes	2
61	204	4620	12	1992	InfServ	Mainfrm	Relatnl	TextUI	Inhouse	Cobol	Telon			2	Yes	3
62	616	7451	15	1990	CustServ	Multi	Relatnl	TextUI	Inhouse	Ai-tools	Cobol	SQL	Telon	4	Yes	2
63	3634	39479	33	1991	CustServ	Multi	Relatnl	TextUI	Inhouse	Cobol	Easytrv	SQL		3	No	2

t02	t03	t04	t05	t06	t07	t08	t09	t10	t11	t12	t13	t14	t15	time	prod
3	3	2	3	4	4	4	3	3	2	4	3	5	3	7	0.52919
3	5	3	3	3	4	5	4	5	4	4	4	4	5	8	0.082201
3	3	3	3	3	2	2	4	3	4	4	4	4	4	9	0.153846
3	2	3	3	4	2	3	4	5	4	3	2	3	3	6	0.109013
2	4	2	2	1	3	5	4	4	5	4	3	2	3	2	0.049643
3	3	4	3	3	4	3	4	4	3	4	5	4	4	4	0.090672
3	3	3	3	3	2	2	4	4	4	4	4	5	4	8	0.122081
3	5	4	3	2	3	5	5	5	3	4	4	2	3	3	0.028552
3	3	2	2	2	4	5	4	3	3	3	3	2	3	2	0.04011
3	3	2	1	2	4	5	3	2	2	2	3	4	2	3	0.099244
3	2	3	3	3	2	5	3	4	2	3	2	3	3	3	0.042093
3	4	2	3	1	3	3	3	2	2	2	1	1	2	6	0.178072
2	2	4	3	3	1	4	4	3	4	4	1	5	1	7	0.12
3	3	4	2	2	2	4	4	3	5	3	3	4	2	6	0.082333
3	2	4	3	3	3	5	4	3	3	4	2	4	3	7	0.097076
4	3	3	3	3	3	3	5	5	2	4	3	3	3	8	0.091673
3	2	4	3	3	4	4	4	3	2	4	3	3	3	3	0.138816
1	3	3	3	4	4	5	4	4	4	4	3	3	4	7	0.071362
3	4	3	4	4	5	4	5	4	5	5	3	1	4	5	0.066567
2	3	3	3	2	4	5	4	4	4	4	4	2	3	1	0.028833
3	4	4	4	2	3	4	5	5	3	4	4	2	3	3	0.026452
4	2	3	3	3	4	3	4	4	5	3	2	3	3	6	0.159676
3	2	4	3	3	4	4	5	4	3	4	2	4	3	7	0.032447
3	2	3	2	3	2	4	4	4	2	2	3	3	3	5	0.049137
2	2	4	3	3	4	4	5	5	5	4	2	2	4	8	0.054274
3	4	3	3	3	3	3	4	4	3	3	2	3	3	7	0.091569
3	3	4	3	3	4	5	4	4	4	4	4	2	4	8	0.052878
3	3	4	3	4	2	4	4	3	2	4	4	2	4	8	0.153241
4	2	3	3	4	2	3	2	3	2	4	2	4	3	7	0.135172
4	2	3	3	4	3	5	3	3	3	4	4	5	4	8	0.106017
4	3	2	2	2	3	4	5	4	4	4	3	3	4	4	0.215239
3	3	3	3	2	4	5	3	2	3	3	3	4	3	4	0.145418
4	2	3	3	3	3	4	3	4	2	4	3	3	3	5	0.211838
3	3	4	3	3	2	3	4	2	3	4	2	4	3	4	0.057583
2	4	3	5	3	4	5	5	4	3	5	4	4	5	7	0.259259
2	4	3	5	3	5	3	5	5	4	5	3	4	5	6	0.1648
2	4	3	5	3	5	3	5	5	4	5	3	4	5	7	0.152206
2	4	2	3	2	3	4	3	3	3	4	3	3	3	1	0.142338
3	4	4	4	3	3	4	4	4	4	5	5	4	4	7	0.146714
3	2	4	3	3	4	4	3	3	3	3	2	4	3	4	0.052186
2	2	3	4	4	4	2	4	2	4	3	4	3	4	9	0.120825
3	3	2	2	3	3	3	4	3	3	4	4	4	3	7	0.23
4	2	4	3	3	3	3	5	5	3	3	2	3	3	8	0.040696
3	3	3	3	3	2	3	4	3	3	4	3	3	3	8	0.05566
3	4	4	4	4	3	4	4	3	5	4	3	2	3	7	0.05664
3	3	4	3	3	3	3	5	3	4	4	3	2	4	5	0.05199
4	3	5	4	4	5	3	4	4	3	5	2	4	4	6	0.12147
2	2	3	3	2	4	4	4	4	3	4	4	5	4	6	0.081658
5	3	3	2	3	4	5	5	4	4	4	3	4	4	4	0.035381
4	2	3	4	3	2	2	3	3	3	3	2	4	4	6	0.109972
3	2	3	3	3	3	3	4	3	4	4	4	3	3	7	0.257292
3	3	3	3	3	4	2	4	3	4	4	2	3	3	9	0.12904
3	3	4	3	3	3	4	4	3	2	4	4	2	3	3	0.141389
4	4	2	3	3	2	3	2	2	2	4	5	3	3	4	0.127935
3	5	3	3	3	4	5	4	3	3	4	3	3	3	4	0.035992
4	5	3	3	3	3	3	4	4	2	4	4	3	3	5	0.040116
4	3	3	3	3	3	4	4	4	4	4	4	4	3	4	0.129733
3	3	2	2	2	4	5	4	3	3	4	4	2	3	1	0.030876
2	4	3	3	3	3	3	5	3	3	4	3	4	4	7	0.069669
3	3	4	3	3	3	4	4	3	4	3	2	4	3	6	0.091256
3	3	3	3	4	4	5	5	5	5	4	3	2	3	8	0.044156
3	2	3	3	2	3	5	5	4	5	5	1	5	4	6	0.082674
4	3	3	3	3	4	3	5	5	5	4	4	5	4	7	0.092049

Appendix C
Validated Software
Maintenance Project Data

mid	correff	totfp	pcobol	ptelon	peasy	pjcl	t	ageend	avetrans	disksp	cpu	r1	r2
1	130	237	0.62	0	0	0.38	3	77	0	98	340		
2	102	569	0.76	0	0	0.24	3	71	2	0	23		
3	369	165	0.88	0	0	0.12	3	77	7	13	63		
4	171	203	0.98	0	0	0.02	4	36	6	0	1		
5	61	273	0.57	0	0	0.43	3	48	0	68	0	3	1
6	2125	1748	0.3	0	0.18	0.52	4	44	25	39012	1829	4	4
7	155	41	0.1	0	0	0.9	4	55	1	193	102		
8	430	84	0.38	0	0.02	0.6	4	48	0	4	996	1	3
9	108	448	0.18	0	0.42	0.4	4	84	0	574	18	3	4
10	22	167	0	0	0	1	3	8	0	192	189		
11	59	152	0.22	0	0.24	0.54	3	36	0	2163	46	5	4
12	1508	1988	0.01	0.22	0.47	0.3	4	56	32	5431	1216		
13	25	23	1	0	0	0	4	37	0	0	0	4	2
14	85	278	0.1	0	0	0.9	3	19	0	2764	282	5	5
15	350	63	1	0	0	0	3	24	0	0	0	5	4
16	44	24	0.38	0	0	0.63	3	15	0	0	0	5	5
17	235	73	0.26	0	0	0.74	4	50	74	94	132	4	2
18	260	60	0.42	0	0.05	0.55	3	50	7	220	212	2	1
19	67	54	0.93	0	0	0.09	3	50	0	8	0	3	4
20	82	151	0.38	0	0	0.62	3	8	0	109	108	1	1
21	33	49	0.24	0	0.2	0.55	3	50	0	38	19	1	1
22	360	939	0.16	0.44	0.03	0.37	3	24	1	501	443	3	1
23	282	671	0.29	0	0.34	0.37	4	50	3	925	120		
24	312	381	0.29	0	0.07	0.64	4	50	8	677	209	3	1
25	218	177	0.3	0	0.15	0.55	4	50	0	61	35	1	1
26	196	934	0.06	0.8	0	0.13	3	41	1	128	69	3	1
27	29	213	0.51	0	0	0.49	3	39	0	55	36	3	1
28	38	87	0.7	0	0	0.3	4	64	1	6	17	3	2
29	74	347	0.67	0	0	0.33	4	58	143	431	117	5	3
30	214	887	0.79	0	0	0.21		39	3	336	506	2	2
31	112	321	0.01	0.87	0	0.12	4	35	0	11	5	3	2
32	319	481	0.31	0.34	0.04	0.31	3	26	31	154	152	4	2
33	96	252	0.19	0.42	0	0.39	3	8	1	176	276	4	4
34	861	559	0.04	0.34	0.14	0.49	3	21	14	282	63	4	1
35	248	381	0.01	0.69	0	0.31	3	8	3	617	25	4	4
36	3031	471	0.33	0.06	0.27	0.35	4	44	345	418	6	5	4
37	2056	1979	0.23	0	0.23	0.53	4	27	3	30008	1884	5	4
38	2500	274	0	0	0.23	0.77	3	20	0	7789	254	4	4
39	1122	1264	0.68	0.19	0	0.13	3	45	18	1352	50	4	2
40	350	292	0.19	0	0.13	0.68	1	36	0	906	912	5	4
41	463	724	0.76	0	0.03	0.21		40	10	1564	115	1	1
42	96	36	0.42	0	0	0.58		36	0	2	187	4	4
43	292	301	0.24	0	0.2	0.56	4	25	0	1717	1345	5	1
44	260	715	0	0.36	0.19	0.45	3	26	6	877	42	1	2
45	664	1361	0.07	0	0.04	0.89	3	23	0	3249	2197	4	4
46	462	686	0.11	0	0.05	0.84	3	12	0	450	503	2	4
47	309	433	0.02	0	0.02	0.96	4	19	0	2171	1446	5	4
48	535	347	0.17	0	0.04	0.79	4	12	0	77	131	5	1
49	284	69	0.22	0	0.26	0.52	4	8	25	729	40	4	5
50	401	368	0.17	0	0.52	0.31	1	35	0	0	0	5	3
51	319	670	0.65	0	0.01	0.34		44	17	650	36	3	4
52	71	448	0.78	0	0.08	0.13	3	35	6	0	0	3	1
53	304	986	0.55	0	0.03	0.41	2	35	4	76	0	3	3
54	2840	1366	0.86	0	0	0.14	4	35	10	1	0	3	1
55	164	776	0.51	0	0.02	0.47		44	6	430	1267	2	4
56	55	56	0.3	0	0.36	0.32	4	62	23	98	13	1	2
57	2600	68	0.25	0	0	0.74	3	20	0	151	45	4	2
58	1254	801	0.68	0	0.13	0.19	4	35	4	133	46	1	1
59	155	114	0.68	0	0.23	0.09	4	10	0	78	30	4	4
60	490	262	0.63	0	0.01	0.35	3	12	1	409	292		
61	292	237	0.46	0	0.24	0.3	3	76	0	0	0	4	5
62	367	216	0.61	0	0	0.39	1	29	7	98	23	4	3
63	795	238	0.47	0	0.04	0.49		47	8	432	85	3	3
64	1611	2328	0.26	0	0.36	0.38	4	76	89	5914	497	4	2
65	271	18	0	0	0	1	4	85	0	2216	0		
66	278	66	0.05	0	0	0.95		44	0	3	1808	4	1
67	39	81	0	0	0.23	0.77		84	0	4400	39		

r3	r4	r5	r6	r7	r8	r9	r10	appdef	borg	morg	apptype	dbms	tpms
								5	BigCorp	Treasury	BackOff	DB2	IMS
								2	BigCorp	Treasury	BackOff	DB2	IMS
								1	BigCorp	Treasury	Core	DB2	IMS
								12	BigCorp	Treasury	BackOff	DB2	IMS
2	3	2	2	2	1	1	1	2	Retail	Common	BackOff	DB2	IMS
4	2	2	2	4	4	4	3	53	Retail	Deposit	Core	DB2	IMS
								2	Corp	Treasury	Core	DB2	IMS
2	3	2	2	5	1	4	1	1	Retail	Common	BackOff	DB2	BATCH
3	4	3	2	4	2	4	3	1	Corp	Payment	InfServ	DB2	IIMS
								0	Group	Account	BackOff		IMS
4	2	1	3	5	5	5	1	0	Corp	Payment	Connect	DB2	BATCH
								21	Corp	DecSup	InfServ	IDSN	IIMS
3	4	2	2	1	4	1	3	0	Retail	Deposit	Connect		IMS
5	2	1	2	5	5	5	1	1	Corp	Payment	Connect	DB2	IMS
4	2	1	1	4	1	5	2	1	ITServ	Common	Connect	DB2	IMS
5	2	1	2	5	5	5	1	0	Corp	Payment	BackOff	DB2	IMS
1	3	3	2	4	1	4	1	0	Retail	Account	Core	DB2	IMS
1	2	3	2	4	1	4	3	0	Group	Account	BackOff	DB2	IMS
4	2	2	2	4	1	5	2	0	Group	Account	BackOff	DB2	IMS
2	2	2	3	4	1	3	1	0	Group	Account	BackOff	DB2	IMS
1	2	3	2	4	1	4	1	2	Group	Account	BackOff	DB2	IMS
1	1	1	1	2	2	1	1	8	Group	Account	BackOff	DB2	BATCH
								5	Corp	BUC	BackOff		IMS
2	1	1	1	4	3	3	1	4	Group	Account	Core	DB2	IMS
2	2	1	2	4	1	3	1	7	Group	Account	Core	DB2	BATCH
1	3	1	2	3	2	3	1	5	Group	Person	Core	DB2	IMS
2	3	2	2	4	1	2	1	2	InHServ	Resto	Core	IDSN	IIMS
1	2	4	3	3	1	1	3	11	Retail	Account	Connect	DB2	IMS
1	1	2	1	5	4	2	1	0	Retail	CusInt	Connect		PTCICS
1	1	1	2	5	4	5	1	0	BigCorp	CusInt	Connect		PTCICS
2	2	1	2	4	4	4	1	11	ITServ	ITSupp	Core		IMS
3	3	2	2	4	5	4	2	1	Group	Account	Core	DB2	BATCH
4	3	2	2	5	2	4	1	0	Group	Account	Core	DB2	BATCH
1	2	2	2	3	3	2	1	7	Corp	Payment	Core	DB2	BATCH
3	1	1	2	5	5	5	1	0	Corp	Payment	Core	DB2	IMS
4	2	2	2	4	5	4	2	24	Retail	Deposit	Core	DB2	IMS
4	2	2	2	4	5	4	2	59	Retail	Deposit	Core	DB2	IMS
4	2	2	2	4	3	4	2	0	Retail	Deposit	Core	DB2	IMS
3	4	4	3	5	4	4	3	20	BigCorp	Loan	Core	DB2	IMS
3	2	3	1	5	3	5	1	3	Corp	Payment	Connect	DB2	IMS
1	4	4	2	4	1	4	1	3	BigCorp	LetCred	Core		RECICS
3	1	1	1	4	1	4	1	0	Corp	Payment	Connect	DB2	IMS
1	2	2	1	5	1	4	1	5	Corp	Payment	Connect	DB2	IMS
1	1	1	2	4	5	4	1	3	Corp	Payment	Core	DB2	IMS
3	2	3	2	5	1	5	1	11	Corp	Payment	Connect	DB2	IMS
3	2	1	3	5	1	5	1	19	Corp	Payment	Connect	DB2	IMS
5	2	1	3	5	4	5	1	0	Corp	Payment	Connect	DB2	IMS
1	3	2	1	5	1	4	1	20	Corp	Payment	Connect	DB2	IMS
3	2	1	2	5	5	5	3	11	Corp	Payment	Core	DB2	IMS
1	3	3	4	5	1	5	2	1	Retail	SecTrade	Connect	DB2	IMS
2	3	3	1	4	3	3	3	32	Retail	SecTrade	Core	DB2	IMS
2	4	3	3	3	4	1	3	8	Retail	SecTrade	Core	DB2	IMS
2	4	3	3	3	4	1	3	16	Retail	SecTrade	Core	DB2	IMS
1	3	3	1	5	3	4	3	39	Retail	SecTrade	Core	DB2	IMS
4	3	3	1	4	3	5	3	163	Retail	SecTrade	Core	DB2	IMS
1	4	3	2	2	2	2	3	1	Retail	SecTrade	Core	DB2	IMS
1	3	3	3	2	5	5	3	0	Retail	SecTrade	Connect	DB2	IMS
1	3	3	2	4	4	3	3	0	Retail	SecTrade	Core	DB2	IMS
3	2	2	1	4	3	4	3	7	Retail	SecTrade	Connect	DB2	IMS
								6	BigCorp	Treasury	BackOff		
2	1	1	2	5	5	1	3	0	Retail	Common	Core	DB2	IMS
2	1	2	2	5	5	4	3	0	BigCorp	Treasury	Core	DB2	IMS
2	4	4	2	4	2	5	1	3	Corp	IntlBank	Connect	DB2	IMS
4	2	3	2	3	5	5	3	4	Retail	Deposit	Core	DB2	IMS
								2	ITServ	ITInfra	Connect	DB2	BATCH
1	2	4	3	4	5	3	3	7	Retail	Account	BackOff	DB2	IMS
								0	ITServ	ITServ	Core	DB2	IMS

Index

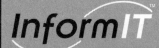